AQA German
Higher

GCSE

Heather Murphy
David Riddell
Alan O'Brien
Helen Kent

OXFORD
UNIVERSITY PRESS

OXFORD
UNIVERSITY PRESS

Great Clarendon Street, Oxford, OX2 6DP, United Kingdom

Oxford University Press is a department of the University of Oxford.
It furthers the University's objective of excellence in research,
scholarship, and education by publishing worldwide. Oxford is a
registered trade mark of Oxford University Press in the UK and in
certain other countries

British Library Cataloguing in Publication Data
Data available

978-0-19-836587-7

10 9 8 7

Paper used in the production of this book is a natural, recyclable
product made from wood grown in sustainable forests.
The manufacturing process conforms to the environmental
regulations of the country of origin.

Printed and bound in Great Britian by Bell and Bain Ltd, Glasgow

MIX
Paper from
responsible sources
FSC® C007785

Approval message from AQA

This textbook has been approved by AQA for use with our
qualification. This means that we have checked that it broadly
covers the specification and we are satisfied with the overall
quality. Full details of our approval process can be found on
our website.

We approve textbooks because we know how important it is
for teachers and students to have the right resources to support
their teaching and learning. However, the publisher is ultimately
responsible for the editorial control and quality of this book.

Please note that when teaching the AQA GCSE German Higher
course, you must refer to AQA's specification as your definitive
source of information. While this book has been written to match
the specification, it cannot provide complete coverage of every
aspect of the course.

A wide range of other useful resources can be found on the
relevant subject pages of our website: www.aqa.org.uk.

Contents

Theme 2 – Local, national, international and global areas of interest, Unit 6 – Social issues
6.1 Charity / voluntary work   6.2 Healthy / unhealthy living

Theme 2 – Local, national, international and global areas of interest, Unit 7 – Global issues
7.1 Environment   7.2 Poverty / homelessness

Theme 2 – Local, national, international and global areas of interest, Unit 8 – Travel and tourism
8.1 Holidays and travel   8.2 Regions of Germany

Introducing AQA GCSE German

Reading • Learning vocabulary • Writing • Translation skills • Building grammar knowledge • Listening • Dealing with authentic texts • Speaking

Understanding how the specification works

The AQA GCSE German specification is divided into three main subject areas, called **Themes**. This book is divided up in the same way, with colour-coding to help you know where you are.

Identity and culture • Local, national, international and global areas of interest • Current and future study and employment

Each Theme is divided into four **Topics**, making a total of twelve Topics to study during the course. The exam is divided up according to the four **Language Skills**: Listening, Speaking, Reading and Writing. Each one of these has its own separate exam, in the form of an end-of-course paper.

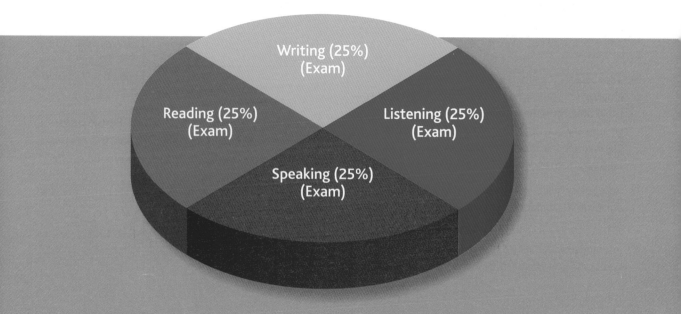

Writing (25%) (Exam) • Reading (25%) (Exam) • Listening (25%) (Exam) • Speaking (25%) (Exam)

Key Stage 3 revision

The Key Stage 3 revision section at the beginning of the book provides an opportunity to recap and practise important grammar and vocabulary from Key Stage 3.

📖 Reading

The Student Book contains plenty of German reading material on the themes and topics included within the specification. The activities that follow the reading passages help develop your comprehension skills so that you can access unfamiliar texts in the future.

🎧 Listening

Activities with a listening icon next to them help you to improve listening comprehension skills. The audio can be accessed through Kerboodle or on the Audio CDs accompanying the course.

🗫 Speaking

The speaking activities are designed to build your confidence in speaking German and to practise using the vocabulary you've learned in the spread or unit. There are also practice role plays and photo card activities throughout the book.

✏️ Writing

The writing icon indicates an activity that will help you to use the language you've learned to build sentences and paragraphs of written German.

🅣 Translation

Translation activities throughout the book develop your ability to tackle translation tasks.

🅥 Learning vocabulary

Vocabulary support is provided in various ways throughout the book and on the accompanying Kerboodle:

- ◼ Vocabulary lists – for each section where new language is introduced, there is a list of useful words that come up in the tasks. Vocabulary in grey is vocabulary that appears in the AQA GCSE 2016 German specification. There are also recordings to help you learn to pronounce each word correctly.

- ◼ Vocabulary tasks – vocabulary activities help to build the vocabulary required in each topic of the specification.

- ◼ Interactive activities – the vocabulary builder on Kerboodle provides activities with instant feedback.*

- ◼ Glossary – the glossary at the back combines the vocabulary from the vocabulary pages. Again, specification vocab is indicated in grey.

🅖 Building grammar knowledge

Understanding grammar is key to building your own phrases. *AQA GCSE German* helps you to consolidate your grammar knowledge in a logical way.

- ◼ Grammar boxes outline key grammar points with accompanying activities on the page to put theory into practice.

> #### Using *haben* and *sein* in the present tense
> The verbs *haben* (to have) and *sein* (to be) are key verbs to know. They are irregular verbs
>
> *Grammatik*

- ◼ Grammar boxes for the subsidiary grammar points can be found on the Grammar practice pages along with practice activities.

- ◼ Worksheets on the Kerboodle for each main and subsidiary grammar point help to reinforce understanding.*

- ◼ Interactive activities on the Kerboodle provide further consolidation with instant feedback.*

- ◼ There is a grammar section at the back of the Student Book, to refer to whenever you need to.

Language structure boxes

These tables provide you with the building blocks you need to construct sentences for speaking and writing.

Ein Handy ist für mich Ich finde mein Handy	wichtig / nötig / toll,	denn	ich ka ich hö
Ja, es gibt auch Probleme,	denn	ich / man soll nicht d man muss auch aktiv	
Mein altes Handy war altmodisch /		und ich konnte	(nur) keine

Accessing Foundation Student Book pages

Where you see this link icon in your book, this means you can access Groundwork pages on Kerboodle, offering extra activities and grammar practice.

> 🔗
>
> 4.1 Groundwork is available in the Foundation book.

Developing learning strategies

Strategy boxes are provided throughout the book to develop the skills required for effective language learning. These are supported by further activities on Kerboodle.*

> ### Understanding questions in German
>
> It's useful if you have a good grasp of the key German question words, so that you know what sort of information is being asked for in reading or listening activities.
>
> Here are the main ones and examples of the types

Strategie

Ongoing revision opportunities

There are regular revision opportunities throughout the book in the five test and revise sections. Each section includes:

- Reading and listening activities
- Writing and translation activities
- Speaking role plays and photo cards

Dictionary skills

At the beginning of each theme there is a page of activities to help you acquire dictionary skills.

Kerboodle offers a range of products to help engage teachers and students alike. Kerboodle for *AQA GCSE German* includes resources focused on developing key grammar, vocabulary, listening, reading, speaking, translation and writing skills. Kerboodle resources include videos of native speakers, self-marking tests, listening activities with downloadable transcripts, interactive vocabulary builders, practice questions and comprehensive teacher support.*

Our *AQA GCSE German* Kerboodle resources are accompanied by online interactive versions of the Student Books. All your Kerboodle resources are embedded to open directly from the book page.

Find out more at www.kerboodle.com.

*These resources are not part of the AQA approval process.

Nouns

The gender of nouns

There are three genders in German: masculine, feminine and neuter.

It's best to try to learn any new nouns you encounter with their gender (and with their plural form), but there are also a few guidelines to help you work out genders. Though there are also exceptions, knowing these general guidelines will help.

Have a look at these examples:

masculine	example	feminine	example	neuter	example
	der / ein		*die / eine*		*das / ein*
male people	*Mann*	female people	*Frau*	most countries	*Deutschland*
seasons	*Sommer*	most fruits	*Erdbeere*	most metals	*Gold*
months	*Mai*	most trees	*Eiche*	infinitive nouns	*Lesen*
days	*Freitag*	-*ung* endings	*Zeitung*	-*chen* endings	*Mädchen*
compass points	*Norden*	-*heit* endings	*Freiheit*	-*lein* endings	*Fräulein*
most -*en* endings	*Morgen*	-*keit* endings	*Wirklichkeit*	most foreign words	*Hotel*
-*ing* endings	*Frühling*	-*schaft* endings	*Freundschaft*	most *Ge-* nouns	*Geschenk*
-*ig* endings	*König*	-*ei* endings	*Bäckerei*		
		-*tät* endings	*Aktivität*		
		-*ik* endings	*Musik*		
		-*in* endings	*Lehrerin*		
		many -*e* endings	*Farbe*		

1 Work out the gender of the words. Then check your answers using a dictionary.

1 Tante
2 Essen
3 Donnerstag
4 Banane
5 Winter
6 Schwester
7 Kaninchen
8 Brötchen
9 Großvater
10 Blume
11 Restaurant
12 Pflaume
13 Oktober
14 Süßigkeit
15 Tochter
16 Mittwoch
17 Stiefvater
18 Schwimmen
19 Gemüse
20 Einladung

Singular and plural nouns

You will meet most nouns in the singular form with *der / die / das* in front to show their gender.

If you want to use a noun in the plural form (more than one), you'll need to know, or check, how that noun changes in the plural. Remember that the plural form will be shown in brackets after the noun: *Banane (-n) / Tische (-e) / Lehrer (–)*. The last of these indicates no change in the plural.

Unlike English, where we usually just put an **s** on the end of the noun (house**s** / dog**s** / brother**s**), German has several different ways of making plurals.

Remember that a few nouns are always plural, because of what they mean: *Eltern* (parents), *Leute* (people)

There are also some nouns which, because of what they mean, will not be used in the plural. Here are a few which you might use: *Obst* (fruit), *Wetter* (weather), *Gepäck* (luggage)

Here are some guidelines to help you get plural forms right:

Masculine
- A large group of masculine nouns add **-e** in the plural: *Tage, Monate*
- A lot add an umlaut and an **-e**: *Söhne, Füße, Gäste*
- A few add an umlaut and **-er**: *Männer, Wälder*
- Masculine nouns with **-er** or **-el** endings don't change: *Finger, Lehrer, Schlüssel*
- A few add an umlaut only: *Vögel, Brüder, Gärten*

Feminine
- A very large number of feminine nouns form their plural with **-n** or **-en**: *Frauen, Familien, Lampen*
- A few add an umlaut and **-e**: *Hände, Städte*
- Nouns ending in **-in** (feminine people) form their plural with **-nen**: *Lehrerinnen, Schülerinnen*
- *Words ending in **-heit** / **-keit** / **-ung** / **-schaft** all add **-en**: *Krankheiten, Schwierigkeiten, Zeitungen, Freundschaften*

Neuter
- Some common neuter nouns add **-er**: *Bilder, Lichter, Kleider*
- Some add an umlaut and **-er**: *Länder, Häuser*
- Those ending in **-er** / **-el** / **-en** don't change, unless an umlaut can be added: *Fenster, Mädchen, Vögel*
- Neuter nouns made from verbs have no plural
- Words of foreign origin (loan words) usually add **-s**: *Sofas, Büros, Kinos*

2 Work with a partner. Write the words in activity 1 in the plural. (One word doesn't have a plural!)

Articles and the case system

Definite and indefinite articles

The **definite articles** (the) in German are **der** / **die** / **das** in the singular. Decide the right word by looking at the gender of the noun: *der Mann* (m), *die Frau* (f), *das Haus* (n). See page 10 for more on genders.

When these nouns are plural, the article is *die*: *die Männer, die Frauen, die Häuser*. See page 10 for more on the plural forms of nouns.

The **indefinite articles** (a / an) in German are **ein** / **eine** / **ein**: *ein Mann* (m), *eine Frau* (f), *ein Haus* (n)

There is obviously no plural of *ein* / *eine* / *ein*, but note the plural endings with *kein* (no / not a): *keine Männer, keine Frauen, keine Häuser*

3 Write the correct definite article for the nouns. You may need to check any genders you're not sure of. Also watch out for changes to the noun which mean it's plural – there are three plurals in this activity (one is underlined for you).

1 … Hund
2 … Haus
3 … <u>Freunde</u>
4 … Klasse
5 … Familie
6 … Garten
7 … Lehrerinnen
8 … Stuhl
9 … Hausaufgaben
10 … Pferd

4 Write the correct indefinite article for the nouns. All the words are singular.

1 … Apfel
2 … Buch
3 … Schultasche
4 … Bruder
5 … Zimmer
6 … Fernseher
7 … Fußballspiel
8 … Instrument
9 … Postkarte
10 … Schule

5 These words are plural. Write the missing word (*keine* or a number word). Then translate the words into English.

Beispiele: … Männer (5) – fünf Männer
… Kinder (0) – keine Kinder

1 … Bücher (7)
2 … Tassen (0)
3 … Schüler (2)
4 … Geschäfte (0)
5 … Stunden (4)
6 … Schlafzimmer (3)
7 … Lehrer (50)
8 … Großeltern (0)
9 … Söhne (2)
10 … Kleider (0)

The case system: nominative and accusative

Unlike English, where the words for 'the / a / an' are always the same, the German articles change according to how they are used in a sentence. This is called the case.

There are four cases in German, and each one has at least one main use.

The **nominative** is used for the subject of the sentence (the person doing the action of the verb).

The **accusative** is used for the direct object in a sentence (the person / thing which has the action done to it).

Remember that some **prepositions** are followed by the accusative case too. See page 180.

The case system: genitive and dative

The **genitive** case is used to express 'of' / possession / belonging (my dad's car / my sister's boyfriend), which we mentally rephrase to make them the car **of my dad** / the boyfriend **of my sister** in German: *das Auto meines Vaters, der Freund meiner Schwester.*

The **dative** case is often used to express the idea of **to / for someone**. This is called an indirect object. In the sentence 'He buys his mother flowers.' **his mother** actually means **for his mother**, so will be dative / the indirect object.

Some verbs are also used with the dative. There is often (but not always) an easy way of recognising these. If they are words which can logically have the word '**to**' added in English, they will probably be used with the dative case, e.g. *sagen* (to say **to**), *geben* (to give **to**), *erklären* (to explain **to**), *zeigen* (to show **to**), *reichen* (to pass **to** / hand **to**), *schicken* / *senden* (to send **to**)

Remember that some **prepositions** are also followed by the dative and some by the genitive case. See pages 180 & 181.

6 Underline and label the subject / nominative and the direct object / accusative noun in the sentences.

Beispiel: Mein Bruder kauft ein Auto.

subject / nominative   direct object / accusative

1 Die Schule hat einen Tennisplatz.
2 Meine Freundin hat keine Brüder.
3 Der Hund beißt den Briefträger.
4 Das Mädchen isst einen Apfel.
5 Die Schülerin hat keinen Bleistift.
6 Mein Onkel schickt eine Postkarte.
7 Der Arzt kauft ein Haus in Leeds.
8 Die Kinder machen die Hausaufgaben.

7 Complete the sentences with the correct form of *der / die / das* (1–5) and *ein / eine / ein* (6–10).

1 … Haus hat … schönsten Garten.
2 … Frau kauft … blaue Kleid.
3 … Katze sieht … Maus.
4 … Schülerinnen haben … Bücher.
5 … Mann trägt … Koffer.
6 Ich habe … Bruder.
7 Wir essen … Eis.
8 Bekommst du … Geschenk?
9 Max hat heute … Fußballspiel.
10 Hast du … Computer?

8 Identify the nouns that would use the genitive or dative when translated into German.

Example: My brother's friend is sporty. (the friend of my brother, so genitive)

1 My sister's house is enormous.
2 I'm sending my friend a birthday card.
3 The teacher gives the pupils too much homework.
4 His dad's new car is an Audi.
5 The professor shows the students an interesting experiment.

9 Complete the German translations of the sentences in activity 8 by adding the missing nouns in the genitive or dative.

1 Das Haus … ist riesengroß.
2 Ich schicke … eine Geburtstagskarte.
3 Der Lehrer gibt … zu viele Hausaufgaben.
4 Das neue Auto … ist eine Audi.
5 Der Professor zeigt … ein interessantes Experiment.

The full case system

Revise how the whole case system looks together.

The best advice is to learn it as soon as you can – knowing it will make a huge difference to the quality of your spoken and written German, and not knowing it means lots of avoidable errors. Try setting it to a tune, recording it and listening to it on your phone.

The good news is that if you know the *der / die / das* system, the *ein / eine / ein* one follows almost exactly the same pattern.

	masculine	feminine	neuter	plural
nominative	der	die	das	die
accusative	**den**	die	das	die
genitive	des + -s	der	des + -s	der
dative	dem	der	dem	den + -n

	masculine	feminine	neuter	plural
nominative	ein	eine	ein	keine
accusative	**einen**	eine	ein	keine
genitive	eines + -s	einer	eines + -s	keiner
dative	einem	einer	einem	keinen + -n

10 Identify which cases have been used with the definite and indefinite articles. Write N (nominative), A (accusative), G (genitive) or D (dative) above them.

1 Der Tisch ist braun.
2 Der Junge bestellt eine Tasse Kaffee.
3 Die Band einer Freundin ist toll.
4 Der Hund meiner Tante ist sehr klein.
5 Die Frau gibt meiner Mutter einen Pullover.
6 Die Wohnung meines Großvaters ist klein.
7 Hat dein Bruder ein Handy?
8 Die Schüler tragen eine Uniform.
9 Das Mädchen zeigt den Touristen das Rathaus.
10 Das Kleid des Mädchens ist rot.

11 Complete the sentences with the correct form of *der / die / das* (1–5) and *ein / eine / ein* (6–10).

1 … Junge sieht … Film.
2 … Buch … Lehrerin ist hier.
3 … Bahnhof ist ziemlich weit weg.
4 … Hausaufgaben … Schülers sind zu Hause.
5 … Mann kauft … Auto.
6 Das ist … gute Idee.
7 Hast du … Schwester oder … Bruder?
8 Er trinkt … Bier und isst … Apfel.
9 … Zug kommt in zwei Minuten.
10 Wir haben … große Familie.

12 Translate the sentences into German.

1 My name is Anna. My mum is called Jane.
2 I have a brother and two sisters.
3 We also have a dog.
4 My family's house is in a village.
5 My parents love the house and the garden.
6 I help my mum in the garden.
7 The rooms in the house are quite small.
8 My dad's car is always dirty.
9 My brother sometimes washes the car.
10 I often take the dog for a walk. (*spazieren gehen mit*)

Verbs

Verbs hold together everything that you say and write, making clear who does particular actions and in which time frame. You can't make a sentence without a verb.

This section revises the basics of verbs in the present tense, so that you can begin the course with confidence. For more information about verbs and tenses, see the main grammar section on page 176.

Regular / weak verbs in the present tense form according to a clear pattern and show a characteristic ending for each person of the verb.

Form regular present tenses by removing **-en** from the infinitive and then adding the endings shown below.

The verb *machen* (to do / make) looks like this:

ich mach**e**	wir mach**en**
du mach**st**	ihr mach**t**
er / sie / es mach**t**	sie / Sie mach**en**

Irregular / strong verbs follow the same process BUT, in the *du / er / sie / es* forms the vowel sound changes in the middle of the verb. The endings are the same as for regular verbs.

There are three ways for the vowel change to happen: the addition of an umlaut (*fahren* – *fährst*), the addition of an extra vowel (*sehen* – *siehst*) or the replacement of the original vowel with another one (*geben* – *gibst*).

Remember that the change only happens in the two forms mentioned, and the plurals follow the regular pattern.

change *a > ä*	change *e > ie*	change *e > i*
ich fahre	ich sehe	ich gebe
du f**ä**hrst	du s**ie**hst	du g**i**bst
er / sie / es f**ä**hrt	er / sie / es s**ie**ht	er / sie / es g**i**bt

Check the verb tables on page 192 to see what happens to other irregular verbs in the present tense.

Sein (to be) and **haben (to have)** are perhaps the verbs we use most, and they are irregular, so worth learning early.

sein	haben
ich bin	ich habe
du bist	du hast
er / sie / es ist	er / sie / es hat
wir sind	wir haben
ihr seid	ihr habt
sie / Sie sind	sie / Sie haben

13 Complete the sentences with the correct form of the regular / weak verb given in brackets.

1 Ich … gern Tennis. (*spielen*)
2 Wir … die Musik. (*hören*)
3 Er … seine Hausaufgaben. (*machen*)
4 Die Jungen … laut. (*lachen*)
5 … du gern Deutsch? (*lernen*)

14 Complete the sentences with the correct form of the irregular / strong verb given in brackets.

1 Wir … nach Spanien. (*fahren*)
2 Meine Mutter … mir Taschengeld. (*geben*)
3 Ich … keine Filme. (*sehen*)
4 Was … du zum Frühstück? (*essen*)
5 … Sie Italienisch, Frau Dunst? (*sprechen*)

15 Translate the sentences into German. Use the correct forms of *haben* or *sein*.

1 My uncle is very tall and has blond hair.
2 She is very pretty and is 18.
3 At school we have eight lessons a day.
4 That's too much for me!
5 I am tired and I have too much homework.
6 Do you have my exercise book, Miss Smith?
7 Do you have a new mobile phone? (*du* form)
8 Are you intelligent? (*du* form)
9 There are four of us in the family. (We are four …)
10 My town is not very interesting.

Numbers and dates

Numbers

Numbers are very logical in German, and it's best to revise them in three stages.

Stage 1: Start with the numbers 1–12, which you should just learn if you haven't done so already.

1 *eins*	4 *vier*	7 *sieben*	10 *zehn*
2 *zwei*	5 *fünf*	8 *acht*	11 *elf*
3 *drei*	6 *sechs*	9 *neun*	12 *zwölf*

Stage 2: Once you have mastered these basics, the rest is easy and is done by **combining** what you already know. So 13 = 3+10 > *dreizehn*. The other numbers up to 19 follow this pattern: *vierzehn, fünfzehn, sechzehn, siebzehn, achtzehn, neunzehn.* Though note that with *sechzehn* and *siebzehn,* the *s* from *sechs* and the *en* from *sieben* have been dropped.

The combining process continues throughout the formation of German numbers. Remember the nursery rhyme about 'four and twenty blackbirds', as this will remind you that the combining happens the opposite way round to that in English. The units and tens are joined by **und** and numbers are written as **one word**.

21	*ein**und**zwanzig*	26	*sechs**und**zwanzig*
22	*zwei**und**zwanzig*	27	*sieben**und**zwanzig*
23	*drei**und**zwanzig*	28	*acht**und**zwanzig*
24	*vier**und**zwanzig*	29	*neun**und**zwanzig*
25	*fünf**und**zwanzig*		

Stage 3: After this, you only need to know the tens numbers to make any number you need up to 100 and beyond. For example, *einundzwanzig* (21), *vierhundertneunundneuzig* (499).

30	*dreißig*	70	*siebzig*
40	*vierzig*	80	*achtzig*
50	*fünfzig*	90	*neunzig*
60	*sechzig*	100	*hundert*

16 Write the numbers as German words.

1	7	6	89
2	19	7	105
3	26	8	275
4	33	9	515
5	58	10	999

Dates

Remember the days of the week: *Montag, Dienstag, Mittwoch, Donnerstag, Freitag, Samstag, Sonntag.*

And the months of the year: *Januar, Februar, März, April, Mai, Juni, Juli, August, September, Oktober, November, Dezember.*

Days and months are all masculine nouns and are always written with a capital letter.

To say dates, you need also to adapt the basic numbers to say 2nd / 6th / 28th etc. The way to do this, for numbers up to and including 19, is to add **-te** to the end of the number (*der elf**te** Januar, der sech**ste** Juni*), and for numbers from 20 onwards, add **-ste** to the end of the number (*der achtundzwanzig**ste** September, der dreißig**ste** März*). When we write a date in German with digits, we add a full stop, eg. *der 4. März.*

Note that there are a couple of important exceptions: *erste* (first), *dritte* (third) and *siebte* (seventh).

To say **on a particular day**, for example to say your birthday, you need to use **am** (on the) and add an **-n** to the end of the number: *Ich habe **am** vierten März Geburtstag.*

17 Write the dates in German in full.

Beispiel: 14th February – der vierzehnte Februar
(der 14. Februar)

1   1st April
2   9th May
3   17th July
4   20th August
5   29th October
6   31st December

18 Write the dates in German in full.

Beispiel: on 26th June – am
sechsundzwangisten Juni

1   on 10th January
2   on 20th March
3   on 21st April
4   on 1st June
5   on 30th September
6   on 11th November

① Identity and culture

1 Me, my family and friends

1.1 F In meiner Familie
- Using regular and irregular verbs in the present tense
- Looking for clues when listening

1.1 H Beziehungen zu Familie und Freunden
- Using reflexive verbs
- Learning to distinguish word types

1.2 F Heiraten oder nicht?
- Using the future tense
- Understanding questions in German

1.2 H Glücklich ohne Ehe?
- Using comparative and superlative adjectives
- Spotting patterns in German and English

2 Technology in everyday life

2.1 F Bist du Facebook-Fan?
- Using direct and indirect object pronouns
- Spotting grammatical signposts

2.1 H Sicherheit im Internet
- Deciding when to use *wann*, *wenn* and *als*
- Making the most of near-cognates

2.2 F Trends in der mobilen Handywelt
- Using the imperfect tense
- Thinking creatively in speaking

2.2 H Handys – das Gute, das Schlechte und das Hässliche
- Using the imperfect tense
- Achieving a fluent English translation

3 Free-time activities

3.1 F Musikfan oder Filmfreak?
- Using separable verbs in the perfect tense
- Listening for key information

3.1 H Leinwand oder Flimmerkiste?
- Using separable and reflexive verbs in the perfect tense
- Working out the meaning of new words

3.2 F Wo wollen wir essen?
- Revising the present tense
- Asking for clarification

3.2 H Essen fassen!
- Using the correct word order with adverbial phrases
- Spotting more common patterns in German / English words

3.3 F Sport – für alle?
- Using separable and reflexive verbs in the future tense
- Listening for essential words

3.3 H Hast du Mumm?
- Revising the different words for 'when'
- Spotting feminine nouns

4 Customs and festivals

4.1 F Hurra! Die Tradition ist da!
- Using adjectives as nouns
- Paraphrasing when speaking

4.1 H Bräuche braucht das Land
- Revising the verb as second idea in the sentence
- Using infinitives as nouns

4.2 F Das muss gefeiert werden!
- Revising the perfect tense II
- Spotting different words used to express the same idea

4.2 H Feste feiern, wie sie fallen
- Using personal pronouns
- Using the context when listening

Catchwords

Use your dictionary

Trawl through your dictionary entry by entry if you like, but those in the know use the **catchwords** at the top of each page to locate the correct page quickly.

At the top of the page in your dictionary are the first and last words on the two pages – the catchwords or guidewords. They help you to find words faster.

On these two pages you'll find any word which is in alphabetical order between *kitzlig* and *Kloster*.

On these pages:

- you'll find *Klang*
- you won't find *Klugheit*.

---

kitzlig   **klauen**

kitzlig *adjective*
  ticklish
die **Kiwi** (*plural die* **Kiwis**)
  kiwi fruit
klagen *verb* (*perfect* **hat geklagt**)
  to complain
die **Klammer** (*plural die* **Klammern**)
  1 **peg** (*for washing*)
  2 **grip** (*for hair*)
  3 **bracket**

die **Klarinette** (*plural die* **Klarinetten**)
  clarinet
  Annika spielt Klarinette. Annika plays the clarinet.
♂ die **Klasse** (*plural die* **Klassen**)
  1 **class**
     Sie reist immer erster Klasse. She always travels first class.
  2 **year**
     Ich gehe in die sechste Klasse. I'm in year six.

Klavier   **Kloster**

♂ das **Klavier** (*plural die* **Klaviere**)
  piano
  Dennis spielt Klavier. Dennis plays the piano.
kleben *verb* (*perfect* **hat geklebt**)
  1 **to stick**
  2 **to glue**
  3 **jemandem eine kleben** (*informal*) to belt somebody
klebrig *adjective*
  sticky

klettern *verb* (*perfect* **ist geklettert**)
  to climb
  Sie kletterten auf den Baum. They climbed the tree.
der **Klick** (*plural die* **Klicks**)
  click (*with mouse*)
das **Klicken**
  click (*noise*)
der **Klient** (*plural die* **Klienten**)
  client (*male*)

German-English

---

1 Two pages of the dictionary

- Would you find the words on the two pages of the dictionary shown above?
- Look up the words and translate them into English.

	ja / nein	Englisch
Beispiel: Klingel	ja	bell
1 Klatsch		
2 Knall		
3 Kirsche		
4 Klagen		
5 Klippe		

2 Break the code!

- Break the code by putting the letters of each word in alphabetical order to make a German word. The first one has been done for you.
- Now look up the German words in your dictionary. What do they mean in English? Use the catchwords to help you locate the correct dictionary page.

	Deutsch	Englisch
Beispiel: REBA	aber	but
1 NINGEB		
2 SNIET		
3 TROD		
4 ETBE		

Tip

Use the catchwords to help you locate the correct dictionary page!

1.1 F   In meiner Familie

1 **V** Finde die Paare. Schreib zwei Listen: maskuline Wörter (der / ein) und feminine Wörter (die / eine).

Find the pairs. Write two lists: masculine words (der / ein) and feminine words (die / eine).

| Großmutter | Partner | Onkel | Tante | Cousine |
| Vater | Oma | Frau | Mutter | Witwe |

| aunt | grandmother | partner (masculine) | cousin (feminine) |
| father | widow | uncle | mother | gran / granny | woman / wife |

2 📖 Read the texts. Petra and her brother Moritz are describing their family. Choose the five correct statements.

Hallo! Ich stelle mich vor. Ich heiße Petra und ich wohne in Bremen, in Norddeutschland. Wir sind zu dritt in der Familie. Ich habe einen Zwillingsbruder, der Moritz heißt, aber wir sind keine traditionelle Familie. Meine Eltern sind geschieden und wir wohnen nur mit Mutti zusammen. Mein Vater hat eine neue Frau und ich sehe ihn nicht so oft, nur in den Schulferien. Das ist aber kein Problem. Ich habe ein sehr gutes Verhältnis zu meiner Mutter. Sie ist eine tolle Frau und sehr liebevoll. Obwohl sie viel arbeitet, hat sie immer Zeit für uns.

Mutti hat einen neuen Partner, der Richard heißt und auch in Bremen wohnt. Meine Schwester und ich verstehen uns gut mit Richard und wir machen viel zusammen. Das gefällt mir. Meine Mutter sieht immer glücklich aus, wenn Richard da ist. Wir haben auch eine Großmutter, die Witwe ist. Meine Oma wohnt nicht weit weg von uns und kommt oft vorbei, um uns zu sehen. Ich liebe sie sehr und spreche mit ihr über alles.

Petra

Moritz

1   Petra has a younger brother.
2   Petra and her brother live with their mother.
3   Petra's father has remarried.
4   Petra is very upset that she sees so little of her father.
5   Moritz and Petra get on well with Richard.
6   Moritz is happy that his mother has a new partner.
7   Their grandmother is married.
8   Moritz has a close relationship with his grandmother.

3 🎧 Listen to three young people talking about family life and relationships. Choose the correct answer.

1   Lea is **15 / 16** years old.
2   Lea lives with **one parent and her brother / both parents and her brother**.
3   Lea thinks her family life is **normal / unusual**.
4   Sven has **one sister / no siblings**.
5   Sven's parents are **divorced / separated**.
6   Sven would like to **live in Berlin / see his father more**.
7   Olivia considers herself **lucky / special**.
8   Olivia's parents are **elderly / healthy**.
9   Olivia **often / rarely** does things with her family.

Looking for clues when listening

You are not expected to understand every single word in a recording. Read the questions carefully first so that you know the context.

If unfamiliar words occur, focus on 'surrounding' key words which you **do** know. For example, even if you don't recognize *Familiengemeinschaft* (family community / family group), you will know the *Familie-* part of the word and also surrounding words like *zusammen*, *Bruder* and *Eltern*, which will help you.

Challenge: When you do activity 3, try out this tactic and start working out what words might mean.

Strategie

4 **G** Complete the sentences with the correct verb form. Do you need *geben* (to give), *fahren* (to go / travel) or *sehen* (to see)?

1 Wir … nach Berlin.
2 Es … vier Personen in der Familie.
3 Ich … meinen Vater am Samstag.
4 Mein Vater … mit.
5 … du oft deinen Großvater?
6 Ich … mit meiner Schwester Rad.
7 Er … seiner Tante ein Geschenk.
8 … du in die Stadt?
9 Meine Eltern … mir Taschengeld.
10 Mein Freund … oft Filme.

5 **T** Translate the paragraph into English.

> Mein bester Freund, Peter, wohnt nicht weit weg von mir. Jeden Morgen gehen wir zusammen zur Schule und sind in derselben Klasse. Wir verstehen uns gut und spielen gern Fußball im Park. Peter hat keine Geschwister.

6 Partnerarbeit. Stellt Fragen über die Familie. Dann tauscht die Rollen.

Work with a partner. Ask questions about their family. Then swap roles.

Wie heißt du?
Wie alt bist du?
Wo wohnst du?
Wie viele Personen gibt es in deiner Familie?
Wer sind sie?
Wie alt ist dein Bruder / deine Schwester? Wie heißt er / sie?
Wie alt sind deine Eltern / Brüder / Schwestern? Wie heißen sie?
Hast du Großeltern? Wie alt sind sie? Wo wohnen sie?

7 Lies noch einmal die Fragen in Aufgabe 6 und beantworte sie in einem Absatz mit dem Titel „Meine Familie und ich".

Read the questions in activity 6 again and write your answers in a paragraph with the title *Meine Familie und ich*.

In meiner Familie Bei mir zu Hause Bei uns	gibt es	vier Personen.
Es gibt	meinen Vater / Bruder / Stiefbruder / Halbbruder / Großvater (Opa) / Onkel. meine Mutter / Schwester / Tante / Großmutter (Oma) / Stiefschwester.	
Mein Vater (Vati) Meine Mutter (Mutti)	ist heißt wohnt	… Jahre alt. John / Jenny. in London / Manchester.
Meine Eltern Meine Großeltern	sind leben	getrennt / geschieden.
Mein Bruder / Onkel Meine Schwester / Tante	ist heißt	… Jahre alt. ledig / verheiratet / verlobt. Dan / Debbie.

Grammatik *page 184*

Using regular and irregular verbs in the present tense

Many verbs in German follow a **regular pattern** in the present tense. For example, *wohnen* (to live): *ich wohne, du wohnst, er / sie / es wohnt, wir wohnen, ihr wohnt, sie / Sie wohnen*.

Most **irregular** verbs have the same endings as regular verbs, but the vowel sound changes in the *du* and the *er / sie / es* forms. For example, *fahren* (to go / travel): *ich fahre, du fährst, er / sie / es fährt, wir fahren, ihr fahrt, sie / Sie fahren*.

There are three ways for the vowel sound to be changed:
• the original vowel is replaced by a different one (*geben – gibt*)
• an umlaut is added to the vowel (*fahren – fährt*)
• a second vowel is added to the original one (*sehen – sieht*).

Remember that this only happens in the *du* and the *er / sie / es* forms. The other forms follow the usual pattern.

Also learn how to use reflexive and separable verbs. See page 26.

Beziehungen zu Familie und Freunden

1 📖 Lies die Texte und beantworte die Fragen.

Ich habe Glück, dass ich ein ruhiges Familienleben habe und dass ich ganz zufrieden bin. Meine Eltern leben glücklich zusammen und ich habe ein gutes Verhältnis zu beiden Elternteilen. Mit meiner Mutter kann ich über alles sprechen, was ich sehr positiv finde. Wir interessieren uns beide für Musik und spielen manchmal zusammen Geige. Mein Vater ist ganz zuverlässig und kann dann und wann etwas streng sein, aber ich weiß, er will nur mein Bestes. **Tobias (15)**

Wir haben zu Hause ständig Krach und die Atmosphäre ist oft ganz angespannt. Das finde ich schwierig, besonders wenn ich schon unter Schulstress leide. Meine Eltern sind zwar nicht getrennt oder geschieden, aber sie streiten sich fast täglich und das ist unerträglich für mich. Ich muss zugeben, ich habe manchmal Angst, dass ihre Ehe in die Brüche geht. Aus diesem Grund sind meine Freunde für mich absolut notwendig und ehrlich gesagt, ich bin lieber bei meinen Freunden als zu Hause. Ich kann mich auf sie verlassen und fühle mich entspannter, wenn ich mit ihnen zusammen bin. **Marko (14)**

Meine Eltern sind seit langem geschieden und ich wohne mit meiner Mutter, ihrem neuen Mann und meiner Stiefschwester, Katja, zusammen. Unser Verhältnis ist meistens gut und es freut mich sehr, dass meine Mutter nicht mehr allein ist. Katja ist zwei Jahre älter als ich und wir kommen meistens sehr gut miteinander aus. Das einzige Problem ist, dass Katja oft raucht und Alkohol trinkt, wenn wir abends ausgehen, und ich will nicht mitmachen. Dann meckert sie und sagt, dass ich eine Miesmacherin bin. Ich finde das gemein von ihr und es verdirbt unsere Freundschaft. **Sabine (16)**

Krach haben – to have an argument / a row
angespannt – tense
in die Brüche gehen – to break up
meckern – to moan
die Miesmacherin – spoilsport (f)

Wer …

1 macht sich Sorgen über seine Eltern?
2 findet seinen Vater manchmal streng?
3 hat ein sehr glückliches Familienleben?
4 hat dasselbe Hobby wie ein Elternteil?
5 hängt sehr von Freunden ab?
6 hat eine Stiefschwester?
7 spielt Geige?
8 will schlechte Angewohnheiten vermeiden?

2a 🎧 Listen to Barbara talking about her friends. Complete the sentences in English.

1 Barbara can't imagine …
2 Her relationship with her family is …
3 Friends are important to her because … and …
4 With her friends Barbara sometimes … and …
5 She turns to her friends when …
6 There are some things she would rather …
7 Problems among friends happen when …
8 These problems can be dealt with by …

2b 🎧 Hör noch einmal zu. Wie sagt man auf Deutsch …?

1 to imagine
2 relationship
3 group of friends
4 solution
5 to share
6 to admit
7 easy
8 jealous

3 **G** **T** Complete the sentences with the correct form of the verb and reflexive pronoun given in brackets. Then translate the sentences into English.

1 Ich … … meistens gut mit meiner Mutter. (*sich verstehen*)
2 Er … … oft mit seinen Geschwistern. (*sich streiten*)
3 … du … für Filme? (*sich interessieren*)
4 Mein Vater und ich … … sehr gut. (*sich verstehen*)
5 Seine Eltern … … (*sich trennen*)
6 Ich … … total auf meine Freunde. (*sich verlassen*)
7 … ihr … heute abend? (*sich treffen*)
8 Mein Onkel … … auf das Wochenende. (*sich freuen*)

4 **T** Translate the paragraph into English.

> Man sagt oft, dass Freunde die Familie sind, die man sich selber aussucht. Aber ich denke, dass Freunde wie Schuhe sind. Wenn man jung ist, will man so viele wie möglich haben und, wenn man älter wird, lernt man, dass man sich immer mit den gleichen am wohlsten fühlt.

5 **T** Translate the paragraph into German.

> I have a good circle of friends and friends are very important to me. We get on well because we have lots in common. I love my parents but they sometimes get on my nerves and we argue because they are too strict and don't give me enough freedom.

6 Gruppenarbeit. Sprich eine Minute lang über deine Familienverhältnisse. Gib so viele Infos wie möglich.

Ich verstehe mich (meistens / nicht / sehr) gut mit	meinem Bruder / Vater / Halbbruder, meiner Mutter / Schwester / Stiefschwester,		
Ich streite mich (nicht) oft mit			
Ich komme mit	meinem Bruder / meiner Mutter / meinen Geschwistern / Eltern	(nicht / sehr) gut	aus,
weil / da	er / sie er / sie	immer Zeit für mich hat. (so / zu / sehr) streng / laut / faul / nervig ist. mir auf die Nerven geht.		
	sie	immer freundlich / nett / hilfsbereit sind.		
denn ich	habe keine Freiheit / muss immer im Haushalt helfen / darf nur am Wochenende ausgehen.		
denn er / sie	ist zu streng / gibt mir keine Freiheit / mag meine Freunde nicht / hilft mir mit Hausaufgaben / hat dieselben Interessen wie ich.		

7 Schreib den Text deiner Präsentation mit dem Titel „Familienverhältnisse". Erkläre deine Ideen und gib Gründe, indem du „da" / „weil" / „denn" verwendest. Schreib etwa 100 Wörter.

Grammatik page 183

Using reflexive verbs

These are verbs which have an extra part, called the reflexive pronoun, which relates to the person of the verb. For example, *sich waschen* (to get washed):

ich wasche **mich**	wir waschen **uns**
du wäschst **dich**	ihr wascht **euch**
er / sie / es wäscht **sich**	sie / Sie waschen **sich**

Other reflexive verbs follow the same pattern:
*Ich kümmere **mich** um …* (I look after …)
*Er interessiert **sich** für …* (He is interested in …)
Remember that reflexive pronouns in German cannot always be translated using 'myself', 'yourself', etc.
In the *wir* form, the reflexive pronoun may be used to express 'each other'. So *wir sehen uns.* may mean 'We see ourselves.', but is more likely to mean 'We see each other.'.

Also learn how to use possessive adjectives in the nominative, accusative and dative cases. See page 26.

Learning to distinguish word types

It's useful to be able to spot whether a word is a noun, a verb or an adjective.

German nouns always start with a capital letter, e.g. *Haus*, *Bruder*, *Freund*, *Onkel*.

Verbs have different endings following different persons, so *verstehen* may also appear as, e.g. *ich verstehe* or *er versteht*.

Adjectives (descriptive words) may appear just before the noun (*ein gutes Verhältnis*) or after *ist* or *sind*, e.g. *Meine Freunde sind sehr wichtig für mich.* / *Mein Vater ist streng*.

noun — verb

Meine Freunde und ich unternehmen viele sportliche Aktivitäten.

adjective — noun

Challenge: Look back through the reading texts in activity 1. How many nouns, verbs and adjectives can you note down? Your targets to beat are: 30+ nouns, 45+ verbs and 15+ adjectives. (You can count the same word as many times as it appears in the text.)

1.1 Groundwork is available in the Foundation book.

1.2 F Heiraten oder nicht?

1a 📖📖 Read the texts and complete sentences 1–5 in English.

> Ich bin seit zwei Monaten verlobt und werde in zwei Jahren heiraten. Ich kann es kaum erwarten! Mein Verlobter Lutz ist vielleicht nicht so aufgeregt wie ich, aber wir sind beide sehr glücklich und freuen uns auf unsere Hochzeit. Wir leben nicht zusammen – ich bin dagegen – und ich finde, dass es besser ist, die Tradition zu respektieren. Wir werden auch später Kinder haben und wir glauben, dass sie die Stabilität der Ehe brauchen.
>
> **Laura**

mein Verlobter – my fiancé

> Ich werde bestimmt nie heiraten! Das ist sicher. Bei uns zu Hause gibt es täglich Streit zwischen meinen Eltern, und es ist klar, dass sie unglücklich sind. Also für mich heißt Heiraten nicht automatisch Glück, und ich werde anders leben als meine Eltern. Ich habe aber eine tolle, schöne Freundin. Ihre Eltern sind geschieden und sie denkt auch, dass die Ehe ein veralteter Lebensstil ist. Später werden wir eine Wohnung haben und zusammen leben.
>
> **Benjamin**

1 In two years, Laura …
2 Lutz is less …
3 Laura is not in favour of …
4 In Benjamin's opinion, marriage doesn't mean …
5 His girlfriend's parents are …

1b 📖 Lies die Texte noch einmal. Beantworte die Fragen auf Deutsch.

Read the texts again. Answer the questions in German.

1 Seit wann ist Laura verlobt?
2 Warum leben Laura und Lutz nicht zusammen?
3 Wie ist Benjamins Leben zu Hause?
4 Wie findet Benjamin seine Freundin?
5 Was wird Benjamin später tun?

2 🎧 Hör dir das folgende Gespräch an. Vier Jugendliche sprechen über das Heiraten. Sind die Aussagen richtig (R), falsch (F) oder nicht im Text (NT)?

Listen to four young people talking about marriage. Are the statements true (R), false (F) or not in the text (NT)?

Frank
1 Es gibt manchmal Probleme in einer Ehe – das ist normal.
2 Ehepaare sind oft unglücklich.
3 Es ist besser, verheiratet zu sein, wenn man Kinder hat.

Lotte
4 Wenige Leute lassen sich scheiden.
5 Heiraten ist ein großes Risiko.
6 Alle Kinder sollen bei ihrer Mutter wohnen.

Daniel
7 Viele Ehen dauern nicht lange.
8 Eine Hochzeit kann teuer sein.

Gudrun
9 Man soll nicht zu jung heiraten.
10 Sie will mit 25 Jahren heiraten.
11 Man soll viel reisen, bevor man heiratet.

Understanding questions in German

It's useful if you have a good grasp of the key German question words, so that you know what sort of information is being asked for in reading or listening activities.

Here are the main ones and examples of the types of responses needed for different question words:

- *wann?* (information about days, dates or times)
- *wo?* (information about places)
- *warum?* and *wieso?* (reasons)
- *wer?* (the name of a person or people)
- *wie?* and *was für?* (a description of a person or thing)
- *welcher / welche / welches?* (a specific person or thing).

Challenge: Make a note of any question words you can find in the book so far.

Strategie

3 **G** **T** Complete the sentences with the correct form of *werden*. Then translate the sentences into English.

1   Mein Bruder … nächstes Jahr mit seiner Freundin leben.
2   Ich … vielleicht heiraten, wenn ich älter bin.
3   Wir … am Wochenende eine Radtour machen.
4   Meine Großeltern … in zwei Jahren ihre goldene Hochzeit feiern.
5   Meine Schwester … immer ledig bleiben.
6   … du eines Tages heiraten?
7   Meine Geschwister … da sein.
8   Ich … heute Abend ausgehen.
9   Was … ihr am Samstag machen?
10 Im Sommer … mein Freund eine Arbeit finden.

4 **📣** Partnerarbeit. Stellt und beantwortet die Fragen.

Work with a partner. Ask and answer the questions.

•   Wirst / Willst du heiraten? Warum (nicht)?
•   Wann wirst / willst du heiraten?
•   Ist Heiraten wichtig für dich? Warum (nicht)?
•   Wie ist dein idealer Partner / deine ideale Partnerin?
•   Wirst / Willst du Kinder haben? Wann? Wie viele?

Ich werde Ich will Ich möchte	eines Tages	heiraten, Kinder haben,	weil	es Tradition / wichtig ist. ich meine(n) Freund(in) liebe. ich nicht allein sein will. ich Kinder haben will. wir Kinder haben wollen.
	nicht / nie			es teuer / schwierig ist. es Probleme gibt. viele Ehen nicht dauern. viele Leute sich trennen.
Mein(e) ideale(r) Partner(in)	ist	intelligent / schön / nett / groß / klein / schlank / ehrlich / geduldig / lustig	und	sportlich / interessant / aktiv / gesund / verständnisvoll / hilfsbereit / humorvoll.

ich möchte – I'd like

5 **T** Translate the sentences into German.

1   I'd like to have four children, two boys and two girls.
2   A big wedding is very expensive.
3   My ideal partner (f) is intelligent, funny and sporty.
4   He will never get married.
5   Manni and Lola are engaged.

Using the future tense

Grammatik · page 187

Form the future tense with the present tense of *werden* + the infinitive of the verb you're using. This infinitive will go to the end of the clause or sentence.

Here are some examples from what you've read:
*Ich **werde** in zwei Jahren **heiraten**.*
*Ich **werde** anders **leben**.*
*Wir **werden** auch später Kinder **haben**.*
*Wir **werden** uns eine Wohnung **suchen**.*

Here's an example of a complete verb:
ich werde … heiraten
du wirst … heiraten
er / sie / es wird … heiraten
wir werden … heiraten
ihr werdet … heiraten
sie / Sie werden … heiraten

Werden is an irregular verb, so watch the *du* and *er / sie / es* forms!

Remember that any other information in your sentence will appear in the gaps (shown above as '…'), or at the very start of the sentence.

Also check out how to use the modal verb *wollen* to say what you want to do. See page 27.

1.2 H Glücklich ohne Ehe?

1 📖 Lies den Artikel und sieh dir die Aussagen an. Sind die Aussagen richtig (R), falsch (F) oder nicht im Text (NT)?

Das große Zögern

Die Hochzeit soll der schönste Tag im Leben sein. Ein Paar möchte für immer zusammenbleiben, und es bekennt dies öffentlich vor Familie und Freunden mit einem großen Fest und oft auch noch in der Kirche. Die Romantik dieses Moments ist immer noch ein beliebter Stoff für Kinofilme. In der Wirklichkeit aber verliert dieser Lebensbund an Attraktion. Immer mehr Paare verzichten auf den formellen Akt der Ehe. Sind die Deutschen ehemüde geworden? Ist Heiraten aus der Mode gekommen? Sicher ist, dass die Paare heute länger zögern. Die Deutschen heiraten immer später und die meisten Paare haben das Zusammenleben schon in einer gemeinsamen Wohnung erprobt.

„Eine Lebensform ohne Ehe ist bei jüngeren und kinderlosen Paaren heute fast schon ein Normalfall", erklärt der Bremer Familienforscher Johannes Huinink. Da der gesellschaftliche Druck zu heiraten nicht mehr da ist, ist das Zusammenleben zu einer Art Vorehe geworden, zu einer modernen Form der Verlobungszeit.

1 Bei Hochzeiten ist ein großes Fest üblich.
2 Wenige Leute heiraten in der Kirche.
3 Hochzeiten werden oft in Filmen dargestellt.
4 Immer mehr Leute wollen heiraten.
5 Heiraten macht immer glücklich.
6 Viele Leute warten länger, bevor sie heiraten.
7 Das Zusammenleben ist die beste Idee.
8 Viele Paare leben zusammen, bevor sie heiraten.
9 Johannes Huinink ist ledig.
10 Das Zusammenleben ist wie eine Verlobung.

> *bekennen* – to profess, to state
> *der Lebensbund* – bond, union for life
> *verzichten auf* – to do without, to give up
> *aus der Mode kommen* – to go out of style
> *zögern* – to hesitate, to take one's time
> *erproben* – to test, to try out

2a 🎧 Listen to Zehra talking about marriage. Answer the questions in English.

1 Who is Zehra?
2 Why doesn't she have a boyfriend?
3 What will happen in three years?
4 How well does Zehra know Erdem?
5 What is Erdem like?
6 What matters most to Zehra's father?
7 What is Zehra's view of arranged marriage?

2b 🎧 Hör dir Lars an. Ergänze die Sätze auf Deutsch.

1 Lars findet Heiraten …
2 Lars hat seit …
3 Der Vater von Lars …
4 Für Lars sind … wichtiger als Liebe und Ehe.

Strategie

Spotting patterns in German and English

It's possible to improve your recognition of some German words even if they are not cognates or near-cognates. Look at these examples, where there is only a small difference between the sound / look of the word in the two languages:

German **ch** / English **k**: *Koch* / cook, *kochen* / cook, *machen* / make

German **d** / English **th**: *dass* / that, *danken* / thank, *Ding* / thing

German **t** / English **d**: *trinken* / drink, *tun* / do, *tanzen* / dance

German **pf** / English **p**: *Pfund* / pound, *Pflanze* / plant, *Pfeffer* / pepper

Challenge: Any time you have a few minutes to spare in class, look through a page of the *Glossar* at the back of the book. How many words can you find which show one of these patterns? Can you spot any more patterns which may be useful?

3 **G** Complete the sentences using the German for the adjective given in brackets.

1 Heute muss ich … warten als gestern. (*longer*)
2 Mein Bruder ist … als meine Schwester. (*younger*)
3 Heute ist es … als gestern. (*warmer*)
4 Glück ist … als ein Trauschein. (*more important*)
5 Mein Kleid ist … als dein Rock. (*more beautiful*)
6 Das Fest ist … … (*most important*)
7 Magda ist das … Mädchen in der Klasse. (*smallest*)
8 Diese ist die … Kirche im Dorf. (*oldest*)
9 Lena ist meine … Freundin. (*best*)
10 Heute ist der … Tag meines Lebens. (*most important*)
11 Das … Problem für ein Ehepaar ist Geld. (*biggest*)
12 Mein … Bruder ist ledig. (*younger*)

4 **T** Translate the paragraph into English.

> Immer wieder fragt man mich nach dem Rezept für meine lange und glückliche Ehe. Nun, meine Frau und ich gehen zweimal die Woche aus. Ein entspannendes Abendessen bei Kerzenlicht und romantischer Musik, ein paar Runden auf der Tanzfläche. Sie geht Dienstag, ich am Freitag. **Henny Youngman**

5 **T** Translate the paragraph into German.

> I have no idea whether I will marry or not in the future. I feel that I'm much too young to decide. At the moment my school subjects and exams are the most important things in my life. Later I want to go to university and find a good job.

6 Schreib sechs Fragen zum Thema Heiraten / Ehe / Zusammenleben. Dann arbeite mit einem Partner / einer Partnerin. Stellt euch die Fragen und beantwortet sie.

Grammatik

Using comparative and superlative adjectives

page 181

You can use adjectives in the comparative and superlative forms to compare things:

| adjective | | comparative form |

wichtig (important), *wichtiger* (more important), *am wichtigsten* (most important)

| superlative form |

*Mir ist die Ehe **wichtig**.*
*Mir ist das Zusammenleben **wichtiger**.*
*Mir ist das Glück am **wichtigsten**.*

The usual rule, as shown above, is to add -er to the adjective for a comparative and -st for a superlative. Think of the English equivalents, which work in the same way (e.g. long, longer, longest).

Single-syllable adjectives often add an umlaut in the comparative and superlative forms (*lang – länger – längst*, *groß – größer – größt*). There are a few exceptions to the rule, notably *gut – besser – best* (like the English).

Add appropriate endings when using the adjective before a noun (*meine ältere Schwester, der schönste Tag, die beste Freundin*), but not when it stands alone (*meine Schulnoten sind wichtiger, diese Schuhe sind am billigsten*).

Check also your understanding of German nouns in the plural. See page 27.

1.2 Groundwork is available in the Foundation book.

G Me, my family and friends

1 Write the sentences in the correct order. Note that sentence 5 is a question! Then translate the sentences into English.

1 Familie – vor – Ich – meine – stelle
2 glücklich – Sie – aus – immer – sieht
3 zusammen – Paare – junge – leben – Viele
4 Freundin – vorbei – Tag – jeden – Meine – kommt
5 du – mit – aus – gut – Eltern – Kommst – deinen?

Separable verbs

When you use separable verbs, the front part (called the separable prefix) moves to the end of the sentence. So, *vorbeikommen* (to call in / drop by) looks like this in a sentence: *Sie kommt oft vorbei.* (She often calls in.)

When you meet a new separable verb, write it like this in your vocabulary book to remind you which part breaks off: *vorstellen*, *vorbeikommen*, *zusammenleben*.

2 Complete the sentences with the correct verb form and reflexive pronoun given in brackets. Then translate the sentences into English.

1 Er … … oft mit seinen Geschwistern. (*sich streiten*)
2 Meine Oma … … um meinen kleinen Bruder. (*sich kümmern*)
3 Meine Schwester … … bei meiner Mutter. (*sich entschuldigen*)
4 Du … … für Filme. (*sich interessieren*)
5 Ich … … meistens gut mit meiner Mutter. (*sich verstehen*)
6 Mein Onkel … … auf das Wochenende. (*sich freuen*)

Reflexive verbs

These are verbs which have an extra part, called the reflexive pronoun, which relates to the person of the verb. For example:

sich waschen (to get washed)
ich wasche **mich**   wir waschen **uns**
du wäschst **dich**   ihr wascht **euch**
er / sie / es wäscht **sich**   sie / Sie waschen **sich**

Reflexive pronouns in German can usually be translated using 'myself', 'yourself', etc.

In the *wir* form, the reflexive pronoun may be used to express 'each other'. (*Wir sehen uns.* – We see each other.)

3 Complete the sentences with the correct German form of the possessive adjective given in brackets. Take care to use the correct case each time.

1 Wir wohnen seit 10 Jahren in … Haus. (*our*)
2 Er sieht oft … Opa. (*his*)
3 Ich gebe … Mutter die Blumen. (*my*)
4 Sie freut sich auf … Hochzeit! (*her*)
5 Haben Sie … Auto? (*your* – polite)
6 Kommst du gut mit … Vater aus? (*your* – familiar singular)
7 … Schwester heißt Freya. (*her*)
8 Wie ist … neues Haus? (*your* – familiar plural)
9 Ich treffe mich oft mit … Freunden. (*my*)

Possessive adjectives

Possessive adjectives are words like *mein* (my), *dein* (your) and *unser* (our). They go in front of a noun and work in exactly the same way as *ein / eine / ein*.

This is how the endings for *mein* look in the three main cases:

	masculine	feminine	neuter	plural
nominative (subject)	mein	meine	mein	meine
accusative (direct object)	meinen	meine	mein	meine
dative (indirect object)	meinem	meiner	meinem	meinen

The other possessive adjectives are: *dein* (your – familiar singular), *sein* (his / its), *ihr* (her), *unser* (our), *euer* (your – familiar plural), *Ihr* (your – polite singular and plural), *ihr* (their). They follow the same pattern as *mein*.

4a Complete the sentences with the correct form of *wollen*. Then translate the sentences into English.

1 Ich … drei Kinder haben.
2 Mein Freund … in den USA arbeiten.
3 Wo … du später wohnen?
4 Martin und Katrin … nächstes Jahr heiraten.
5 Wir … eine große Party haben.

4b Translate the sentences into German. Think about whether you need to use *wollen* or *werden*. Here are the second verbs you need to complete each sentence. Choose the correct one!

kaufen	gehen	haben
sehen	bleiben	

1 I want to see the film.
2 We're going to go to the cinema.
3 My father is going to buy a book.
4 They want to stay at home.
5 I'm going to have four children.

5a Write the plural forms of the nouns. Make a note of any words you don't know.

1 der Besuch   7 die Meinung
2 die Brille   8 der Punkt
3 der Grund   9 der Traum
4 die Hochzeit   10 das Verhältnis
5 der Kuss   11 der Reisepass
6 das Mitglied   12 der Brieffreund

5b Dative plural challenge! Translate the phrases into German. They are all in the dative plural. For how many do you need to add the extra *-n*?

1 in the holidays
2 under the trees
3 for two reasons (*aus* = for)
4 after the weddings
5 with our penfriends
6 in my dreams

Grammatik   page 185

Using *wollen* to say what you want to do

The verb *wollen* (to want to) looks just like the future tense in English, but be careful not to mix them up! *Ich will* means 'I want to' and **not** 'I will' (which is *ich werde*). Like the future tense, *wollen* needs another verb at the end of the sentence to complete the sense.

*Ich will später **heiraten**.* (I want to get married later on.)
*Willst du Kinder **haben**?* (Do you want to have children?)
*Wir wollen einen Film **sehen**.* (We want to see a film.)

It's an irregular verb, so you will need to know its parts:
ich will   *wir wollen*
du willst   *ihr wollt*
er / sie / es will   *sie / Sie wollen*

Grammatik   page 178

German nouns in the plural

It's so easy in English to make a noun plural! We almost always just add -s (e.g. houses, sons, flats), except for odd exceptions like mouse / mice, tooth / teeth and knife / knives.
German nouns form their plurals in many different ways, and the best idea is to try to learn the plural whenever you learn a new noun.

• Most **feminine** nouns which end in *-e* will add *-n* to form their plural (*Schule* → *Schulen*, *Blume* → *Blumen*).

• **Feminine** nouns which end in *-ung*, *-schaft*, *-heit* or *-keit* add *-en* (*Zeitung* → *Zeitungen*, *Freundschaft* → *Freundschaften*).

• One or two words are **always plural** – one you know already is *Eltern* (parents), another is *Leute* (people), not forgetting *Ferien* (holidays).

• The plural form of a noun is shown in brackets in the dictionary and in the vocabulary list in this book, so it's easy to check. For example, if you look up *Schwester*, you'll find (-*n*) after it, so you know that 'two sisters' is *zwei Schwestern*. If you look up *Zimmer*, you'll find (–), which means the word doesn't change in the plural.

• Another fascinating fact is that, when you use a plural noun in the **dative** case, it must always end in *-n*, so you will need to add *-n* if the plural form doesn't have one already. Look at these examples:
mit meinen Freunden (the plural form is *Freunde*, so *-n* has been added)
von seinen Brüdern (the plural form is *Brüder*, so *-n* has been added)
mit meinen Eltern (the plural noun already ends in *-n*)
seit zwei Wochen (the plural noun already ends in *-n*)

Vokabeln

1.1 Relationships with family and friends

1.1 F In meiner Familie
➡ *pages 18–19*

	auskommen (mit)	to get on (with)
	aussehen	to look like, to appear
	beide	both
	beschreiben	to describe
	bestimmt	certainly
der	*Cousin (-s)*	cousin (m)
die	*Cousine (-n)*	cousin (f)
die	*Familie (-n)*	family
die	*Frau (-en)*	woman, wife
die	*Freundin (-nen)*	(girl)friend
	geben	to give
	gefallen	to like, to please
die	*Gemeinschaft (-en)*	community, group
das	*Geschenk (-e)*	present, gift
	geschieden	divorced
	es gibt	there is / are
	Glück haben	to be lucky
	glücklich	happy
die	*Großeltern*	grandparents (pl)
die	*Großmutter (¨)*	grandmother
der	*Großvater (¨)*	grandfather
	jeder / jede / jedes	each, every
	ledig	single, unmarried
	liebevoll	loving, affectionate
der	*Morgen*	morning
	auf die Nerven gehen	to get on one's nerves
die	*Oma (-s)*	granny, grandma
der	*Onkel (–)*	uncle
der	*Opa (-s)*	grandad
der	*Partner (–)*	partner (m)
die	*Partnerin (-nen)*	partner (f)
die	*Person (-en)*	person
die	*Stadt (¨e)*	town
der	*Stiefbruder (¨)*	stepbrother
	Stiefmutter (¨)	stepmother
die	*Stiefschwester (-n)*	stepsister
	Stiefvater (¨)	stepfather
die	*Tante (-n)*	aunt

das	*Taschengeld (-er)*	pocket money
das	*Verhältnis (-se)*	relationship
	verheiratet	married
	verlobt	engaged (to someone)
	sich verstehen (mit)	to get on (with)
	vorbeikommen	to call in, drop by
die	*Witwe (-n)*	widow
	wohnen	to live, reside
	zu dritt	three (of us)
	zusammen	together

1.1 H Beziehungen zu Familie und Freunden
➡ *pages 20–21*

die	*Angewohnheit (-en)*	habit
	sich ärgern (über)	to get annoyed (about)
	besprechen	to discuss
die	*Beziehung (-en)*	relationship
	in die Brüche gehen	to break up
	dann und wann	now and then
die	*Ehe (-n)*	marriage
	eifersüchtig	jealous
der	*Elternteil (-e)*	parent
	eng	tight, close
	sich entschuldigen	to apologise
	entspannt	relaxed
die	*Freiheit*	freedom
der	*Freundeskreis (-e)*	circle of friends
die	*Freundschaft (-en)*	friendship
	sich fühlen	to feel
die	*Geige (-n)*	violin
	gemein	mean
der	*Grund (¨e)*	reason
	hilfsbereit	helpful
	sich interessieren für	to be interested in
	sich kümmern um	to take care of, to look after
	leiden	to suffer, to stand
die	*Lösung (-en)*	solution
	miteinander	with each other, together
	notwendig	necessary, essential
	ruhig	quiet, calm

	sich Sorgen machen	to worry
	ständig	constantly
	sich streiten	to argue
	streng	strict
	teilen	to share
	unerträglich	unbearable
	unternehmen	to do, to undertake
	verderben	to spoil
	sich verlassen auf	to rely on
	sich vorstellen	to introduce oneself, to imagine
	sich wenden an	to turn to
	wichtig	important
	zufrieden	content, happy
	zugeben	to admit
	zuverlässig	reliable

1.2 Marriage and partnership

1.2 F Heiraten oder nicht?
➡ pages 22–23

	anders	different(ly), in a different way
	aufgeregt	excited
	beide	both
	bestimmt	definite(ly), certain(ly)
	brauchen	to need
	dagegen	against, opposed to something
	dauern	to last
das	Ehepaar (-e)	married, couple
	ehrlich	honest
	erwarten	to wait, to expect
	sich freuen auf	to look forward to
	geduldig	patient
die	Gesellschaft (-en)	society
die	goldene Hochzeit	golden wedding
	leben	to live
der	Lebensstil (-e)	lifestyle
	lösen	to solve
	etwas Positives	something good
das	Risiko (Risiken)	risk
	seit	for (a period of time), since

	sich scheiden lassen	to get divorced
	einen Sinn für Humor haben	to have a sense of humour
die	Stabilität	stability
der	Streit (-e)	argument
	suchen	to look for, to search
sich	trennen	to separate
	veraltet	outdated
die	Verschwendung	waste
	verständnisvoll	understanding (adj)
	versuchen	to try
die	Wohnung (-en)	flat, apartment

1.2 H Glücklich ohne Ehe?
➡ pages 24–25

	abnehmen	to decrease, to lose weight
die	Ahnung (-en)	idea
der	Bräutigam (-e)	bridegroom
der	Druck (-e)	pressure
	erproben	to try out
	gemeinsam	shared together, in common
	gesellschaftlich	social
der	Haushalt (-e)	household
	keineswegs	in no way
	kinderlos	childless
	nötig	necessary
	öffentlich	in public
das	Paar (-e)	couple
das	Rezept (-e)	recipe
der	Stoff (-e)	material, subject matter
die	Tanzfläche (-n)	dance floor
	üblich	usual
	verlieren	to lose
die	Verlobung (-en)	engagement
der	Vorteil (-e)	advantage
die	Wirklichkeit (-en)	reality
der	Zeitraum (¨-e)	period of time
	zögern	to hesitate
die	Zukunft	future
	zusammenbleiben	to stay together

2.1 F   Bist du Facebook-Fan?

1a 📖 Lies drei Texte über Aspekte von sozialen Netzwerken. Wähl den passenden Titel (1–3) für jeden Text.

Read three texts about aspects of social networks.
Choose the appropriate title (1–3) for each text.

A

Soziale Netzwerke sind heute sehr beliebt. Wenn man sie benutzt, ist man immer gut informiert, und man kann rund um die Uhr und rund um die Welt kommunizieren. Es ist auch meist kostenlos, diese Netzwerke zu benutzen. Man bekommt schnell Feedback und weiß, was andere Leute denken. Durch YouTube und Myspace kann man sogar berühmt werden!

B

Es gibt verschiedene soziale Netzwerke. Sie haben verschiedene Zwecke – entweder als Treffpunkt für Freunde oder für Beruf und Business oder für Eltern und Familien. Es funktioniert ganz einfach. Man findet Leute mit den gleichen Interessen und schickt ihnen eine Nachricht.

C

Man muss bei Facebook immer vorsichtig sein und gut aufpassen. Daten sind nicht immer sicher und man kann sie missbrauchen. Viele Nutzer sind jung und unerfahren, und der Inhalt ist schwer zu kontrollieren. Deshalb gibt es manchmal Missverständnisse und Probleme. Soziale Netzwerke können Freundschaften auch zerstören!

1   Nachteile von sozialen Medien

2   Definition von sozialen Netzwerken

3   Vorteile von sozialen Medien

1b 📖 Read the texts again and answer the questions in English.

1. Find five advantages of using social networks.
2. According to text B, who, apart from friends, uses social networks?
3. What is said about personal data in text C?
4. Why might problems arise?
5. What might be the result of a misunderstanding on Facebook?

2 🎧 Hör dir einige Ratschläge für die Sicherheit in sozialen Netzwerken an und lies die Aussagen. Sind die Aussagen richtig (R), falsch (F) oder nicht im Text (NT)?

Listen to the advice about security on social networks and read the statements. Are the statements true (R), false (F) or not in the text (NT)?

A
1. Die Sendung heißt „Soziale Medien heute".
2. Man soll neue Internetfreunde nur akzeptieren, wenn man sie kennt.
3. Es ist nicht wichtig, persönliche Informationen zu schützen.
4. Ein Passwort muss auf Deutsch sein.

B
5. Man soll seine Adresse nicht angeben.
6. Private Fotos sollen privat bleiben.
7. Man soll sich mit allen neuen Internetfreunden treffen.
8. Nächste Woche gibt es wieder eine Sendung.

Spotting grammatical signposts

Grammatical signposts can help you understand an unknown word. For example, a word at the end of a sentence that ends in -en is likely to be a verb (*keine privaten Fotos* **hochladen**).

A word between an article (*der / die / das* or *ein / eine / ein* in any of the different forms) and a noun will be an adjective (*ein* **sicheres** *Passwort*).

Challenge: Look for more examples on these two pages. How many verbs can you note down? And how many adjectives?

Strategie

3 🇬 🇹 Complete the sentences using the German for the pronoun given in brackets. Then translate the sentences into English.

1 Meine Freundin? Ich sehe … jeden Tag. (*her*)
2 Das Internet ist großartig. Ich benutze … täglich. (*it*)
3 Er schickt …. eine E-Mail. (*to them*)
4 Er erklärt … morgen das Problem. (*to us*)
5 Ich gebe … die Adresse. (*to you* – Sie *form*)
6 Meine Eltern geben … so viel. (*to me*)
7 Wir geben … kein Geld. (*to you* – du *form*)

4 🗨 Gruppenarbeit. Seht euch das Bild an und macht Notizen. Stellt euch und beantwortet die Fragen. Wechselt euch ab.

Work in groups. Look at the picture and make some notes.
Ask and answer the questions. Take turns.

- Was kannst du auf diesem Bild sehen?
- Wie oft benutzt du das Internet?
- Welche sozialen Netzwerke magst du (nicht)? Warum?
- Wie finden deine Eltern soziale Netzwerke?
- Hast du ein Handy?

5 ✏️ Schreib deine Antworten für die Fragen in Aufgabe 4 auf.

Write your answers to the questions in activity 4.

6 🇹 Translate the paragraph into German.

> I love social media, and my favourite network is Facebook. All my friends use it. We find it useful when we plan activities. I often send them messages in the evenings when we're doing homework.

Grammatik page 183

Using direct and indirect object pronouns

Pronouns are used to replace nouns in a sentence.

Direct object pronouns (DOPs) replace nouns in the accusative case. Indirect object pronouns (IOPs) replace nouns in the dative case.

accusative	dative
mich	mir
dich	dir
ihn / sie / es	ihm / ihr / ihm
uns	uns
euch	euch
sie / Sie	ihnen / Ihnen

Soziale Netzwerke *sind heute sehr beliebt. Wenn man* **sie** *benutzt …* (Social networks are very popular today. When you use them …)

Man findet **Leute** *mit den gleichen Interessen und schickt* **ihnen** *eine Nachricht …* (You find people with the same interests and send them a message …)

Also learn how to make more interesting sentences using *weil* and *wenn*. See page 38.

Ich finde	soziale Medien / soziale Netzwerke / Facebook / Twitter	fantastisch / toll nützlich / gut / interessant,	weil	ich mir gern Fotos ansehe. ich gern Fotos hochlade. ich mit Freunden in Kontakt bleibe.
			wenn	wir Aktivitäten planen.
Ich finde / Meine Eltern finden	sie es	schlecht / ungesund / gefährlich,	weil	es Risiken gibt. die Daten nicht sicher sind. es dort viele unbekannte Menschen gibt.
			wenn	ich lange vor dem Computer sitze.

2.1 H   Sicherheit im Internet

Lernziele

Talking in more detail about social networks

Deciding when to use *wann*, *wenn* and *als*

Making the most of near-cognates

1 📖 Lies den Text über Mobbing im Internet und beantworte die Fragen auf Deutsch.

Cybermobbing

Leider kommen Beleidigungen, Bedrohungen oder andere Gemeinheiten manchmal im Internet vor. Andere zu beleidigen ist eine miese Sache.

Das solltest du zum Thema „Mobbing" wissen:

- Wenn dir im Internet jemand blöd kommt, zum Beispiel in einem sozialen Netzwerk, zeige ihm die kalte Schulter und ignoriere ihn.
- Wenn du gemobbt wirst, erzähle sofort deinen Eltern oder Lehrern davon.
- Mobbing-Erlebnisse zu verheimlichen macht die Situation für dich schlimmer. Vergiss nicht, nicht **du** machst etwas Falsches, sondern der andere!
  - Besprich gemeinsam mit deinen Eltern, was ihr tun könnt, um blöden Typen die rote Karte zu zeigen.
- Melde den Vorfall dem Seitenbetreiber und, wenn es weitergeht, der Polizei.
- Dokumentiere den Vorfall, indem du Screenshots machst, und notiere Datum und Zeit des Vorfalls.
- Der beste Schutz vor Cybermobbing:
  - Halte persönliche Daten wie E-Mail und Adresse geheim.
  - Benutze die Sicherheitseinstellungen des Netzwerks, so dass nur echte Freunde mit dir Kontakt aufnehmen können.
  - Veröffentliche keine Fotos von dir.

🔄 **Strategie**

Making the most of near-cognates

Near-cognates are helpful words which, though they are not absolutely identical, are very similar in English and German. They are quite straightforward to recognise in reading and listening, and knowing the meaning in English helps you to use the German word when speaking and writing.

There are some good examples in the reading activity you have just done. *Thema, Netzwerk, Polizei, notieren, Datum, Daten, Adresse, Foto, privat.*

Challenge: Keep a page or two at the back of your vocabulary book for words which are cognates or near-cognates. The words above give you a start. Aim to add to your list every week.

vorkommen – to occur
die Beleidigung – insult
die Bedrohung – threat
Gemeinheiten – mean tricks (pl)
mies – terrible, lousy
blöd kommen – to mess with
verheimlichen – to keep quiet / secret
der Vorfall – incident
der Seitenbetreiber – website operator
geheim – secret, private
veröffentlichen – to publish

1 Was geschieht manchmal im Internet?
2 Wie sollst du sofort reagieren, wenn dir jemand blöd kommt?
3 Wem sollst du davon erzählen?
4 Was sollst du nicht vergessen?
5 Wann sollst du zur Polizei gehen?
6 Wie kannst du das Mobbing dokumentieren?
7 Welche Information soll man privat halten?
8 Was soll man auf keinen Fall tun?

2 **G** **T** Complete the sentences with *wann* or *wenn*. Then translate the sentences into English.

1 Ich werde alles erklären, … ich sie sehe.
2 … kommt dein Zug an?
3 Wir gehen zum Strand, … das Wetter gut ist.
4 … ich Zeit habe, benutze ich Facebook.
5 Meine Freunde und ich simsen, … wir zu Hause sind.
6 … du Mobbing erlebst, musst du sofort mit deinen Eltern sprechen.
7 Ich bin nicht sicher, … sie Geburtstag hat.
8 Willst du heiraten, … du älter bist?

3 🎧 Listen to the opinions about the pros and cons of social networks. Complete the sentences in English.

| 1 Anna | 2 Sabine |

a Anna is concerned about …
b Her daughter …
c Some experts think that …

d Social media are important for Sabine because …
e You can feel an outsider if …
f Sabine never …

4 💬 Partnerarbeit. Sprecht über die Vor- und Nachteile von sozialen Netzwerken. Eine Person gibt Argumente für soziale Netwerke, die andere gibt die Gegenargumente. Benutzt diese Adjective und erklärt eure Meinung (weil, da, denn).

Pro: gut, nötig, normal, interessant, lebensnotwendig, informativ, sozial, lehrreich, unterhaltsam, lustig

Kontra: schlecht, negativ, gefährlich, isolierend, beunruhigend, alarmierend, riskant, unkontrollierbar

5 ✏️ Schreib einen kurzen Bericht über deine Internetnutzung und deine Meinung zu sozialen Netzwerken.

Deciding when to use *wann*, *wenn* and *als*

Grammatik page 184

Though these words all mean 'when', they are not interchangeable!

Use **wann** to ask a **direct question** (*Wann kommt er nach Hause?*) or to state an **indirect question** (*Ich weiß nicht, wann er nach Hause kommt.*).

Use **wenn** for 'when' in the **present** / **future** tenses or to mean 'whenever' or 'if':
*Ich gehe online, wenn ich Zeit **habe**.* (when – present)
*Er ist glücklich, wenn er bei ihr **ist**.* (when / whenever)
*Wir gehen zur Polizei, wenn das Mobbing **weitergeht**.* (if)

Use **als** to say 'when' in the **past** tense:
*Er war glücklich, als er sie **sah**.* (when – past)

Note than *wenn* and *als* are both **subordinating conjunctions** which move the verb to the end of the clause / sentence!

Also revise your knowledge of the imperative. See page 38.

---

die Fähigkeit – ability, skill
einschränken – to limit
in Verbindung – in touch / contact
auf dem Laufenden sein – to keep up to date

---

6 **T** Translate the paragraph into English.

Heute spielen die neuen Technologien eine wichtige Rolle im Leben der meisten Jugendlichen. Sie suchen im Netz nach aktuellen Informationen, wenn sie Hausaufgaben machen, sie machen Einkäufe online, wenn sie den neusten Modeartikel haben wollen und sie schreiben fast keine Briefe mehr, denn E-Mails sind schneller und einfacher.

7 **T** Translate the paragraph into German.

I like new technology and find the internet very important for my everyday life. I often use social networks to keep in touch with friends. We upload photos and send emails and messages – it's good fun. But we know the dangers and we protect personal data.

2.1 Groundwork is available in the Foundation book.

2.2 F

Trends in der mobilen Handywelt

1a 📖 Lies die Texte und wähle die passende Frage oder Bemerkung (1–4) für jeden Text.

Read the texts and choose the appropriate question or comment (1–4) for each text.

A
Handys waren einmal nur zum Telefonieren da. Heute sind sie multifunktionale Minicomputer zum Fotografieren, Filmen, Surfen im Netz, Radio hören oder Navigieren mit GPS.

B
Handys sind bei Jugendlichen sehr beliebt. Eine Studie zeigte, dass schon 94% der Jugendlichen zwischen 12 und 19 Jahren ein Mobiltelefon haben. Vor fünf Jahren war die Zahl nur 63%.

C
Es gibt besondere Tarife für Kinder und Jugendliche. Damit kann man seine wichtigsten Nummern (z.B. die Nummer der Eltern) kostenlos anrufen.

D
Früher hatte man einen iPod – jetzt braucht man keinen iPod mehr. Ein modernes Handy hat auch einen MP3-Player – man kann also Musik herunterladen und jederzeit hören.

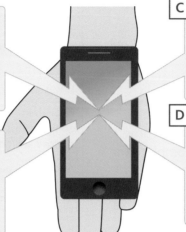

1   „Wenn ich zu Fuß zur Schule gehe, will ich aber meine Lieblingsband hören."
2   „Haben die meisten Kinder und jungen Leute ein Handy?"
3   „Ich hatte eine Kamera, aber sie ist kaputt. Soll ich eine neue kaufen?"
4   „Meine Eltern sagen immer, ein neues Handy ist zu teuer. Stimmt das?"

1b 📖 Lies die Texte noch einmal. Welche fünf Aussagen sind richtig?

Read the texts again. Which five statements are correct?

1   Ein modernes Handy ist nur zum Telefonieren da.
2   Ein modernes Handy funktioniert wie ein Computer.
3   Man kann sein Handy benutzen, um den richtigen Weg zu finden.
4   Vor fünf Jahren hatten nur wenige junge Leute ein eigenes Handy.
5   Jetzt haben 63% der Jugendlichen ein Handy.
6   Mit gewissen Tarifen kann man kostenlos zu Hause anrufen.
7   Ein modernes Handy hat Internetanschluss.
8   Heute haben die meisten Jugendlichen keinen iPod mehr.

2 🎧 Listen to four people talking about mobile phones. Complete the sentences in English.

1   Mehmet had … but now …
2   Jana uses her phone to … but thinks it's stupid to … because …
3   Daniel uses his mobile mainly … and also uses it as …
4   Sandra needs her phone … and she also likes … but she knows …

Grammatik · page 186

3 **G** Complete the sentences with the verb given in brackets in the imperfect tense.

1 Letztes Jahr ... ich in London. (*sein*)
2 Er ... eine nette Freundin. (*haben*)
3 Ich ... gestern keine E-Mails schicken. (*können*)
4 Meine Freundin ... ein neues Smartphone. (*wollen*)
5 Ihre Mutter ... ihr das Geld. (*geben*)
6 Die Jungen ... am Wochenende arbeiten. (*müssen*)

4 **T** Translate the paragraph into English.

> Ein Handy ist heute absolut nötig. Vor ein paar Jahren konnte man mit dem Handy nur telefonieren, simsen und vielleicht Fotos machen, aber moderne Handys sind tolle kleine Geräte. Sie sind Computer – zum Mitnehmen!

5 **T** Translate the sentences into German.

1 Last year I had an old-fashioned mobile phone.
2 It was OK, but it couldn't do much.
3 I could only send texts and make calls.
4 Unfortunately I had no internet connection.
5 My parents are buying me a new phone for my birthday.

6 Gruppenarbeit. Stellt euch und beantwortet die Fragen.

Work in groups. Ask each other the questions and answer them.

• Sind Handys wirklich nötig? Warum (nicht)?
• Gibt es auch Probleme mit dem Handygebrauch? Welche?
• Was für ein Handy hast du jetzt / hattest du letztes Jahr?
• Wofür benutzt du dein Handy?

7 Schreib in einem Absatz deine Antworten auf die vier Fragen in Aufgabe 6. Schreib ungefähr 90 Wörter.

Write your answers to the four questions in activity 6. Write approximately 90 words.

Ein Handy ist für mich Ich finde mein Handy	wichtig / nötig / toll,	denn	ich kann Freunde anrufen und … ich höre gern Musik.
Ja, es gibt auch Probleme,	denn	ich / man soll nicht die ganze Zeit simsen / surfen. man muss auch aktiv sein / direkt kommunizieren.	
Mein altes Handy war altmodisch / nicht gut	und ich konnte	(nur) telefonieren / anrufen. keine Musik hören.	
	und ich hatte	keinen Internetanschluss.	
Mit meinem neuen Handy kann ich	im Internet surfen / online einkaufen / mit Freunden telefonieren / simsen.		
Mein Handy ist auch	mein Wecker / mein Kalender.		

Using the imperfect tense

The imperfect tense is used to refer to the past. You should focus first on the imperfect tense of some very common – and therefore very useful – verbs (*haben*, *sein* and *können*).

Remember these examples from the texts you've read and listened to:
*Ich **hatte** letztes Jahr ein altmodisches Handy.* (Last year I **had** an old-fashioned mobile.)

*Ich **konnte** nur telefonieren und simsen.* (I **could** only make calls and text.)

These are all irregular verbs. Learn the *ich* form and then just learn the endings for other persons of the verb.

ich	war	wir	war**en**
du	war**st**	ihr	war**t**
er / sie / es	war	sie / Sie	war**en**

Note: two of the forms you'll use most (*ich* and *er / sie / es*) are identical in this tense!

Other useful imperfect tense forms are: *ich musste* (I had to), *ich wollte* (I wanted to), *ich gab* (I gave).

Also learn how to use possessive adjectives (*mein*, *dein*, *sein*, etc.). See page 39.

Thinking creatively in speaking

Strategie

If there's a certain word you need to use but don't know, **describe** the thing in question using the German words you **do** know.

For example, if you don't know the word for 'earphones': *Ich stecke kleine Dings* (thingies!) *in die Ohren und höre meine Musik.*

Challenge: Try to explain one of the following items to a partner in German – but without using the actual word, even if you do know it!

a horse   lipstick   a spoon
an electronic whiteboard

2.2 H

Handys – das Gute, das Schlechte und das Hässliche

1 📖 Read the texts and answer the questions in English.

A

Das neue Smartphone K

K heißt Klasse, kompakt und knallrot!

Es ist nicht nur größer und schöner, es ist in allem besser.

Es ist länger, breiter, aber auch dünner, leistungsstärker und unglaublich energieeffizient.

B

Es gibt viele Formen von Handymissbrauch. Mobbing ist an sich nichts Neues, aber Cybermobbing sieht anders aus und gerät durch moderne Medien und Kommunikation schnell außer Kontrolle.

Nach einer Studie hat mindestens jeder fünfte Jugendliche Cybermobbing erlebt. Mädchen sind in der Regel mehr betroffen als Jungen. Solches Mobbing reicht von Missbrauch privater Nachrichten oder Bilder, Bedrohungen und Beleidigungen bis zu „Happy Slapping".

Bei Happy Slapping filmt jemand per Handy eine Schlägerei und veröffentlicht das Video online. Dies ist kein Scherz und kann furchtbare Folgen haben. Es gibt sogar Fälle, wo das Opfer Selbstmord begangen hat.

1 List at least five features of the Smartphone K mentioned in the advertisement.

2 According to the first paragraph of Text B, what's the key difference between bullying and cyberbullying?

3 What has a study discovered?

4 What forms might cyberbullying take?

5 Explain the term 'Happy Slapping', as it's described in the text.

6 Why is so-called Happy Slapping actually very serious?

erleben – to experience
betroffen – affected
das Opfer – victim

2 🎧 Listen to Ralf and Alex talking about the advantages and disadvantages of modern mobiles. Complete the sentences in English.

1 Ralf   2 Alex

a Ralf thinks that modern mobiles are …

b Old-style mobiles …

c Mobiles today are …

d Ralf uses his mobile to … and to …

e He finds the … particularly useful.

f Alex understands why …

g For young people today new technology is …

h But he worries about …

i Young people are careless about internet use. They … and they don't …

j They are running the risk of … and …

Using the imperfect tense

Grammatik

In activity 2, Ralf uses several examples of the imperfect to describe what his life was like when he was younger and had no mobile. Look at these examples:

*Als ich jünger **war**, **hatte** ich kein Handy. Die alten **hatten** keine Anwendungen und **waren** nicht so leistungsstark.*

Apart from verbs like *sein* and *haben*, the imperfect is usually used in writing. The imperfect of regular verbs is formed by adding the following endings to the stem.

*ich spiel**te***   *wir spiel**ten***
*du spiel**test***   *ihr spiel**tet***
*er / sie / es spiel**te***   *sie / Sie spiel**ten***

Also learn when to use the imperfect and perfect tenses. See page 39.

page 186

3 **G** Complete the sentences with the correct form of the verb given in brackets in the imperfect tense.

Regular verbs

1 Ich … immer meine Hausaufgaben. (*machen*)
2 Er … Rockmusik. (*hören*)
3 Die Jungen … manchmal Tennis. (*spielen*)
4 Meine Freundin … oft ihr Handy. (*benutzen*)
5 Mein Vater … keine E-Mails. (*schicken*)
6 Ich … viele Bücher. (*kaufen*)

Sein and haben

7 Er … am Wochenende krank. (*sein*)
8 Wir … in Italien im Urlaub. (*sein*)
9 Er … keine Freundin. (*haben*)
10 Die Kinder … keine Hausaufgaben. (*haben*)

4 Gruppenarbeit: Kettenreaktion. Die erste Person sagt einen Vor- oder Nachteil von Handys, dann kommt der nächste an die Reihe. Könnt ihr einen langen Satz bauen?

Beispiel: Person 1: Ich finde mein Handy sehr nützlich und ich höre oft Musik, wenn …

Person 2: wenn ich zu Fuß zur Schule gehe. Ich mag auch soziale Netzwerke und …

Person 3: und alle meine Freunde sind auch Nutzer bei Facebook. Das …

Person 1: Das finde ich sehr praktisch, weil wir in Kontakt bleiben und …

Person 2: und auch unser Leben organisieren können, zum Beispiel, wenn wir …

Person 3: wir ins Kino oder in die Stadt gehen …

5 Schreib einen kurzen Bericht (90–100 Wörter) über Handys.

- Wie ist dein Handy?
- Wie war dein Leben, bevor du ein Handy hattest?
- Was machst du mit deinem Handy?
- Wie oft / Wie lang benutzt du dein Handy?
- Sag etwas über die Gefahren der Handys / des Internets.

6 **T** Translate the paragraph into English.

> Vor vier Jahren, als ich 12 Jahre alt war, hatte ich kein Handy, aber das war damals total normal. Jetzt ist es anders.
>
> Fast alle Jugendlichen, die ich kenne, haben heute ein modernes Handy und sie benutzen es täglich. Ein Leben ohne Handy kann man sich nicht mehr vorstellen.

7 **T** Translate the paragraph into German.

> My mobile phone is old-fashioned. It's not very powerful and it is too big and very ugly. But it has a camera and I like that, as I'm interested in photography. I can also text friends. That's useful when we plan our free time. Last weekend we played football in the park.

Achieving a fluent English translation

When translating from German into English, you're aiming to get as close as you can to the original language while producing an English version which sounds natural! If your version sounds unnatural or awkward and you've written things you can't ever imagine saying in English, it probably needs improving.

Consider this example: *Das neue Smartphone ist nicht nur größer, es ist einfach in allem besser.*
A word-for-word (literal) translation would be: 'The new smartphone is not only bigger, it's simply in all better.' But 'in all better' is not natural or fluent English, so you'd think again and say instead: 'The new smartphone is not only bigger – it's simply better in every way.' This is good translation!

Challenge: Can you improve on the translation of this sentence, taken from the listening test?

Ich telefonierte mit meinen Freunden über das Festnetz. (I telephoned with my friends over the landline.)

Strategie

2.2 Groundwork is available in the Foundation book.

G Technology in everyday life

1a Link the sentences using *weil*. Then translate the sentences into English.

1 Ich bleibe heute zu Hause. Es ist sehr kalt.
2 Er kommt nicht zur Schule. Er ist krank.
3 Ich hasse Facebook. Es gibt zu viele dumme Fotos.

1b Link the sentences using *wenn*. Then translate the sentences into English.

1 Meine Eltern ärgern sich. Ich simse die ganze Zeit.
2 Ich helfe meiner Mutter. Sie ist müde.
3 Wir gehen zum Strand. Das Wetter ist schön.

1c Write the sentences in the correct order, starting with the underlined word. Then translate the sentences into English.

1 Wetter – schön – nicht – viel – benutze – wenn – meinen – Computer – <u>Ich</u> – das – ist
2 Bruder – weil – immer – <u>Mein</u> – er – ist – ist – toll – lustig

2a Copy and complete the grid with the three imperative forms and the meanings.

	Sie form	*ihr* form	*du* form	meaning
Beispiel:	Lesen Sie den Text!	Lest den Text!	Lies den Text!	Read the text.
1	Bleiben Sie hier!			
2		Kommt nach Hause!		
3			Melde den Vorfall!	
4				Eat the apple.

2b Write three more instructions you might give your dog, your two younger brothers and your German teacher. Take care to use the appropriate form of address.

Grammatik page 189

Using *weil* and *wenn*

Another great way to link ideas together is to use **weil** (because) or **when** (when / if). They are called **subordinating conjunctions**. This type of conjunction (also called 'connective') has an effect on the position of the verb. Look at these examples:
*Ich liebe mein Handy. Ich **telefoniere** oft mit meinen Freunden.*
*Ich liebe mein Handy, **weil** ich oft mit meinen Freunden **telefoniere**.* (I love my mobile phone because I often phone my friends.)

*Ich benutze Facebook. Ich **habe** Zeit.*
*Ich benutze Facebook, **wenn** ich Zeit **habe**.* (I use Facebook when I've got time.)

Note that the verbs *telefoniere* and *habe* have slipped to the end and that a comma has been placed in front of *weil* and *wenn* to mark the start of the new clause (part of the sentence).

Grammatik page 189

The imperative

The imperative is used to give someone instructions or commands. There are three forms – one for each of the forms of 'you'. These are all formed differently.

- ***Sie* form** – to give an instruction in the formal / polite *Sie* form, simply invert (swap around) the verb and the subject, just as you do to form a simple question: *Kommen Sie mit! Geben Sie mir das Handy!*
- ***ihr* form** – to give an instruction to more than one person in the familiar form (a teacher telling a class what to do, for example), use the verb form alone, and drop the word *ihr*: *Kommt mit! Gebt mir das Handy!*
- ***du* form** – to address just one person, use the *du* form of the verb, drop the *du* and the *-st* verb ending: d̶u̶ komms̶t̶. *Komm mit! Gib mir das Handy!*

Note that:
- it's usual to use an exclamation mark after an imperative.
- irregular verbs which add an umlaut in the *du* form of the present tense will lose this again in the imperative form (*du fährst* becomes *fahr*).
- *Sein* is irregular in the imperative and looks like this: *seien Sie …! / seid …! / sei …!*)

3a Translate the words into English.

1 deine Freundin, ihre Freundin,
    unsere Freundinnen
2 Ihr Haus, unser Haus, sein Haus
3 eure Bücher, euer Hund, eure Passwörter
4 meine Meinung, mein Klassenzimmer,
    mein Stiefvater

3b Complete the sentences with the German
for the possessive adjective given in brackets.
Take care to use the correct case each time.
Then translate the sentences into English.

1 … Familie ist nicht so groß. (*my*)
2 Ich mag … Freunde. (*her*)
3 Hast du … Laptop mit? (*your* – du *form*)
4 Ich gebe … Mutter Blumen. (*to my*)
5 … Computer ist ziemlich alt. (*our*)
6 Sie liebt … neues Handy. (*her*)
7 Ich finde … Vater sehr streng. (*his*)
8 Das Auto … Freundes ist rot. (*of my*)
9 Wir geben … Tante ein Geschenk. (*to our*)
10 Er vermisst … Eltern. (*his*)

4 Translate the sentences into German.

1 When I was younger, I used to read the Harry
    Potter books.
2 Yesterday I bought this lovely dress.
3 I haven't done my German homework!
4 When he was a little boy, he used to play
    Super Mario games.
5 What did you do on Saturday?
6 We played tennis and then had a picnic in
    the park.

Grammatik · page 179

Possessive adjectives

Possessive adjectives (*mein*, *meine*, *mein*, etc.) are
used instead of *ein / eine / ein* when showing who
something belongs to and they work in the same way.

The other possessives which work like *mein* are *dein*
(your – familiar singular), *sein* (his / its), *ihr* (her),
unser (our), *euer* (your – familiar plural),
Ihr (your – formal) and *ihr* (their).

Look at these examples, using *mein* in the four cases:

nominative *Mein Bruder ist sehr intelligent.*
                (My brother is very intelligent.)
accusative *Ich mag **meinen** Bruder sehr.*
                (I like my brother very much.)
genitive   *Die Freundin **meines** Bruders
                heißt Natascha.*
                (My brother's girlfriend is called
                Natascha. Literally: The girlfriend **of my
                brother** is called Natascha.)
dative   *Ich kaufe **meinem** Bruder eine DVD
                zum Geburtstag.*
                (I'm buying my brother a DVD for his
                birthday. Literally: I'm buying a DVD **for
                my brother** for his birthday.)

Grammatik · pages 185 & 186

When to use the imperfect and perfect tenses

You know that the imperfect and perfect tenses are
both past tenses.

The **imperfect tense**:
- is used mostly in written German, though some of
  the most common verbs are often used in spoken
  language too (*ich war*, *er hatte*, *wir konnten*, *ich
  musste*, *sie wollten*).
- is also often used to refer back to how something
  used to be, where the past event has little
  connection with present time: *Als er jünger war,
  wohnte er lange in der Schweiz.*

The **perfect tense**:
- is used when speaking about past events: *Hast du
  gestern das Spiel gesehen?*
- makes more of a connection between past events
  and the present: *Ich habe mir letzte Woche den Arm
  gebrochen!* (suggesting 'so now, as you see, I am
  in plaster')

Vokabeln

2.1 Social media

2.1 F Bist du Facebook-Fan?
➡ *pages 30–31*

	akzeptieren	to accept
	ändern	to change
	aufpassen	to pay attention, to watch out, to take care
	beliebt	popular
der	Beruf (-e)	job, profession
	berühmt	famous
	Daten	data (pl)
	deshalb	therefore, because of that
	ebenfalls	as well
	entweder … oder …	either … or …
die	Gefahr (-en)	danger
	gleich	(the) same, equal, immediately
	informiert	informed
der	Inhalt (-e)	content
	kommunizieren	to communicate
	kontrollieren	to control
	kostenlos	free of charge
	meist	mostly, usually
	missbrauchen	to misuse, to abuse
das	Missverständnis (-se)	misunderstanding
die	Nachricht (-en)	message, news
der	Nutzer (–)	user
das	Passwort (¨er)	password
	peinlich	embarrassing
	privat	private
der	Ratschlag (¨e)	piece of advice
	regelmäßig	regular, regularly
	rund um die Uhr	24/7
	rund um die Welt	all around the world
	schicken	to send
	schützen	to protect
	sicher	sure, safe, secure
die	SMS	text
der	Spitzname (-n)	nickname
	täglich	every day, daily

	unbekannt	unknown
	unerfahren	inexperienced
	verschieden	various, different
	vorsichtig	careful
das	Zeichen (–)	character (in text)
	zerstören	to destroy
der	Zweck (-e)	purpose

2.1 H Sicherheit im Internet
➡ *pages 32–33*

	alarmierend	alarming
der	Außenseiter (–)	outsider
die	Bedrohung (-en)	threat
die	Beleidigung (-en)	insult
	beunruhigend	worrying
der	Brief (-e)	letter
das	Datum (Daten)	date
der	Einfluss (¨e)	influence
der	Einkauf (¨e)	purchase
die	E-Mail (-s)	email
das	Erlebnis (-se)	experience
	erzählen	to tell, to narrate
	geheim halten	to keep secret
	ignorieren	to ignore
	isolierend	isolating
die	kalte Schulter	the cold shoulder
	lebensnotwendig	vital
	lehrreich	educational, informative
	leider	unfortunately
	mobben	to bully
das	Netzwerk (-e)	network
	neulich	recently
	riskant	risky
die	Rolle (-n)	role
	schlimm	bad
der	Schutz	protection
die	Sicherheitseinstellungen	security settings (pl)
	sofort	immediately, straight away
die	Technologie (-n)	technology
	unkontrollierbar	uncontrollable

	unterhaltsam	entertaining
	in Verbindung (mit)	in contact (with)
	verheimlichen	to conceal, to hide
	veröffentlichen	to publish
	zeigen	to show

2.2 Mobile technology

2.2 F Trends in der mobilen Handywelt
➡ *pages 34–35*

	altmodisch	old-fashioned
der	Anschluss (¨e)	connection
	besonders	special, particularly, especially
	blöd	stupid
das	Dings	thingy
die	Dummheit (-en)	stupid thing, foolishness
	einmal	once
das	Geld	money
das	Gerät (-e)	device, gadget, appliance
	gewiss	certain
	jederzeit	at any time
der	Kalender (–)	diary, calendar
der	Klingelton (¨e)	ringtone
sich	konzentrieren	to concentrate
	mitnehmen	to take with (you)
	nötig	necessary
	das stimmt	that's right / correct
die	Studie	study, research
der	Tarif (-e)	tariff, scale of charges
	vielleicht	perhaps
der	Wecker (–)	alarm clock
der	Weg (-e)	route, way, path
	zeigen	to show

2.2 H Handys – das Gute, das Schlechte und das Hässliche
➡ *pages 36–37*

	in allem	in every way
der	Anrufebeantworter (–)	answering machine, messaging service
die	Anwendung (-en)	application, app
	beherrschen	to master, to manage, to control
	betroffen	affected
·	breit	wide, broad
	damals	then, in those days
	dünn	slim
die	Erfindung (-en)	invention
das	Festnetz (-e)	landline
	filmen	to film
die	Folge (-n)	consequence, result, outcome
	glatt	smooth, sleek
	hässlich	ugly
der	Identitätsklau	identity theft
die	Kette (-n)	chain
die	Kettenreaktion (-en)	chain reaction
	leistungsstark	powerful (battery, processor)
der	Maßstab (¨e)	standard
der	Missbrauch (¨e)	misuse, abuse
die	Oberfläche (-n)	surface
das	Opfer (–)	victim
	prüfen	to check
	in der Regel	in general
	reichen	to range
die	Sache (-n)	thing, stuff
der	Scherz (-e)	joke
die	Schlägerei (-en)	fight, brawl
	Selbstmord begehen	to commit suicide
	unerwünscht	unwanted
	wechseln	to change

Higher – Reading and listening

1 📖 Lies Millies Blog über Beziehungen zu Familie und Freunden. Ergänze die Sätze auf Deutsch.

> **Millie**   6 Kommmentare
>
> Es läuft in meiner Familie nicht immer gut, aber ich halte das für völlig normal. Teenager sind nicht die einfachsten Mitbewohner! Und Eltern haben ihre eigenen Ideen, wie das Familienleben aussehen soll …
>
> Bei mir heißt es, ich soll mehr im Haushalt helfen, soll mein Zimmer regelmäßig aufräumen UND soll auch auf meinen kleinen Bruder aufpassen, wenn meine Eltern ausgehen! Sie spinnen, meine Eltern! Haben sie nicht verstanden, dass ich mein eigenes Leben haben will, und dass ich sowieso wenig Freizeit habe?
>
> Meine beste Freundin, Eva, hat aber Glück! Ich bin etwas neidisch, weil die Eltern ihr mehr Freiheit geben. Sie haben also bessere Familienverhältnisse und weniger Streit. Ich finde mein Leben zu Hause ganz stressig und freue mich auf mein Studium.

es läuft – it works out / goes well
spinnen – to be crazy / nuts

1 Millie findet es normal, dass …

2 Es kann schwer sein, mit …

3 Ihre Eltern erwarten, dass sie …

4 Millie findet das nervig, weil sie …

5 Eva hat …

6 Millie kann ihr Studium kaum erwarten, weil …

[10 marks]

2 📖 Read these ten comments taken from Facebook. Then answer the questions by writing the number of the correct comment.

Which comment mentions …

a rumours?

b a door?

c dreams?

d getting up early?

e fruit?

In which comment does the writer say that …

f films are responsible for disappointments?

g he / she wants to escape into a private world of sound?

h he / she has been let down by a Facebook friend?

i What is the message in comment 4?

j What does comment 10 say?

[10 marks]

10 Facebook-Sprüche – die besten Einträge

1 Kopfhörer rein. Musik an. Welt aus.

2 Disney hat mir unrealistische Vorstellungen von Liebe gegeben!

3 Lebe deine Träume und verträume nicht dein Leben!

4 Wenn jemand aus meinem Leben geht und hofft, ich renne hinterher, dann tut's mir leid. So sportlich bin ich nicht.

5 Jeder Mensch ist eine neue Tür zu einer anderen Welt.

6 Ein Mathebuch ist der einzige Ort, wo es normal ist, 53 Melonen zu kaufen.

7 Früh aufstehen ist der erste Schritt in die falsche Richtung …

8 Vor kurzem dachte ich noch, du wärst jemand dem ich vertrauen kann, doch jetzt bist du nichts weiter als ein Name in meiner Facebook-Liste.

9 Gerüchte über mich!? WOW! … muss mein Leben interessant sein …

10 Haltet die Welt an … ich will aussteigen!!!

3 📖 Read these short poems about friendship and answer the questions in **English**.

> A Wenn es dir im Leben gut geht,
> lernen deine Freunde kennen, wer du bist.
> Und wenn es dir schlecht geht,
> lernst du kennen, wer deine Freunde sind.

> C Wenn uns viele Meilen trennen,
> bin ich froh, dass wir uns kennen.
> Du bist jemand, den man nie vergisst,
> weil du etwas Besonderes bist …

> B dein Leben ist wie eine Zugfahrt
> viele Menschen steigen ein
> einige steigen wieder aus;
> nur ganz wenige begleiten
> dich bis ans Ziel

1 In which poem does the author mention a journey?
2 Why is the friend in Poem C unforgettable?
3 According to Poem A, what happens when our life is going smoothly?
4 And what happens when things are not going well?
5 Why does it seem that the friends in Poem C don't see much of each other?   **[5 marks]**

> **Strategie**
>
> Always read the questions and any answer options **before** you listen to the recording for the first time. They are your early warning system and tell you which specific information to listen out for.
>
> If any vocabulary is provided in a glossary for you, it's there for a good reason. Look at these words and imagine the sounds of them before you listen.
>
> When listening to longer texts or conversations involving more than one person, train yourself to scribble the occasional note in German as you listen so that you'll remember the order of ideas you've heard. The listening test shouldn't become a memory test!

4 🎧 Listen to this radio report about cyberbullying. Which **four** statements are correct? Write the correct letters.

A	Bullying is more serious than some people think.
B	Victims of bullying are usually girls.
C	Bullying always takes place in private.
D	A bullying campaign often lasts a long time.
E	Mobile phones and the internet can play a part in bullying.
F	Bullies send nasty emails to their victims.
G	Cyberbullies publish embarrassing pictures of their victims on the internet.
H	Facebook has security measures which prevent this.

[4 marks]

> *der Ärger* – irritation, bother
> *der Angriff* – attack
> *schikanieren* – to hassle / bully
> *der Täter* – culprit

> **Strategie**
>
> When the questions for a listening task are in German, it's important to look first at the specific question words used, and make a connection between them and the sort of information they are directing you towards. For example:
> • *wo?* (where?) – a place
> • *wie?* (how? / what … like?) – a description
> • *was?* (what?) – an object or action
> • *wann?* (when?) – a time or day or date
> Looking at the questions before you listen will mean you are aware in advance of where your focus should be.

5 🎧 Hör dir an, was Max über seine Freunde sagt. Beantworte die Fragen auf **Deutsch**.

1 Wann sieht Max seine Freunde? (**zwei** Details)
2 Was hat er mit seinen Freunden gemeinsam?
3 Wo spielen sie Fußball? (**zwei** Details)
4 Wie ist Thomas? (**zwei** Details)
5 Was ist auch wichtig bei dieser Freundschaft?
6 Was hofft Max?

[9 marks]

> ⧟
> Foundation test and revise tasks are available in the Foundation book.

Higher – Writing and translation

Either:

1a Du schreibst ein Blog über Familienverhältnisse.

Schreib:

- wer deine Familienmitglieder sind
- wie du mit ihnen auskommst
- über einen Streit, den du gehabt hast
- über deine Pläne für nächstes Wochenende.

Du musst ungefähr **90** Wörter auf **Deutsch** schreiben. Schreib etwas über alle Punkte der Aufgabe.

[16 marks]

Or:

1b Dein Freund aus der Schweiz hat dich über neue Technologien gefragt. Schreib eine E-Mail.

Schreib:

- etwas über Computer in deiner Schule
- deine Meinung über soziale Netzwerke
- was du gestern mit deinem Handy gemacht hast
- warum das Internet manchmal gefährlich ist.

Du musst ungefähr **90** Wörter auf **Deutsch** schreiben. Schreib etwas über alle Punkte der Aufgabe.

[16 marks]

Strategie

Your writing will be more fluent and coherent if you can link your ideas together into more flowing sentences.

As an example, let's look at how to answer the second bullet point in activity 1a. A basic response would be:

Ich komme gut mit meinen Eltern aus. Mein Vater ist streng. Meine Mutter ist liebevoll. Sie ist nett. Meine Schwestern gehen mir auf die Nerven. Sie sind laut.

Although the messages are clearly conveyed and the German is all correct, this still doesn't sound very good. There are too many short and unconnected sentences.

A rather better response would be something like this:

*Ich komme gut mit meinen Eltern aus, **aber** mein Vater ist streng. Meine Mutter ist liebevoll **und** sie ist nett. Meine Schwestern gehen mir auf die Nerven, **denn** sie sind laut.*

The flow of language has been improved by the use of coordinating conjunctions.

Let's take it one step further and look at an even better response:

*Ich komme **meistens** gut mit meinen Eltern aus, **aber** mein Vater ist **manchmal etwas** streng. Meine Mutter ist **ganz** liebevoll **und immer** nett. Meine beiden Schwestern gehen mir auf die Nerven, **denn** sie sind **unglaublich** laut und frech.*

> *sie ist* has been deleted here to avoid repetition

Note what has changed:

- Time expressions have been added to most ideas.
- Other adverbs have been added to intensify the effect of the adjectives.
- Unnecessary repetition (*sie ist* …) has been removed.
- A couple of additional words have been added. Can you find them?

Either:

2a ✎ Du schreibst einen Eintrag für ein Internet-Forum: Heiraten gegen Zusammenleben.

Schreib:

* deine Meinung über Heiraten und Zusammenleben – pro und kontra
* deine eigenen Zukunftspläne – heiraten oder nicht?

Du musst ungefähr **150** Wörter auf **Deutsch** schreiben. Schreib etwas über alle Punkte der Aufgabe.

[32 marks]

Or:

2b ✎ Du schreibst ein Flugblatt für jüngere Kinder über das Internet – pro und kontra.

Schreib:

* was am Internet gut ist und wie du neulich das Internet benutzt hast
* über Risiken im Internet und wie man online sicher bleiben kann.

Du musst ungefähr **150** Wörter auf **Deutsch** schreiben. Schreib etwas über alle Punkte der Aufgabe.

[32 marks]

3 ⊤ Translate the paragraph into German.

> I usually get on well with my parents. We have only one problem – and it's the internet! I spend a lot of time in my room with my laptop and they don't like this. There was an argument yesterday because I wanted to use Facebook. They think social networks are too dangerous.

[12 marks]

Foundation test and revise tasks are available in the Foundation book.

Higher – Speaking

1 Role play

Your teacher or partner will play the part of your friend and will speak first.

You should address your friend as *du*.

When you see this – **!** – you will have to respond to something you have not prepared.

When you see this – **?** – you will have to ask a question.

> Du besprichst Beziehungen mit einem / einer neuen deutschen Freund / Freundin.
>
> - Verhältnis zu Eltern (**ein** Detail).
> - Streit worüber (**zwei** Details).
> - **!**
> - neulich Aktivitäten Clique (**zwei** Details).
> - **?** Freunde wichtig.

[15 marks]

2 Role play

Your teacher or partner will play the part of the parent and will speak first.

You should address the German parent as *Sie*.

When you see this – **!** – you will have to respond to something you have not prepared.

When you see this – **?** – you will have to ask a question.

> Sie besprechen soziale Netzwerke mit der Mutter / dem Vater Ihres deutschen Partners.
>
> - soziale Netzwerke: positive Aspekte (**ein** Detail).
> - soziale Netzwerke: Probleme (**zwei** Details).
> - **!**
> - neulich Facebook Benutzung (**zwei** Details).
> - **?** Facebook: Benutzung.

[15 marks]

Strategie

As you know, there's a '**!**' (**unexpected question**) in every role play. Don't just ignore this during the preparation time! Try to leave a few minutes to work out two or three things it **could** be – and write some brief notes accordingly.

In activity 2, for example, the conversation is about social networks, and you already **know** you will be asked what the plus points are, what the problems are, and what you've done recently on Facebook. So, what might the unknown question be?

3 📁 Photo card

- Look at the photo during the preparation period.
- Make any notes you wish to on an Additional Answer Sheet.
- Your teacher or partner will then ask you questions about the photo and related to the topic of **Me, my family and friends**.

Your teacher or partner will ask you the following three questions and then **two more questions** which you have not prepared.

- Was gibt es auf dem Foto?
- Was ist besser – Heiraten oder Zusammenleben?
- Wirst du eines Tages heiraten und Kinder haben?   **[15 marks]**

4 📁 Photo card

- Look at the photo during the preparation period.
- Make any notes you wish to on an Additional Answer Sheet.
- Your teacher or partner will then ask you questions about the photo and related to the topic of **Technology in everyday life**.

Your teacher or partner will ask you the following three questions and then **two more questions** which you have not prepared.

- Was gibt es auf dem Foto?
- Wie hast du neulich das Internet benutzt?
- Was sind die Gefahren des Internets?   **[15 marks]**

> **Strategie**
>
> Use the preparation time before your speaking test to get to grips with the photo card.
>
> The card tells you exactly what the first three questions will be, so can shape your responses.
>
> Make notes which will give you the prompts you need.
>
> Comment on as many aspects of the photo as possible! Don't just say how many people there are. Say whether they are male or female, young or old, what they look like, what they are wearing, where they are, what they're doing.

> **GGG**
>
> Foundation test and revise tasks are available in the Foundation book.

3.1 F Musikfan oder Filmfreak?

1 📖 Lies diesen Artikel über die deutsche Band Tokio Hotel und beantworte die Fragen auf Deutsch.

Read the article about the German band Tokio Hotel and answer the questions in German.

Biografie einer Band

Tokio Hotel ist eine deutsche Band aus Magdeburg. Mit bisher vier Nummer-eins-Singles in Deutschland und Österreich ist Tokio Hotel in deutschsprachigen Ländern eine der kommerziell erfolgreichsten Bands der letzten Jahre.

Die Mitglieder der Band kennen sich seit der Kindheit. Sie sind: Sänger Bill Kaulitz, Gitarrist Tom Kaulitz, Bassist Georg Listing und Schlagzeuger Gustav Schäfer.

Die Plattenfirma Universal Music vermarktet die Band seit 2007 über ganz Europa und seit 2008 auch in Nord- und Südamerika. Anfang Oktober 2014 hat die Band ihr fünftes Studio-Album *Kings of Suburbia* herausgebracht. Bis heute hat die Band über 6 Millionen Platten weltweit verkauft.

Ihre Welttournee (2015) war total ausverkauft.

1 Woher kommt die Band Tokio Hotel?
2 Wie weiß man, dass die Band erfolgreich ist?
3 Wie viele Mitglieder hat Tokio Hotel?
4 Wer spielt Schlagzeug?

5 Seit wann hört man ihre Musik in den Vereinigten Staaten?
6 Was hat die Band 2014 gemacht?
7 Wie weiß man, dass die Band 2015 viele Fans hat?

2 🎧 Listen to the people talking about films they have seen. Copy and complete the grid in English.

1 Frank   3 Faruk
2 Natascha   4 Elma

Listening for key information

Practise focusing on the essentials you need to answer the question. Have a look at this excerpt from activity 2. The bold bits are the essentials, and the rest is – in terms of the question to be answered – filler:

*Meine Freundinnen und ich machen **Filmabende**, wo wir uns **zu Hause** eine **DVD** ansehen. Das ist billiger als eine Eintrittskarte! Gestern haben wir uns den **neuen Twilight-Film** angesehen und waren ganz **aufgereg**t! So eine **tolle Liebesgeschichte** – und **mit Vampiren**!*

Challenge: Now look at another of the excerpts from activity 2. Work out for yourself which bits are the essentials!

Ich bin ein großer Filmfan und gehe regelmäßig ins Kino. Der letzte Film, den ich gesehen habe, war Ein streng geheimes Leben. Benedict Cumberbatch spielt die Hauptrolle, Alan Turing, einen britischen Codeknacker im Zweiten Weltkrieg. Ich habe den Film toll gefunden.

Strategie

	where film was seen	name of film	2 details about film	opinion of film
Example: 1 Frank	cinema	Ein streng geheimes Leben (*The Imitation Game*)	*stars Benedict Cumberbatch* *about a codebreaker in WW2*	*great*

3 **G** **T** Complete the sentences in the perfect tense using the verb given in brackets. Then translate the sentences into English.

Beispiel: Meine Schwester hat ihren Freund vorgestellt. (*vorstellen*)

1 Ich … mir gestern Abend den neuen James Bond Film … (*ansehen*)
2 Der Film … um 20 Uhr … (*anfangen*)
3 Joel und Ethan Coen … einen tollen Film … (*herausbringen*)
4 Er … sich die Sportsendung schon … (*angucken*)
5 Die Mitglieder der Band … sich auf der Uni … (*kennenlernen*)
6 … du gestern …? (*fernsehen*)

4 ◖◗ Rollenspiel. Partnerarbeit. Tauscht die Rollen.

Role play. Work with a partner. Swap roles.

Partner / Partnerin A		Partner / Partnerin B	
1	Was ist dein Lieblingsfilm?	1	Say what your favourite film is.
2	Was für ein Film ist das?	2	Say what kind of film it is.
3	Wer spielt die Hauptrolle(n)?	3	Say who stars in the film.
4	Worum geht es?	4	Say what the film's about.
5	Warum magst du diesen Film?	5	Say why you like this film.

5 ✎ Schreib deine Antworten für die Fragen in Aufgabe 4 in einem Absatz auf. Schreib ungefähr 90 Wörter.

Write your answers to the questions in activity 4 in a paragraph. Write about 90 words.

6 **T** Translate the paragraph into English.

> Man sagt oft, dass moderne deutsche Musik schlecht ist. Aber das stimmt nicht. Ich mag die deutsche Band Tokio Hotel und sie sind auch weltweit erfolgreich. Leider mag ich Rammstein nicht. Hardrock ist nicht meine Art von Musik.

Grammatik — page 186

Using separable verbs in the perfect tense

You'll remember that in the present tense, the front bit (prefix) breaks off the separable verb and slips to the end. In the perfect tense, where the **past participle** also slips to the end of the sentence, they meet up again to form the past participle of the separable verb. Look at these examples:

Die Band hat ein Studio-Album **herausgebracht**. (*herausbringen* – to release)
Ich habe mir den Film Hunger Games **angeguckt**. (*angucken* – to watch)

Here are the past participles of some other useful verbs: *angefangen* (started), *kennengelernt* (got to know / met), *ferngesehen* (watched TV).

Learn about the verb as second idea in the perfect tense. See page 60.

7 **T** Translate the sentences into German.

1 I often go to the cinema.
2 The tickets are quite expensive.
3 I watched a DVD yesterday evening. (*ansehen* or *angucken*)
4 I met my best friend at school. (*kennenlernen*)
5 We watch television every evening.

Mein Lieblingsfilm	ist …		
Das ist	ein Science-Fiction-Film / Horrorfilm / Abenteuerfilm / Actionfilm / Fantasyfilm / Liebesfilm / Zeichentrickfilm / Krimi	mit Benedict Cumberbatch / Rosamund Pike	in der Hauptrolle.
	eine (romantische) Komödie		
Es geht um	eine Liebesgeschichte / eine Gruppe Teenager / einen Kampf zwischen Gut und Böse / Vampire.		
Ich mag den Film,	weil er	aufregend / spannend / lustig / traurig / faszinierend	ist.
		gute Spezialeffekte / tolle Musik	hat.

3.1 H   Leinwand oder Flimmerkiste?

Lernziele

Talking more about music, cinema and TV

Using separable and reflexive verbs in the perfect tense

Working out the meaning of new words

1a 📖 Read the film review. Choose the five correct statements.

SKYFALL – ein hervorragendes James Bond Jubiläum

50 Jahre James Bond im Kino, und die Filme werden nur besser. *Skyfall* fängt spannend an. Bei einer Mission in Istanbul wird der MI6-Doppelnull-Agent (Daniel Craig) angeschossen und stürzt in eine Schlucht – man hält ihn für tot. Kurz darauf sterben sechs Menschen bei einem Bombenanschlag auf das MI6-Hauptquartier. England steht unter Attacke. Erste Spuren führen zum mysteriösen Cyber-Terroristen Silva (Javier Bardem).

Der Film handelt von der allgegenwärtigen **Bedrohung** globalen Terrors und konfrontiert Bond mit den Konflikten des 21. Jahrhunderts. *Skyfall* bietet alles, was man von der Bond-Filmreihe erwartet – Action, Abenteuer und charismatische Schauspieler, obwohl der Stil etwas anders ist – Bond ist diesmal kühler, **zeitgemäßer** und zeigt mehr Emotionen.

Was mir an *Skyfall* am besten gefallen hat? Erstens die Figuren, die die Schauspieler toll dargestellt haben, zweitens die aktionsgeladene Handlung, und dann den spektakulären Showdown, der in der Dunkelheit Schottlands stattgefunden hat. Der Film hat **fesselnd** angefangen und hat sich genauso spannend entwickelt. Total empfehlenswert!

anschießen – to shoot somebody	
stürzen – to fall	
die Schlucht – gorge, ravine	
tot – dead	
sterben – to die	
die Spur – trace	
handeln von – to be about, to deal with	
allgegenwärtig – ever-present	
bieten – to offer	
erwarten – to expect	
zeitgemäß – contemporary	
zeigen – to show	
darstellen – to portray, to represent	
aktionsgeladen – action-packed	
fesselnd – gripping	
entwickeln – to unfold	

1. Bond films are not as good as they used to be.
2. Bond is killed on a mission in Istanbul.
3. The MI6 headquarters are bombed.
4. Silva is a terrorist.
5. The film deals with a serious modern-day issue.
6. The style of *Skyfall* is the same as other Bond films.
7. The critic didn't find the characters very convincing.
8. The final scene took place in dark surroundings.
9. The film started quite slowly but got better.
10. The critic recommends the film highly.

1b 📖 Lies die Filmkritik nochmal. Wie sagt man auf Deutsch?

Verben: to begin, to be about, to offer, to expect, to take place, to portray, to unfold

Nomen: character, plot, series, actor, adventure

Adjektive: exciting, up to date, action-packed, gripping, recommended

Working out the meaning of new words

Sometimes you will need to infer (make an informed guess about) the likely meaning of unfamiliar words you encounter in reading texts. The surrounding words / context can help you with this.

Before you do the *Skyfall* reading activity, look at the words in bold in the text. What is there in each sentence which might help you get to grips with this word?

***Bedrohung** globalen Terrors* – a negative word / something which has to be confronted / to do with terrorism

***zeitgemäßer** und zeigt mehr Emotionen* – an aspect of Bond's character / behaviour / something to do with time / era (*Zeit*)

***fesselnd** angefangen … spannend entwickelt* – something about the feel of the film related to *spannend*

Challenge: As you read the film review, try out this tactic, rather than looking up all the words you don't know.

Strategie

2 **G** Complete the sentences with the correct form of the separable or reflexive verb given in brackets in the perfect tense.

1   Der Film … um 20 Uhr … (*anfangen*)
2   Ich … die Musik … (*aufnehmen*)
3   … du gestern …? (*fernsehen*)
4   Die Band … eine neue Single … (*herausbringen*)
5   Der Regisseur … die Atmosphäre gut … (*darstellen*)
6   Die Schauspieler … … in Schottland … (*sich erkälten*)
7   Daniel Craig … … schnell … (*sich erholen*)
8   Meine Eltern … … darüber … (*sich freuen*)
9   Ich … … über meinen Freund … (*sich ärgern*)
10 Die Verlobten … … … (*sich küssen*)

3 **T** Translate the sentences in activity 2 into English.

4 🎧 Listen to three people talking about TV programmes. Answer the questions in English.

Part A

1   Why doesn't Silke's mum agree to watch TV?
2   Which programme does Silke want to watch? Why?
3   What does she say about the last series?

Part B

4   What does her mum think Silke should be doing?
5   How does Silke respond?
6   What convinces her mum to give in?
7   How does Silke's dad spoil their plans?

Grammatik · page 186

Using separable and reflexive verbs in the perfect tense

In the perfect tense, the two bits of a separable verb join up again in the past participle (PP) at the end of the sentence.
Two things to remember:
• all reflexive verbs take *haben* in the perfect tense
• the reflexive pronoun immediately follows the bit of *haben*.

This example is both a reflexive and a separable verb:
*Ich habe **mir** einen Film **an**gesehen.*
You can see that the separable prefix *an* has linked up with the main PP of the verb (*gesehen*) and that *mir* follows *habe*.
Look at some more examples of either separable or reflexive verbs in the review of *Skyfall*. Can you say what each means?

Also learn about word order using the time – manner – place rule. See page 60.

---

5 💬 Rollenspiel. Partnerarbeit.

Partner / Partnerin A		Partner / Partnerin B	
1	Wie oft siehst du fern? Und wann?	1	Say how often and when you watch TV.
2	Welche Sendungen magst du?	2	Say which programmes you like.
3	Was ist deine Lieblingssendung?	3	Say what your favourite TV programme is.
4	Was für eine Sendung ist das? Ich habe … nie gesehen.	4	Describe what the programme is about.
5	Warum magst du …?	5	Explain why you like it.

6 ✏️ Schreib eine Rezension über einen Film oder eine Sendung, der / die dir gefallen hat. Begründe deine Meinung.

7 **T** Translate the paragraph into German.

I like films, but I don't often go to the cinema because it's expensive. I watch lots of films on DVD or online. That's cheaper! In my free time, I also listen to music. That can be either relaxing or exciting, and I can buy music on the internet. Today I've downloaded the new Tokio Hotel album.

3.1 Groundwork is available in the Foundation book.

3.2 F Wo wollen wir essen?

1 📖 Welches Bild passt zu welcher Werbung?

Which picture goes with which advert?

Restaurants

A **Würzig und schmackhaft!**
Gegrillte Fleisch-Spezialitäten!
Erleben Sie authentische
türkische Küche!

B **Restaurant Fischer bietet
täglich frischen Fisch.**
Kreative Küche in der
alten Fischhalle.

C **Tacos und Steaks.** Genießen Sie
die vielseitigen Landesküchen
aus Lateinamerika in Hamburg!

D **Ja, die Currywurst kommt
aus Hamburg!**
Hier ist sie am leckersten!

E **Von Aalsuppe bis rote Grütze**
Rezepte von echten Hamburger
Klassikern!

die Aalsuppe – eel soup
rote Grütze – a dessert made with
    red berries, red wine and cream

2 **G** Complete the sentences with the correct form of the verb given in brackets. Note that there are both regular and irregular verbs here!

1 Ich ... gern Federball. (*spielen*)
2 Er ... nach Hamburg. (*fahren*)
3 Wir ... das Auto. (*waschen*)
4 Ich ... eine E-Mail. (*schreiben*)
5 Er ... eine gelbe Hose! (*tragen*)
6 Meine Freund ... mir Blumen. (*geben*)
7 Die Lehrer ... uns viel. (*helfen*)
8 ... er Deutsch? (*sprechen*)
9 Er ... seinen Laptop. (*nehmen*)
10 Meine Mutter ... gern Wurst. (*essen*)

Grammatik

page 184

Revising the present tense

You will remember that some verbs are regular (weak) and some are irregular (strong).

- Regular verbs follow a neat pattern of endings – examples are **ich** *wohne*, **du** *spiel**st***, **er** *lieb**t**,* **wir** *kochen*. Look at the verb tables on pages 192–195 to check the different endings used.

- The verbs *haben* and *sein* are totally irregular and need to be known by heart.

- Remember that irregular verbs usually use the same endings, but they change their vowel sound in the *du* and *er / sie / es* forms:
  – replacing one vowel with another: *ich gebe* but *er gibt*
  – adding an umlaut: *ich fahre* but *du fährst*
  – adding an extra vowel: *ich sehe* but *sie sieht*.

- Here are a few of the irregular verbs you should know at this stage – in the *ich* and the *er / sie / es* forms.

infinitive	ich	er / sie / es
empfehlen	empfehle	empfiehlt
essen	esse	isst
fallen	falle	fällt
helfen	helfe	hilft
laufen	laufe	läuft
nehmen	nehme	nimmt ◄
schlafen	schlafe	schläft
sprechen	spreche	spricht
tragen	trage	trägt
waschen	wasche	wäscht

This verb loses the *h* and doubles the *m*!

Also learn about when to use different modes of address with the three words for 'you': *du*, *Sie* and *ihr*. See page 61.

3 🎧 Hör dir das folgende Gespräch an. Magda und Max sprechen über das Abendessen. Ergänze die Sätze auf Deutsch.

Listen to Magda and Max talking about dinner.
Complete the sentences in German.

1   Magda fragt, was sie …
2   Max hat …
3   Es ist nicht viel …
4   Sie gehen in …
5   Dort kann man …

4 🗨 In Gruppen von sechs Personen, spielt das Würfelspiel. Die erste Person würfelt und stellt die Frage mit dieser Nummer. Die zweite Person antwortet auf Deutsch, würfelt und stellt die nächste Frage, usw.

In groups of six, play the dice game. The first person throws the dice and asks the question with that number. The second person answers the question in German, then throws the dice and asks the question, etc.

Asking for clarification

When speaking another language, you will sometimes need to ask for help, explanation or clarification. Never be afraid to ask! As long as you can ask in German, you are keeping the communication going! Here are a couple of ways to ask for information:

Wie sagt man 'gravy' auf Deutsch? (How do you say 'gravy' in German?)

Wie heißt das auf Englisch? (What's that in English?)

Challenge: Now use these questions when doing the group speaking activity. If one of you doesn't know the word for e.g. strawberry, someone in the group may be able to help!

Strategie

⚀	Beschreib dein Lieblingsessen.	⚁	Was isst du nicht gern und warum?	⚂	Magst du Fastfood? Welches? Warum (nicht)?
⚃	Wer kocht bei dir zu Hause? Kocht er / sie gut?	⚄	Wie oft isst du im Restaurant? In welchem Restaurant?	⚅	Was hast du gestern (zum Frühstück / Mittagessen / Abendessen) gegessen?

5 ✏ Schreib deine Antworten für die Fragen vom Würfelspiel in Aufgabe 4 auf. Schreib jedes Mal mindestens einen Satz.

Write your answers to the dice game questions in activity 4.
Write at least one full sentence for each response.

6 🇹 Translate the paragraph into English.

Mein Lieblingsrestaurant ist eine kleine italienische Gaststätte in der Altstadt. Das Essen schmeckt spitze und die Leute sind immer freundlich und hilfsbereit. Gestern Abend habe ich Frikadellen mit einem grünen Salat gegessen und ein Glas Rotwein getrunken.

Ich mag (keinen / keine / kein) / liebe / hasse	Brot / Käse / Brokkoli.
Ich esse viel(e)	Kekse / Kuchen / Obst.
Ich trinke (keinen / keine / kein)	Alkohol / Milch / Tee / Kaffee.
Ich esse (keinen / keine / kein)	Fleisch / Bananen / Gemüse.
Mein Lieblingsessen ist	Hähnchen / Fisch mit Pommes.
Zum Frühstück / Abendessen esse ich	Frühstücksflocken / Salat.
In der Mittagspause esse ich	ein Schinkenbrot / einen Salat.

7 🇹 Translate the sentences into German.

1   We eat dinner at 8 o'clock.
2   My favourite breakfast is bread with honey and a cup of tea.
3   He often drives to Hamburg and goes to a restaurant.
4   My sister is a vegetarian and doesn't eat meat.
5   I am not a good cook!

3.2 H   Essen fassen!

1  Lies die Blogs über Essgewohnheiten. Welche fünf Aussagen sind richtig?

Ich ernähre mich gesund, weil ich nicht dick werden will. Ich benutze immer nur Magermilch, die weniger Fett enthält und esse regelmäßig Obst und Gemüse. Fleisch schmeckt mir meistens nicht, deshalb esse ich selten Fleischgerichte. **Nadja 17**

Ich muss zugeben, ich bin ein richtiger Vielfraß. Ich habe immer Hunger und mir gefallen allerlei Lebensmittel. Täglich esse ich drei umfangreiche Mahlzeiten (völlig in Ordnung), aber ich knabbere auch zwischendurch … einige Chips oder Kekse … das schmeckt immer gut! **Tobias 16**

Ich finde, man soll nicht zu hastig essen, wenn man richtig essen will. Man setzt sich hin, man isst in aller Ruhe, man nimmt sich Zeit, das Essen zu genießen. Eine Mahlzeit soll eine kleine Pause von der Hektik des Lebens sein. **Bernd 26**

Ich bin ledig und ich finde es wirklich zu mühsam, für mich allein zu kochen. Ich kaufe gewöhnlich im Supermarkt Fertiggerichte, oder ich esse mit Freunden oder Kollegen im Restaurant. Fastfood vermeide ich aber, weil es fettig und salzig ist und relativ wenig Nährwert hat. **Kristin 24**

1 Nadja will schlank bleiben.
2 Nadja isst oft Fleisch.
3 Essen gefällt Tobias.
4 Tobias isst nichts zwischen Mahlzeiten.
5 Bernd isst oft vor dem Fernseher.
6 Bernd mag ruhige Mahlzeiten.
7 Kristin kocht nicht oft zu Hause.
8 Kristin findet Fastfood nicht sehr gut.

sich ernähren – to eat
Lebensmittel – food
umfangreich – substantial
knabbern – to snack, to nibble
Nährwert – nutritional value

2a Listen to the conversation in a restaurant. Then answer the questions in English.

1 Where does the customer want to sit?
2 What does he order to drink?
3 What does he get to drink?
4 What's sold out?
5 What's in the 'treasure chest'?
6 What's the problem with his order for fish and chips?
7 What does the waitress say is 'not bad'?

2b Hör noch einmal zu. Wie sagt man das auf Deutsch?

1 Do you have a table free?
2 menu
3 Here we are!
4 I'm sorry.
5 Have you chosen?
6 One moment, please.
7 to order
8 What would you like?
9 starter
10 main course
11 sold out
12 selection
13 I don't believe it!
14 one …
15 another beer
16 the bill

Strategie

Spotting more common patterns in German / English words

These patterns of repeated slight differences can help you to recognise unknown words and to make sense of them. This skill is particularly helpful in reading and listening where the range of vocabulary you encounter can be quite varied. Consider these examples, some of which come from the activity on this page.

German **ch** / English k: *Milch* / mil**k**
German **z** / English t: *Salz* / sal**t**, *zehn* / **t**en
German **t** / English d: *trinken* / **d**rink, *tun* / **d**o
German **d** / English th: *Durst* / **th**irst, *danken* / **th**ank, *denken* / **th**ink

Challenge: Look back through your vocabulary book and see whether you can find further examples to add to these. You can also look through the *Glossar* in this book.

Speisekarte

der Sekt – German sparkling wine
die Austern – oysters (pl)
die Schatzkiste – a mixed tasting dish (literally: treasure chest)
die Garnelen – prawns (pl)
der Lachs – salmon
der Kabeljau – cod
die Forelle – trout

3 🔲 Rollenspiel im Restaurant. Partnerarbeit. Tauscht die Rollen.

Kunde / Kundin		Kellner / Kellnerin	
1	Greet the waiter / waitress and ask whether they have a table for two.	1	Ja, wir haben Tische frei. Wo möchten Sie sitzen?
2	Say you'd like to be near the window.	2	Natürlich. Kommen Sie bitte mit. Hier ist die Speisekarte.
3	Say you would like one salmon with salad and one steak and chips.	3	Ja, gerne. Und zu trinken?
4	Order a glass of white wine and a glass of red, also a bottle of mineral water.	4	Kommt sofort …
5	Ask for the bill.	5	Einen Augenblick, meine Damen und Herren. Ich komme gleich …

4 🟢 🔵 Translate the sentences into German, starting with the underlined part of the sentence.

Beispiel: **1** <u>Jeden Tag um 6 Uhr</u> mache ich meine Hausaufgaben.

1 I do my homework <u>every day at 6 o'clock</u>.
2 We eat in a Chinese restaurant <u>every weekend</u>.
3 <u>In the summer holidays</u> I'm going to work as a waiter / waitress in a café.
4 He plays football <u>every afternoon after school</u>.
5 I'm not going to eat any sweets <u>tomorrow</u>.
6 There are good shops <u>in the town centre</u>.
7 I'm going to Germany <u>next month</u>.
8 <u>Unfortunately</u> I can't go to the cinema today.

5 ✏️ Du schreibst einen Bericht über deine Essgewohnheiten. Schreib ungefähr 90 Wörter auf Deutsch.

- Was isst du normalerweise?
- Beschreibe dein Lieblingsessen.
- Was isst du nicht gern? Warum?
- Wie oft isst du in einem Restaurant? Warum? Mit wem?
- Beschreib einen Besuch im Restaurant. Wie war es?

6 🔵 Translate the paragraph into German.

> I usually eat well and I always have breakfast because I think it's the most important meal of the day. Every morning I eat cereals and drink fruit juice. That gives me energy for the school day. Last weekend was my mum's birthday and we had dinner in a French restaurant in town.

Grammatik — *page 182*

Using the correct word order with adverbial phrases

You'll remember that German is notoriously strict about where verbs appear. Once you know the rules, you will see the logic.

- In a main clause / basic sentence, the verb must be the **second idea**, and very often it will naturally be in second position because it has a subject pronoun (*ich, er, wir*, etc.) in front of it.
  *Ich **esse** heute nur Gemüse.*
  *Wir **lieben** Meeresfrüchte.*
  *Er **arbeitet** als Kellner.*

- If you add something else to the front of the sentence, as very often happens in German with time expressions (*heute, morgen, gestern Abend, später, nächsten Monat, im April*) and other adverbial phrases, you need to return the verb to its **second idea** position by inverting (swapping around) the verb and its subject. Look at these examples:
  *Jeden Tag **esse** ich viel Obst und Gemüse.*
  *In diesem Restaurant **essen** wir immer Meeresfrüchte.*
  *In den Sommerferien **arbeitet** er als Kellner.*

- Bear in mind that **second idea** does not necessarily mean the same as second word. Many expressions added to the front of a sentence will be made up of several words, but they are connected as **one** idea (e.g. *in den Sommerferien*).

Also learn more about forming questions with the different modes of address. See page 61.

🔗

3.2 Groundwork is available in the Foundation book.

Sport – für alle?

Lernziele

Talking about sports activities

Using separable and reflexive verbs in the future tense

Listening for essential words

1 📖 Read the poster in a youth club and answer the questions in English.

Datum	Vormittag (10–13 Uhr)	Nachmittag (14–18 Uhr)	Abend (ab 18 Uhr)
Mo 1.8	Musik – Blockflöte oder Schlagzeug	Führung durch die Kunstgalerie	
Di 2.8	Tennis im Stadtpark	Kochkurs	Jonglieren
Mi 3.8	Basketball im Stadtpark	Tischtennisturnier	
Do 4.8	Schachturnier	Kegelbahnbesuch	
Fr 5.8	Handball im Stadtpark	Basketball im Stadtpark	Filmabend
Sa 6.8	Federballturnier	Federballturnier	Diskoabend
Mo 8.8	Fußballturnier im Stadion	Fußballturnier im Stadion	
Di 9.8	Handball	Fechten oder Korbball	
Mi 10.8	Fechten oder Korbball	Handball	
Do 11.8	Tageswanderung im Taunus	Tageswanderung im Taunus	
Fr 12.8	Zumba	Volksmusikkonzert	Grillabend

EUER JUGENDKLUB SACHSENHAUSEN BIETET EIN TOLLES UND VOLLES PROGRAMM FÜR DIE SOMMERFERIEN!
VERMEIDE ENTTÄUSCHUNG UND RESERVIERE RECHTZEITIG DEINEN PLATZ!

1 What does the heading of the poster tell you to do?
2 How many different sports are mentioned here, and what are they?
3 What is the day trip?
4 Which sessions involve dancing?
5 On which day can you visit an art gallery?
6 Which session would you book if you love bowling?
7 And if you want to learn to cook?
8 When could you take part in a chess tournament?
9 What would you expect at the evening session on Friday 12th August?
10 Which new skill could you learn on the evening of 2nd August?

2 🎧 Listen to two people talking about plans for the coming week. Answer the questions in English.

1 What does Martin think of the youth club summer programme?
2 What does Jutta think about it?
3 Which day trip does Martin say Jutta should join in with?
4 What does Jutta say about day trips? (2 details)
5 What does Martin say they'll do on Saturday? (3 details)
6 What does Jutta say in the end?

Listening for essential words

Unless you happen to be a native speaker, there will always be some words you don't recognise when listening. The skill is to work out which words are essential and which are not. Once you know what information each question is asking for, you can focus on what you need to pick up from the recording in order to give an answer.

Remember also that the key idea may be repeated but in different words, so that you have more than one chance of grasping the essentials.

Challenge: Think about this as you do activity 2. Did you find examples of 'filler' (non-essential) words in the listening? Were there any instances of the key idea being repeated using different words?

Strategie

Grammatik *page 187*

3a **G** **T** Write the sentences in the correct order, starting with the underlined word. Then translate the sentences into English.

1   morgen – werde – mitfahren – <u>Ich</u>
2   wird – am Samstag – früh – <u>Er</u> – aufstehen
3   teilnehmen – an der Tanzstunde – wird – <u>Jutta</u>
4   sich – am Freitag – <u>Er</u> – amüsieren – wird
5   <u>Sie</u> – putzen – werden – die Zähne – sich

3b **T** Translate the sentences into German.

1   I'm going to sunbathe today.
2   We will enjoy ourselves at the weekend.
3   My brother will get up late.
4   Will you come with (us) tomorrow?
5   She'll watch TV later.

4 Partnerarbeit. Stellt euch und beantwortet die Fragen.

Work with a partner. Take turns to ask and answer the questions.

• Treibst du Sport?
• Was ist deine Lieblingssportart? Warum?
• Siehst du oft Sport im Fernsehen?
• Was wirst du dieses Wochenende machen?

5 Schreib deine Antworten auf die Fragen in Aufgabe 4.

Write your answers to the questions in activity 4.

6 **T** Translate the sentences into German.

1   I like sport. I'm interested in cricket, but my favourite sport is tennis.
2   I prefer playing basketball.
3   Best of all I like swimming. I find swimming relaxing.
4   Football is not my thing. It's stupid.
5   I'm not interested in hiking. It's hard work / tiring.
6   I can't stand badminton!

Using separable and reflexive verbs in the future tense

Remember that the future tense uses the right form of *werden* + infinitive at the end. Anything else in the sentence sits between these two key parts.

Wir werden	eine Wanderung	machen.
Wir werden	am Freibad	picknicken.

When the future tense verb is separable, the front part (separable prefix) and the main verb simply join up again at the end.

Ich werde	nicht	**teil**nehmen.
Du wirst		**mit**fahren.
Wir werden	um 10 Uhr	**ab**fahren.

When the future tense verb is reflexive, there is an extra part (the reflexive pronoun) which immediately follows the part of *werden*.

Wir werden	**uns**	gut	amüsieren.
Wir werden	**uns**	morgen	sonnen.

Also learn how to use modal verbs. See page 61.

Deine Meinung sagen (Giving your opinion)	
😊	🙁
Ich mag … … gefällt mir. Ich liebe … Ich … gern / lieber / am liebsten. Mein(e) Lieblings … Ich interessiere mich für … Ich habe Interesse an … … interessiert mich. … ist das Beste. … ist toll / spitze / fantastisch / spannend / entspannend. Ich finde … super / großartig.	Ich mag … nicht. … gefällt mir nicht. Ich … nicht gern. Ich interessiere mich nicht für … Ich habe kein Interesse an … … interessiert mich nicht. Ich finde … nicht gut / blöd. … ist langweilig / anstrengend / ermüdend. … ist nichts für mich. … ist nicht mein Ding. … kann ich nicht leiden.

Hast du Mumm?

Lernziele

Talking in more detail about sport

Revising the different words
for 'when'

Spotting feminine nouns

WM-Torschützenkönigin Sasic beendet Karriere

Im besten Fußballer-Alter beendet Celia Sasic ihre Karriere. Die 27 Jahre alte Nationalstürmerin teilte ihre Entscheidung via Facebook mit.

Fußball-Nationalspielerin Celia Sasic hat ihre aktive Karriere beendet. „Fußball ist meine Leidenschaft. Fußball begleitet mich schon mein ganzes Leben und wird auch immer ein Teil von mir sein", schrieb die 27 Jahre alte Stürmerin auf ihrer Facebookseite: „Ich habe mich entschieden, neue Wege zu gehen und meine aktive Laufbahn im Profifußball zu beenden." Sasic begann ihre Karriere in der Nationalmannschaft, damals noch unter ihrem Mädchennamen Okoyino da Mbabi, im Jahr 2005. Am 28. Januar spielte sie gegen Australien ihr erstes Länderspiel. Insgesamt spielte sie 111 Mal für die DFB-Frauen und erzielte dabei 63 Treffer. Zuletzt im Juni 2015 war die Angreiferin bei der WM-Endrunde in Kanada sechsmal erfolgreich und wurde WM-Torschützenkönigin. Mit den DFB-Frauen gewann Sasic auch Olympiabronze 2008 in Peking.

Bundestrainerin Neid versteht Sasic

„Ich bedauere die Entscheidung von Celia, kann sie aber verstehen, denn Fußball ist nicht alles im Leben, und irgendwann kommt der Zeitpunkt, wo man andere Prioritäten setzen muss", sagte Bundestrainerin Silvia Neid: „Für uns ist das ein echter Verlust, weil Celia eine bedeutende Persönlichkeit ist, die große Fußspuren hinterlässt. Sie war immer ein Vorbild, auf und neben dem Platz."

WM = Weltmeisterschaft – World Championships / World Cup
DFB = Deutscher Fußball-Bund – German Football Association

Spotting feminine nouns

You will already know some ways of guessing the gender of unfamiliar words. It's worth having a look at nouns which are always (or almost always) feminine, as these have the most reliable guidelines and the fewest exceptions. They are:

- most nouns ending in -e: *Karriere, Seite, Bronze, Endrunde (-n)*
- all nouns ending in *-in*: *Spielerin, Stürmerin, Angreiferin, Königin (-nen)*
- all nouns ending in *-ung*: *Entscheidung, Herausforderung (-en)*
- all nouns ending in *-schaft*: *Leidenschaft, Mannschaft (-en)*
- all nouns ending in *-heit / -keit*: *Persönlichkeit, Möglichkeit (-en)*
- all nouns ending in *-tät*: *Priorität (-en)*.

These feminine nouns always have a plural ending in *-n*, shown above in brackets.

Challenge: Which of the groups refers to female people? Which group is largely abstract nouns (things like love, hope, friendship)? Which other nouns do you already know which could be added to one of these groups?

Strategie

1 📖 Lies den Artikel und beantworte die Fragen auf Deutsch.

1 Was teilte Celia Sasic via Facebook mit?
2 Wie erklärte sie ihre Entscheidung?
3 Wird Fußball immer wichtig für sie bleiben?
4 Wann fing Sasic bei der Nationalmannschaft an?
5 Warum war das Spiel gegen Australien für Sasic wichtig?

2 🎧 Listen to the young people talking about extreme sports and answer the questions in English.

1 What sort of holiday has Alex booked?
2 Which sport does he not intend to do? Why?
3 Which sport does he want to try? Why?
4 Where and when has Jana done abseiling?
5 Which other activity appeals to her?
6 What does Tom say you need for this?
7 What is Alex's good idea?
8 Why has he suggested this? (2 details)

3 **G** **T** Complete the sentences with *wann*, *wenn* or *als* and translate them into English.

1   … hast du Freiwasserschwimmen gemacht?
2   Ich habe Fallschirmspringen probiert, … ich in Neuseeland war.
3   Wir können wandern gehen, … das Wetter schön ist.
4   Ich habe keine Ahnung, … sie nach Spanien fahren.
5   … er in den Urlaub fährt, fahren wir mit.
6   Ich habe Abseilen gemacht, … ich letztes Jahr in Frankreich war.

4 **T** Translate the paragraph into German.

> I like many different sports, and often go swimming. When I have time I like going to the gym. But last weekend, when I was studying for a maths test, I couldn't go. When I'm older I want to try skiing. It is sometimes dangerous, but it's very exciting!

5 🗨 Gruppenarbeit (drei oder vier Personen). Diskutiert Extremsportarten – pro und kontra. Seht euch die Tabelle unten an.

positive Aspekte	negative Aspekte
aufregend	die Risiken / Gefahren
aktiv	gefährlich
sportlich	riskant
gesund (körperlich / psychisch)	man riskiert sein Leben
draußen	viel Ausrüstung
im Freien	spezifische Kleidung
in der Natur	kann teuer sein
eine Herausforderung	unverantwortlich
ein richtiges Erlebnis	Eltern machen sich Sorgen
persönliche Leistung	egoistisch
Teamgeist	
stärkt den Charakter	
man überwindet Angst	
man überwindet Schwierigkeiten	
macht mutig	
man lernt Selbstständigkeit	

Revising the different words for 'when'

German has three words for 'when', and each is used differently!

- **wann** is used either to ask a **direct** question: *Wann fährst du in die Alpen?* or to refer to a question which has been asked (an **indirect** question): *Ich weiß nicht, wann er abfährt.*
- **wenn** is used to say 'when' in the present or future tense: *Wenn man in den Alpen ist, …* It is also used to say 'whenever' and 'if': *Wenn man nicht frieren will, … Man braucht einen Neoprenanzug, wenn man im Meer schwimmt.*
- **als** is used to say 'when' in the past tense: *Als ich in Australien war …* (When I was in Australia …)

One very important thing to bear in mind is that *wenn* and *als* are subordinating conjunctions, so move the verb to the end, and they need a comma to divide the two clauses.

Also learn about using past, present and future time frames. See page 61.

page 184

6 🖊 Schreib ein Blog über Sport auf Deutsch (ungefähr 90 Wörter).

- Sag, welchen Sport du gern machst.
- Beschreibe deinen Lieblingssport.
- Welchen Sport machst du in der Schule? Wie ist er?
- Was denkst du über Extremsport?
- Welchen Sport möchtest du in der Zukunft machen?

3.3 Groundwork is available in the Foundation book.

G   Free-time activities

1 Write the sentences in the correct order. The first idea is underlined each time. Then translate the sentences into English.

1   Restaurant – türkisches – in – ein – gegangen – wir – sind – <u>Am Freitag</u>

2   gegessen – ich – <u>Zum Frühstück</u> – habe – Müsli

3   Bruder – hat – mein – gespielt – Basketballturnier – <u>Im Sommer</u> – im

4   Mutter – meine – Brathähnchen – Pommes – <u>Gestern</u> – gemacht – mit – hat

5   Freunde – <u>Am Nachmittag</u> – gegangen – kegeln – sind – meine

2 Translate the sentences into German. Then label each expression in the sentences with 'time', 'manner' or 'place'.

1   I'm going into town by bus this afternoon.

2   We played football in the park with friends last Saturday.

3   She's having a film evening at home this evening.

4   Tomorrow we're having a basketball tournament at school.

5   I like to go to the cinema at the weekend.

6   Last year I was on holiday with my grandparents.

3 Which form of address would you use to speak to the following people?

1   your brother

2   your mum

3   your maths teacher

4   the waiter in a restaurant

5   two of your friends

6   the doctor

7   your best friend

8   your dog

9   your whole football or netball team

The verb as second idea in the perfect tense

Grammatik — page 185

Exactly the same rules apply in the perfect as in the present – or indeed any other tense! The 'working' verb (the verb which matches its subject) will be the second idea in any normal sentence.

In the perfect tense, the 'working' verb will always be a form of *haben* or *sein*.

*Gestern **haben** wir im Restaurant gegessen.*
*Letzte Woche **ist** er nach Berlin gefahren.*

Word order using the time – manner – place rule

Grammatik — page 190

The time – manner – place rule is another important rule about word order. It simply tells you the order for different expressions in a sentence: a time expression (**when**) comes before a manner expression (**how**), which comes before a place expression (**where**):
Ich gehe am Freitagabend mit Freunden auf ein Ed Sheeran Konzert.
Am Freitagabend gehe ich mit Freunden auf ein Ed Sheeran Konzert.

If in the sentence there are only two types of expression, the respective order is still observed.

Modes of address (the three words for 'you')

Grammatik — page 182

Unlike English, where we simply say 'you' no matter whom we're speaking to, in German you need to vary the word according to who that person is and according to how many people you're talking to.

• Use the *du* form to speak to one person you know well – this is a familiar form. You can use it to speak to friends, family and pets!

• There is also a polite / formal mode of address. This is the *Sie* form. You will need this form to speak to your teacher and other adults. *Sie* is always written with a capital letter when it means 'you' and can be singular or plural.

• You also need to be able to recognise the *ihr* form. This is the plural familiar form, used to speak to two or more people you know.

Grammatik

4a Complete the sentences with the correct form of the verb given in brackets.

1   Wann … Sie zurück? (*kommen*)
2   Ihr … hier! (*bleiben*)
3   Du … heute Geburtstag! (*haben*)
4   … ihr gern Musik? (*hören*)
5   … du ins Restaurant? (*gehen*)
6   Sie … hier warten. (*sollen*)
7   … ihr mit ins Kino? (*kommen*)
8   Sie … gut Geige, Herr Kennedy! (*spielen*)
9   … du in der Cricketmannschaft? (*sein*)
10 … Sie mir helfen, Frau Schmidt? (*können*)

Forming questions with the different modes of address

You will need to be able to actively use all three modes of address (*du*, *Sie*, *ihr*).
The most likely scenario for using these will be when asking questions in a role play.
Remember that to ask a question which has a yes / no response, you simply need to invert the verb and its subject:
Kommst du heute Abend mit?
If you are using an interrogative (question word), the same inversion takes place following the question word:
Wie kommst du nach Hause?

page 182

4b Combine the words to form questions. Use the correct form of the verb and the form of address given in brackets (*du*, *ihr* or *Sie*).

1   Wann   fahren   in die Schweiz   (*du*)
2   Warum   kommen   nicht mit ins Kino   (*ihr*)
3   Wie   finden   den Film   (*Sie*)
4   Wie oft   gehen   schwimmen   (*du*)
5   Wie viele bekommen   Hausaufgaben   (*du*)
6   Warum   fahren   nach London   (*Sie*)
7   Wohin   gehen   am Samstag   (*ihr*)
8   Woher   kommen   (*du*)

5 Complete the sentences using the German for the words given in brackets.

1   … … später ins Kino gehen. (*I want to*)
2   … … mitkommen? (*Do you want to*)
3   … … Deutsch sprechen. (*We can*)
4   … Rugby … (*I can play*)
5   Ich … im Haushalt … (*I have to help*)
6   Wir … uns … (*We'll have to text*)
7   … … ins Kino …? (*Are you allowed to go*)
8   Er … mir … (*He is supposed to write*)

Using modal verbs

Modal verbs are a special group of verbs which use the <u>infinitive</u> of another verb to complete their sense: *müssen* (to have to), *wollen* (to want to), *können* (to be able to), *sollen* (to be supposed to), *dürfen* (to be allowed to).
Ich **will** heute Abend <u>fernsehen</u>.
Kannst du <u>schwimmen</u>?
Ich **muss** jetzt Hausaufgaben <u>machen</u>.
Man **soll** viel mehr Sport <u>treiben</u>.
Ich **darf** am Wochenende nicht <u>ausgehen</u>.

page 185

6 Translate the sentences into German.

1   I know that I probably watch too much television. I spend at least three hours every evening in front of the 'box'.
2   On Saturday evening I watched *The X Factor* with my friends, and we had great fun together. Some of the singers were really awful!
3   Tomorrow I'm going to watch a documentary film about Egypt and its history. My mum will be happy, because this time it will be educational!

Using past, present and future time frames

It's important for you to be able to express yourself clearly in all three time frames and to be able to use a range of tenses in your speaking and writing.

Check on the rules for forming the perfect and future tenses.
See pages 184–187.

pages 184–187

Vokabeln

3.1 Music, cinema and TV

3.1 F Musikfan oder Filmfreak?
➡ *pages 48–49*

	anfangen	to start, to begin
	angucken / ansehen	to watch, to look at
	ausverkauft	sold out
	deutschsprachig	German-speaking
	erfolgreich	successful
	es geht um	it's about
die	*Hauptrolle (-n)*	starring role, main role
	herausbringen	to release (record etc.)
	kennenlernen	to meet, to get to know
die	*Komödie (-n)*	comedy
das	*Mitglied (-er)*	member
die	*Plattenfirma (-en)*	record company
das	*Schlagzeug*	drum kit
die	*Tournee (-s)*	tour
	verkaufen	to sell
	weltweit	worldwide

3.1 H Leinwand oder Flimmerkiste?
➡ *pages 50–51*

das	*Abenteuer (–)*	adventure
	aufnehmen	to record
	einladen	to invite
	entspannend	relaxing
die	*Flimmerkiste (-en)*	box, TV
	sich freuen (über)	to be happy (about)
	hervorragend	excellent, outstanding
das	*Jahrhundert (-e)*	century
die	*Leinwand (¨e)*	the big screen, cinema
	Lust haben, etwas zu tun	to feel like doing something
	der *Regisseur (-e)*	director
die	*Reihe (-n)*	series (films / books)
der	*Schauspieler (–)*	actor
die	*Schauspielerin (-nen)*	actress
der	*Teilnehmer (–)*	participant
	tot	dead
	zeitgemäß	contemporary, up to date

3.2 Food and eating out

3.2 F Wo wollen wir essen?
➡ *pages 52–53*

die	*Aalsuppe*	eel soup
das	*Abendessen (–)*	dinner, evening meal
	keine Ahnung haben	to have no idea
die	*Altstadt*	the old part of town
das	*Brathähnchen (–)*	roast chicken
die	*Currywurst (¨e)*	spicy sausage
die	*Frikadelle (-n)*	meatball
das	*Frühstück (-e)*	breakfast
	genießen	to enjoy
das	*Hähnchen (–)*	chicken
die	*Himbeere (-n)*	raspberry
der	*Honig*	honey
	Hunger haben	to be hungry
die	*Kartoffel (-n)*	potato
die	*Küche (-n)*	cuisine, kitchen
der	*Kühlschrank (¨e)*	fridge
das	*Mittagessen (–)*	lunch
die	*Sahne*	cream
das	*Schinkenbrot (-e)*	ham sandwich
die	*Suppe (-n)*	soup

3.2 H Essen fassen!
➡ *pages 54–55*

	allerlei	all sorts of
der	*Augenblick (-e)*	moment
die	*Auswahl (-en)*	selection, choice
	bestellen	to order
	Chips	crisps (pl)
	Was darf es sein?	what would you like? (in a shop / restaurant)
	dick	thick, fat
	draußen	outside, outdoors
	drinnen	inside, indoors
	Durst haben	to be thirsty
die	*Ecke (-n)*	corner
	empfehlen	to recommend
	enthalten	to contain
das	*Fett (-e)*	fat

das	Fertiggericht (-e)	ready meal
das	Gericht (-e)	dish, meal
das	Hauptgericht (-e)	main course
	holen	to get, to fetch
der	Kellner (–)	waiter
die	Kellnerin (-nen)	waitress
	es macht nichts	it's OK, it doesn't matter
die	Magermilch	skimmed milk
der	Meeresblick (-e)	sea view
die	Meeresfrüchte	seafood (pl)
	mühsam	arduous, hard work
	Muscheln	mussels (pl)
die	Rechnung (-en)	bill
die	Speisekarte (-n)	menu
das	Stück (-e)	piece
	Das tut mir leid.	I'm sorry.
	vermeiden	to avoid
der	Vielfraß (-e)	a greedy eater / glutton
die	Vorspeise (-n)	starter
	wählen	to choose
	sich die Zeit nehmen	to take your time

3.3 Sport

3.3 F Sport – für alle?
➡ pages 56–57

	abfahren	to leave, to depart, to go off
	sich amüsieren	to enjoy oneself
	anstrengend	hard work, effortful
der	Ausflug (¨e)	trip, excursion
	baden gehen	to bathe, to swim
der	Besuch (-e)	visit
die	Blockflöte (-n)	recorder
das	Ding (-e)	thing
	ermüdend	tiring
das	Fechten	fencing
	frische Luft schnappen	to get a breath of fresh air
die	Führung (-en)	guided tour
der	Grillabend (-e)	barbecue
	großartig	great
	jonglieren	to juggle
der	Jugendklub (-s)	youth club

die	Kegelbahn (-en)	bowling alley
	kegeln	to bowl
die	Kochkurs (-e)	cookery course
die	Kunstgalerie (-n)	art gallery
der	Reisebus (-se)	coach
das	Schach	chess
	sich sonnen	to sunbathe
	teilnehmen	to take part, to join in
das	Tischtennis	table tennis
das	Turnier (-e)	tournament
	wandern	to hike, to walk
die	Wanderung (-en)	hike

3.3 H Hast du Mumm?
➡ pages 58–59

die	Angst (¨e)	fear
	aufregend	exciting
die	Ausrüstung (-en)	equipment, kit
	begleiten	to accompany, to be with
	sich entscheiden	to decide
	erleben	to experience
das	Fallschirmspringen	parachuting
	im Freien	outside, in the open air
die	Fußspur (-en)	footprint
der	Gebirgssee (-n)	mountain lake
	gefährlich	dangerous
die	Herausforderung (-en)	challenge
	körperlich	physical
die	Leistung (-en)	achievement
die	Möglichkeit (-en)	possibility
	Mumm haben	to have the courage
	mutig	brave, courageous
der	Neoprenanzug (¨e)	wetsuit
	probieren, ausprobieren	to try out
	tauchen	to dive
	überwinden	to overcome
	unternehmungslustig	adventurous
das	Wildwasserschwimmen	white-water swimming
der	Zeitpunkt (-e)	point in time, moment

4.1 F

Hurra! Die Tradition ist da!

Lernziele

Talking about customs and traditions

Using adjectives as nouns

Paraphrasing when speaking

1 📖 Lies die Texte. Welche vier Aussagen sind richtig?

Read the texts. Which four statements are correct?

1 Zuckertüten

Am ersten Schultag bekommen Kinder in Deutschland, Österreich und in der Schweiz eine große bunte Tüte aus Karton voller Süßigkeiten und Geschenke! Das Gute daran ist, dass der erste Schultag gut schmeckt! Nicht nur die Deutschen, sondern auch Amerikaner haben diese schöne Tradition.

2 Valentinstag

Am 14. Februar soll man romantisch sein! Man kauft eine Valentinskarte – oder mehr als eine – und schickt sie anonym an die Geliebte oder den Geliebten. Rote Rosen, Pralinen in Form von Herzen, oder ein Plüschbär sind auch gute Valentinsgeschenke.

3 Halloween

Am Tag vor Allerheiligen, am 31. Oktober, verkleiden sich Kinder als Hexen oder Gespenster, basteln Laternen aus Kürbissen und gehen von Tür zu Tür, um von Bekannten und Nachbarn Süßigkeiten oder Geld zu bekommen. Dabei sagen sie: „Süßes oder Saures!"

4 Der 1. April

An diesem Tag im Frühling muss man gut aufpassen! Es ist ein Tag voller Scherze und komischer Streiche. Dieser Tag existiert in ganz Europa und vielleicht weltweit. In Frankreich klebt man einen Fisch aus Papier auf Freunde und in England hat einmal die BBC über Spaghettibäume berichtet!

1 Wenn sie zum ersten Mal zur Schule gehen, bekommen viele deutsche Kinder Bonbons.

2 Diese Tradition existiert nur in deutschsprachigen Ländern.

3 Valentinstag findet im Herbst statt.

4 Am Valentinstag kauft man romantische Karten und Geschenke.

5 Zu Halloween trägt man gruselige Kostüme.

6 In Frankreich isst man am 1. April Fisch.

7 Am ersten April gibt es viele Scherze und Streiche.

8 In England gibt es Spaghettibäume.

basteln – to make, to do handicrafts
die Kürbisse – pumpkins (pl)

2a 🄶 Write the adjectival nouns using the basic adjective given in brackets.

1 the old man (*alt*)
2 an old lady (*alt*)
3 the strangers (*fremd*)
4 the patient / sick person (m) (*krank*)
5 the rich man (*reich*)
6 the blind man (*blind*)
7 the poor woman (*arm*)
8 my dear (f) (*lieb*)
9 the young people (*jugendlich*)
10 the adults (*erwachsen*)

2b 🄶 Add the correct ending to the adjectival nouns.

1 Die Deutsch__ haben viele schöne Traditionen.
2 Kennst du den Deutsch__?
3 Mein Bekannt__ gibt den Kindern Bonbons.
4 Wir sehen heute unsere neuen Bekannt__.

Using adjectives as nouns

German adjectives can be transformed into nouns. They have features of nouns (capital letter, gender, case) **and** of adjectives (endings which change according to case).

Examples: *der Deutsche, die Bekannte, das Gute, ein Deutscher, ein Bekannter.*

They are used with a definite (*der / die / das*) or an indefinite (*ein / eine / ein / (k)ein*) article and you need to use the right endings. Follow the patterns given in the adjective endings tables on page 181.

Also learn about the names of countries and places in German. See page 72.

Grammatik   *page 181*

3 🎧 Listen to Mike and Marta discussing their favourite traditions and read the statements. Are the statements true (T), false (F) or not in the text (NT)?

1　There's a Halloween street party every year in Mike's street.
2　Some people dress up as magicians.
3　Last year Mike went as Voldemort.
4　They eat in someone's house.
5　Sometimes they have a firework display.
6　Marta agrees that Halloween is a fantastic tradition.

7　She sends her boyfriend an expensive Valentine's present.
8　She writes a poem for her boyfriend.
9　Sebastian bought her a heart-shaped cushion this year.
10　Mike thinks that Valentine's Day is all a bit cheesy.

4 🗨 Partnerarbeit. Sieh das Bild an und mach Notizen. Wechselt euch ab, die Fragen zu stellen und zu beantworten.

Work with a partner. Look at the picture and make some notes. Take turns to ask and answer the questions.

- Was gibt es auf dem Foto?
- Wann isst du mit der ganzen Familie?
- Was isst du gern / nicht gern und warum?

5 🖊 Du schreibst eine E-Mail an deinen deutschen Onkel. Schreib ungefähr 40 Wörter über die Themen.

You're writing an email to your German uncle. Write approximately 40 words about the topics.

- eine Wanderung
- ein Picknick
- Halloween
- einen Grillabend

Prost! / Zum Wohl! – Cheers!

6 🅣 Translate the paragraph into English.

> Am ersten Mai habe ich mit meiner Familie die traditionelle Wanderung im Wald gemacht. Es war ein sonniger Tag und zu Mittag haben wir unser Picknick neben einem See gemacht. Ich finde es großartig, im Freien zu essen.

7 🅣 Translate the sentences into German.

1　My favourite tradition is Halloween because we have a big party.
2　Are you going for a walk on May Day?
3　I hope the weather will be fine.
4　We would like to have a picnic in the woods.
5　Last year it rained and was very cold.

Paraphrasing when speaking

There may be a word you would like to use in the speaking test but don't know in German. You can try using **another word** which you do know and which is **similar** to the word you want.

If, for example, you are talking about Christmas lunch, you may not know the word for 'turkey', but could say instead *ein sehr großes Hähnchen* (a very large chicken) and add something like *Das ist ein traditionelles Essen zu Weihnachten*. This would convey your meaning absolutely clearly.

Challenge: Try out this technique when you do activity 4. Can you find a cunning way to talk about things in the picture that you don't know in German? Try this out with 'tablecloth', 'bread basket', etc.

Strategie

4.1 H   Bräuche braucht das Land

1 📖 Lies diesen Text über eine deutsche Tradition und beantworte die Fragen auf Deutsch.

Bleigießen zu Silvester – das Silvester-Orakel

Das Bleigießen ist einer der beliebtesten Silvesterbräuche zum Vorhersagen der Zukunft im neuen Jahr. Tatsächlich handelt es sich nicht wirklich um das Gießen von Blei, sondern von Zinn. Blei ist hochgiftig und daher zu gefährlich. Zinn schmilzt leicht und ist sicherer.

Man braucht:

* Zinn, zum Beispiel von der Rolle
* eine Kerze
* einen Schmelzlöffel
* eine Schüssel mit Wasser zum Abkühlen.

Zum Bleigießen erhitzt man das Metall in einem Löffel über einer Kerze, bis es flüssig ist. Das geschmolzene Zinn gießt man dann in die Schüssel. Durch die Kälte des Wassers erstarrt das Metall sofort wieder und bildet interessante Formen. Es macht Spaß, diese Formen zu deuten!

das Bleigießen – lead-pouring
das Vorhersagen – predicting
das Zinn – tin, pewter
giftig – poisonous
schmelzen – to melt
die Schüssel – bowl
erstarren – to set
deuten – to interpret, to read

Using infinitives as nouns   Strategie

Once the basics of German grammar are in place, you can enjoy developing a broader range of structures and vocabulary.

One good way to boost your vocabulary is to know how some words are formed in German. A good example is the use of the infinitive of a verb as a neuter noun. This means that *lesen* (to read) can easily be tweaked to become the noun *das Lesen* (reading), simply by capitalising the word and adding an article.

Challenge: There are several examples in activity 1 of this handy little linguistic conjuring trick. *Das Bleigießen* (lead-pouring) is the first one. Can you find three more?

1 Warum nennt man Bleigießen das „Silvester-Orakel"?
2 Warum benutzt man lieber Zinn als Blei?
3 Was braucht man (außer Zinn)?
4 Wie erhitzt man das Metall?
5 Warum braucht man kaltes Wasser?
6 Was macht Spaß?

2 🎧 Hör dir den Anfang dieses Märchens an. Welche vier Aussagen sind richtig?

1 Der Prinz wohnte in einem Schloss im Wald.
2 Der Prinz war reich und schön.
3 Im Tiergarten gab es einen Bären und zwei Elefanten.
4 Der Löwe war mutig.
5 Der Papagei war grün.
6 Der Fink sang jeden Morgen.
7 Niemand wusste, warum der Prinz nicht glücklich war.
8 Ein Mann kam zum Schloss.

verwöhnt – spoiled (child)
gehören (+ dative) – to belong to
die Sammlung – collection
merkwürdig – remarkable
der Papagei – parrot
der Fink – finch

3 ⓖ Write the sentences in the correct order, starting with the underlined word.

1 Prinz – <u>Trotzdem</u> – immer – war – traurig – der
2 waren – <u>Letztes</u> – Italien – wir – Jahr – in
3 Zukunft – dem – man – <u>Mit</u> – vorhersagen – Silvester-Orakel – die – kann
4 Garten – es – uns – gibt – <u>Bei</u> – großen – auch – einen
5 meiner – Mutter – ich – Rosen – <u>Zum</u> – kaufte – Muttertag – rote

4 ⓣ Translate the paragraph into English.

In diesem merkwürdigen Tiergarten hatte der Prinz nicht nur einen mutigen Bären, sondern auch einen klugen Löwen und einen starken Elefanten, und in dem Vogelhaus des Prinzen gab es nicht nur einen goldenen Papageien, sondern auch einen silbernen Finken. Der schöne Vogelgesang des magischen Finken erfüllte jeden Morgen die sonnenreiche duftende Luft.

5 ⓣ Translate the text into German.

Stille Tage

There are special days in Germany which are called 'quiet days'. These days are different from one *Land** to another. (say: from *Land* to *Land*) On these days, there are certain restrictions which one should respect. On Good Friday, for example, one should not dance – there's a dancing ban.

Other quiet days are Ash Wednesday, Easter Sunday and Remembrance Day.

*das Land = a state / federal division of Germany, like Bayern (Bavaria)

Grammatik

Revising the verb as second idea in the sentence

Remember this key German word-order rule and train yourself to check that you are respecting it when you speak and write the language.
Basic sentences should have one of these two forms:

normal word order		
subject	verb	rest of sentence
Er	*war*	*reich und schön …*

inverted word order			
first idea	verb	subject	rest of sentence
Im Schlossgelände	*gab*	*es*	*einen wunderbaren Garten …*

In this example a **first idea** (*Im Schlossgelände*) has been added to the front of the sentence, so that the <u>subject</u> (*es*) and **verb** (*gab*) have inverted (swapped positions) to allow the verb to return to being second idea. Here are two more examples showing inversion:
*In diesem merkwürdigen Tiergarten **hatte** <u>der Prinz</u> nicht nur einen mutigen Bären …*
*Eines Tages **kam** <u>ein Reisender</u> vorbei und klopfte an das Schlosstor …*

Learn also how to use weak masculine nouns. See page 72.

die Einschränkung – restriction
Karfreitag – Good Friday
das Verbot – ban
Aschermittwoch – Ash Wednesday
Volkstrauertag – Remembrance Day

page 189

---

6 🗣 Bereite einen kleinen Vortrag zum Thema Traditionen vor.

Du sollst über mindestens zwei Bräuche aus dieser Liste sprechen.

Sag:
- wie du feierst
- was es zu essen gibt
- was du letztes Jahr gemacht hast.

der erste April	*Halloween*
Silvester	*Muttertag*
Valentinstag	*Ostersonntag*

7 ✏ Schreib den Text deines Vortrags, indem du zwei Traditionen beschreibst. Schreib ungefähr 90 Wörter.

4.1 Groundwork is available in the Foundation book.

4.2 F

Das muss gefeiert werden!

1 📖 Lies den Artikel über zwei Feste in Deutschland und die Aussagen. Welches Fest ist das: Karneval oder Eid al-Fitr?

Read the article about two festivals in Germany and the sentences. Which festival is it: carnival or Eid al-Fitr?

Karneval

Karneval gibt es in vielen Teilen Deutschlands, der Schweiz und Österreichs. In Südwestdeutschland heißt es Fastnacht, und in Südostdeutschland Fasching. Der berühmteste Karneval findet im Rheinland statt und beginnt im Februar.

Viele Leute verkleiden sich und tragen bunte Kleider und Masken. Auf den Straßen sieht man Umzüge mit bunt geschmückten Wagen.

Es ist eine sehr alte Tradition und stammt aus dem 13 Jahrhundert. Die alte Idee des Karnevals war, die bösen Geister des Winters zu vertreiben und die guten Geister des Frühlings zu wecken. Nach zwei Tagen ist die Feier zu Ende. Am Aschermittwoch beginnt die vierzigtägige Fastenzeit vor Ostern.

Eid al-Fitr

Die Feier am Ende des heiligen Fastenmonats Ramadan heißt Eid al-Fitr. Das genaue Datum berechnet man nach dem islamischen Mondkalender.

An diesem Tag gibt es das Festgebet und alle tragen besonders schöne Kleider, um in die Moschee oder auf den Gebetsplatz zu gehen. Einige Frauen dekorieren ihre Hände mit Henna.

Die Festlichkeiten geschehen zu Hause mit Verwandten und Familie. Zu dieser Zeit schmückt man das Haus mit Lichtern, gibt Geschenke und bereitet viele Süßigkeiten vor.

Eid Al-Fitr

Spotting different words used to express the same idea

🔄 Strategie

When reading and listening, it's useful to spot different ways of saying the same thing.

In the text for activity 1, you'll see *Viele Leute verkleiden sich*, which is immediately explained by what follows … *tragen bunte Kleider und Masken*, so you know the key idea concerns dressing up / disguising oneself.

In the listening, activity 2, this same verb occurs, and is explained as follows: *Richard hatte eine Soldatenuniform an. / Ich habe mein Piratenkostüm getragen.*

Challenge: Work with a partner to suggest other ways of expressing these key ideas: *dekorieren / Verwandte / Fastenzeit / Süßigkeiten.*

---

sich verkleiden – to wear fancy dress
die Umzüge – processions (pl)
die Wagen – floats (pl)
vertreiben – to drive away
Fastenzeit – Lent
das Gebet – prayer

1	Man schmückt die Häuser mit Lichtern.	
2	Es gibt bunte Umzüge auf der Straße.	
3	Es ist das Ende der Fastenzeit.	
4	Man geht in die Moschee.	
5	Es ist der Anfang einer Fastenzeit.	

6 Man verkleidet sich.
7 Man trägt schöne Kleider.
8 Das Datum des Fests ist anders jedes Jahr.
9 Das Fest beginnt im Februar.
10 Man feiert zu Hause.

2 🎧 Listen to two friends talking about *Karneval* and answer the questions in English.

1 Why couldn't Kathrin go to *Karneval* today?
2 What did Thomas eat at the party?
3 What did the three friends dress up as?
4 What does Thomas say about the procession? (2 details)
5 What made the event so noisy? (2 details)
6 What do they plan to do tomorrow?

neidisch – envious
Berliner (Pfannkuchen) – a sweet doughnut (traditional *Karneval* food)
vor Lachen platzen – to fall about laughing

3 **G** Complete the sentences with the correct form of the verb given in brackets in the perfect tense.

1 Wir … einen tollen Umzug … (*sehen*)
2 Dieter … zu viel … (*essen*)
3 Sie … eine Hexenkostüm … (*tragen*)
4 Was … du …? (*trinken*)
5 Ich … durch die ganze Stadt … (*gehen*)
6 Was … Sie am Karneval …? (*tun*)
7 Hermine … sehr laut … (*singen*)
8 Wir … dann nach Köln … (*fahren*)

4 **T** Translate the six example sentences from the *Grammatik* box into English.

5 Partnerarbeit. Seht euch das Bild und die Fragen an und macht Notizen. Stellt euch und beantwortet die Fragen.

Work with a partner. Look at the picture and the questions and make notes. Ask and answer the questions.

* Was gibt es auf dem Foto?
* Welche Feier magst du?
* Was hast du zu Weihnachten gemacht?

6 Schreib eine E-Mail an deine deutsche Freundin / deinen deutschen Freund. Beantworte ihre / seine Fragen.

Write an email to your German friend. Answer her / his questions.

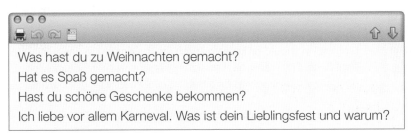

Was hast du zu Weihnachten gemacht?
Hat es Spaß gemacht?
Hast du schöne Geschenke bekommen?
Ich liebe vor allem Karneval. Was ist dein Lieblingsfest und warum?

Grammatik · page 185

Revising the perfect tense II

Always use the same pattern to make the past participle of **regular / weak** verbs:

arbeiten → *arbeit* → **ge**arbeit**t**

If the stem ends in **-t** or **-d** you need to add an extra 'e' to make it possible to pronounce the past participle.

You will need to learn the past participles of **irregular / strong** verbs. Remember that they usually end in **-en** rather than **-t**. Here are some examples from the listening in activity 2:

> *Wir sind weit **gegangen**.*
> *Was hast du dann **getan** und **gesehen**?*
> *Da haben wir etwas **gegessen** und **getrunken**.*
> *Ich habe zu viele Berliner **gegessen**.*
> *Ich habe mein Piratenkostüm **getragen**.*
> *Einige Bands haben **gesungen**.*

Note the use of *haben* or *sein* and the form of the past participle each time. In the first example, *sein* is used to form the perfect tense of *gehen*.

For a list of irregular / strong verbs, see pages 192–195.

Also practise describing past activities and saying what you thought of them. See page 73.

7 **T** Translate the sentences into German.

1 Is there *Karneval* in England?
2 In Germany *Karneval* is an important festival.
3 *Karneval* takes place before Easter.
4 This year I saw a procession in town.
5 The procession was great, colourful and very loud.

4.2 H Feste feiern, wie sie fallen

Finding out more about traditions in German-speaking countries

Using personal pronouns

Using the context when listening

1 📖 Lies Martas Aufgabenliste und beantworte die Fragen auf Deutsch.

die Aufgabenliste –
to-do list

1 Was muss Marta am Freitag, 5. Dezember tun?
2 Wann ist der zweite Advent?
3 Wann sendet Marta festliche Grüßkarten?
4 Wann und ab wie viel Uhr kann sie die Gans abholen?
5 Wann und wo gibt es ein Konzert?
6 Wann und bei wem isst Marta am Abend?
7 Was muss sie am 22. Dezember tun?
8 Wo befindet sich vielleicht der Adventskranz?
9 Was passiert am Heiligabend bei Marta?
10 Welches Geschenk hat Marta noch nicht gekauft?

DEZEMBER

MO	**1**	Adventskranz suchen … (Abstellraum?)	**MI**	**17**	Baum schmücken Glühwein machen!!
DI	**2**	Weihnachtskarten schicken!	**DO**	**18**	Gans abholen … ab 10.00 Uhr
MI	**3**	Kerzen kaufen!	**FR**	**19**	19.30 Abendessen bei Hanna
DO	**4**	Süßigkeiten / Bonbons …	**SA**	**20**	Einkaufen – Supermarkt!!
FR	**5**	Stiefel putzen!	**SO**	**21**	vierter ADVENT
SA	**6**	SANKT NIKOLAUS Party bei Schmidt	**MO**	**22**	Einkaufen – Markt: Rotkohl!
SO	**7**	zweiter ADVENT	**DI**	**23**	Kochen: Kartoffelklöße vorbereiten
MO	**8**		**MI**	**24**	HEILIGABEND großes Abendessen hier!
DI	**9**		**DO**	**25**	erster WEIHNACHTSTAG
MI	**10**	Weihnachtsbaum kaufen!	**FR**	**26**	zweiter WEIHNACHTSTAG
DO	**11**		**SA**	**27**	
FR	**12**		**SO**	**28**	
SA	**13**	Geschenk für Mutti kaufen Steh-Party bei Nachbarn 20.00	**MO**	**29**	
SO	**14**	dritter ADVENT	**DI**	**30**	
MO	**15**	18.00 Weihnachtskonzert Grundschule	**MI**	**31**	SILVESTER
DI	**16**				

2 🎧 Listen to Katja and Fredi. The siblings are talking about Christmas presents for their family. Complete the sentences in English.

1 Fredi and Katja want to give their parents …
2 Fredi hasn't …
3 For their father, Katja suggests …
4 Fredi doesn't agree because …
5 It's Fredi's task to …
6 Last year Katja bought …
7 Fredi reminds her that their mum …
8 Katja thinks Fredi is amazing because …
9 For their grandad, Katja has seen …
10 She's going to go and buy it …

Using the context when listening

When listening to German, always remember that the **context** can give you some ideas about what you might logically expect to hear. Look at titles, questions and any pictures to pick up clues! It's useful to think about context during the **reading time** before the listening test starts.

In activity 2, you can infer (guess / work out) from the pictures below that you're going to be hearing people talking about Christmas shopping and choosing presents. The rubric confirms this.

They may well be discussing possible presents for parents. A rapid brainstorm should provide you with ideas along these lines …
Vati: Buch, CD, Krawatte, Hausschuhe, Taschentücher, Süßigkeiten, Bonbons, Pullover, etwas für das Auto, eine Pflanze für den Garten, ein Kochbuch
Challenge: Do your own brainstorm about what might be mentioned in a discussion about Christmas presents for a mum …

Strategie

3a 🄶 🅣 🎧 Translate the sentences from activity 2 into English. Then listen again. Which noun(s) does the underlined pronoun replace?

Beispiel: **1** We want to give <u>them</u> something nice.
(den Eltern und dem Opa)

1 Wir wollen <u>ihnen</u> etwas Schönes geben.
2 Für <u>ihn</u> ist es immer schwierig, gute Geschenkideen zu haben.
3 Wir kaufen <u>ihm</u> …
4 Du gehst später in die Stadt und kaufst <u>sie</u> …
5 Letztes Jahr habe ich <u>ihr</u> Ohrringe gegeben.
6 Sie hat <u>sie</u> gestern in der Stadt verloren.
7 Er wird <u>es</u> lieben.
8 Ich kaufe <u>es</u> heute Nachmittag.

3b 🄶 Rewrite the sentences, replacing the underlined nouns with pronouns.

1 Hast du <u>den Tannenbaum</u> gesehen?
2 Mutti kann <u>den Adventskranz</u> nicht finden.
3 Ich esse <u>die Lebkuchen</u> sofort.
4 Wir haben <u>die Kartoffeln</u> gekauft.
5 Wir kaufen <u>unserer Großmutter</u> Blumen.
6 Er gibt <u>seiner Schwester</u> einen Hamster.
7 Ich kaufe <u>meinen Freunden</u> Zeitschriften.
8 Hast du <u>deinem Vater</u> eine Krawatte gekauft?

4 🗩 Partnerarbeit. Stellt und beantwortet euch die Fragen.

- Wo verbringst du die Weihnachtszeit und mit wem?
- Was hast du letztes Jahr am Heiligabend gemacht?
- Was wird man bei dir zu Weihnachten essen?
- Kaufst du viele Geschenke für Freunde / Freundinnen?
- Was hast du schon gekauft?
- Was steht auf deinem Wunschzettel?
- Was machst du, um Silvester zu feiern?
- Hast du gute Vorsätze für das neue Jahr? Welche?

5 🖎 Schreib deine Antworten auf die Fragen aus Aufgabe 4. Schreib ungefähr 120 Wörter.

6 🅣 Translate the paragraph into German.

> I love the Christmas period, mainly because it's the time when the whole family can get together. Last year we had our house full of people, and it was great fun. In the afternoon we ate a big Christmas lunch. The traditional turkey was delicious – we all ate too much!

Grammatik | page 183

Using personal pronouns

Every noun can be replaced with a pronoun, and using pronouns often helps avoid repetition.

Meine Mutter ist toll und ich liebe meine Mutter sehr. Zu Weihnachten kaufe ich meiner Mutter Handschuhe, weil meine Mutter ihre Lieblingshandschuhe verloren hat.
The repetition of *meine(r) Mutter* makes the writing sound dull, awkward and unnatural. Try reading it aloud …

Look at this much better version, where pronouns have been used to replace the repeated noun:
*Meine Mutter ist toll und ich liebe **sie** sehr. Zu Weihnachten kaufe ich **ihr** Handschuhe, weil **sie** ihre Lieblingshandschuhe verloren hat.*
Note that a pronoun must **match** in all ways the noun it's replacing (**singular** / **plural**, **gender**, **case**):

nominative (subject)	accusative (direct object)	dative (indirect object)
ich	mich	mir
du	dich	dir
er / sie / es	ihn / sie / es	ihm / ihr / ihm
wir	uns	uns
ihr	euch	euch
sie / Sie	sie / Sie	ihnen / Ihnen

Revise also word order with time – manner – place. See page 73.

Wunschzettel – Christmas wish list
gute Vorsätze für das neue Jahr – New Year's resolutions

🔗 4.2 Groundwork is available in the Foundation book.

G Customs and festivals

1a Translate the sentences into English.

1 Frankfurt liegt am Main.
2 Wann fliegst du in die Türkei?
3 Ich bin in den Sommerferien nach Rom gefahren.
4 In den Niederlanden gibt es viele Frühlingstraditionen.
5 Das Oktoberfest findet in Bayern statt.
6 Im Rheinland ist der Karneval am besten.

1b Translate the sentences into German.

1 There's a big carnival in Venice.
2 This festival happens in Austria and Switzerland too.
3 Advent is the start of the Christmas period in Germany.
4 Children in Europe and the USA love Halloween.
5 Today is a public holiday in the whole (of) Germany.

The names of countries and places

The names of most **countries**, **groups of countries** and **continents** are actually **neuter** nouns, though we rarely use an article with them: *Afrika, Asien, Amerika, Europa, Deutschland, Frankreich, Griechenland, Großbritannien.*

There are some **feminine** countries: *die Türkei, die Schweiz,* **and note also** *die BRD (die Bundesrepublik Deutschland).* The feminine countries are **always used with the definite article**.

A few countries are **masculine**, and are also usually used with the article: *der Sudan, der Kongo.*

There are also a few **plural** countries, which work like normal plural nouns: *die Vereinigten Staaten, die Niederlande.*

Most native German rivers are **feminine** nouns: *die Donau* (the Danube), *die Elbe*, and note also: *die Themse* (the Thames). But some important rivers are **masculine**: *der Rhein* (the Rhine), *der Main.*

Some cities have a **German form** of the name. Here are some you should know: *Köln* (Cologne), *München* (Munich), *Rom* (Rome), *Athen* (Athens), *Warschau* (Warsaw), *Moskau* (Moscow), *Venedig* (Venice).

2 Read the excerpt from a fairytale. Find the nine weak masculine nouns.

Es war einmal ein Prinz, der in einem wunderschönen Schloss am Ende der Welt lebte. Er war reich und schön und hatte alles, was er sich wünschen konnte.
Auf dem Schlossgelände gab es einen wunderbaren Garten, der dem Prinzen alleine gehörte und wo er seine fantastische Tieresammlung hatte. Der Prinz hatte sogar einen Hirten und einen alten Bauern, die auf die Tiere aufpassten.
In diesem merkwürdigen Tiergarten hatte der Prinz nicht nur einen mutigen Bären, sondern auch einen klugen Löwen und einen starken Elefanten, und in dem Vogelhaus des Prinzen gab es nicht nur einen goldenen Papageien, sondern auch einen silbernen Finken. Der schöne Vogelgesang des magischen Finken erfüllte jeden Morgen die sonnenreiche duftende Luft.
Trotzdem war der Prinz traurig und er lachte nie. Warum? Das kann man wohl fragen. Das Leben des Prinzen war in jeder Hinsicht perfekt und es gab keinen Menschen im ganzen Königreich, der dieses Rätsel lösen konnte.

Weak masculine nouns

Weak masculine (WM) is the name given to a small group of nouns in German which add the ending *-n* / *-en* in the different cases, except in the nominative singular form. Most of these nouns denote living beings – people or animals, e.g. *der Junge* (boy), *der Mensch* (person), *der Held* (hero), *der Herr* (gentleman / sir).

	singular	plural
nominative	*der / ein Junge*	*die / keine Jungen*
accusative	*den / einen Jungen*	*die / keine Jungen*
genitive	*des / eines Jungen*	*der / keiner Jungen*
dative	*dem / einem Jungen*	*den / keinen Jungen*

In WM nouns, no *-s* is added to the end of the noun in the genitive. *Herr* adds *-n* in the singular, but *-en* in the plural.

der Hirte – shepherd
der Bauer – farmer, peasant

3a Translate the two example sentences in the *Grammatik* box into English.

3b Translate the sentences into German.

1 We did a long hike on May Day. It was hard work but really great.
2 On 1st April we played a trick on our teacher. That was brilliant and so funny!
3 On Valentine's Day my dad cooked dinner for my mum. That was sweet of him.
4 On Christmas Day we ate turkey and roast potatoes. That was really delicious.
5 Mum and Dad danced in the living room yesterday. That was so embarrassing!

jemandem (dative) *einen Streich spielen* – to play a trick on someone
lieb – sweet

Grammatik · pages 185 & 186

Describing past activities and saying what you thought of them

As you know, it's important in the exam to be able to demonstrate a good grasp of tenses **and** to be able to express opinions, so what better way to showcase skills than to combine these two?

When speaking or writing in the past, this allows you to use both the perfect tense (for the past action) and the imperfect (to say what it was like).

*Wir **haben** in Köln einen riesengroßen Umzug **gesehen**. Das **war** toll!*
*Zu Halloween **habe** ich mit Freunden **gegrillt**. Das Essen **war** würzig und schmackhaft.*

4a Label each word / phrase with T (time), M (manner) or P (place).

1 mit dem Auto
2 vorgestern
3 am 1. April
4 zu Ostern
5 mit dem Rad
6 früher
7 vor ein paar Tagen
8 nach Hause
9 in Bayern
10 mit Freunden
11 in der Türkei
12 entlang der Themse

Grammatik · page 190

Word order with time – manner – place (revision)

The T – M – P rule reminds you of the order in which certain types of information should occur within a German sentence. You will recall that …

| 1 Time | any expression relating to time (**when** something happens) | *heute, in zehn Minuten, nächstes Jahr, letzten Monat* |

needs to come before …

| 2 Manner | any expression denoting manner (**how** something happens) | *schnell, langsam, zu Fuß, mit Freunden* |

and that both of these come before …

| 3 Place | any expression relating to place (**where** it happens) | *nach Mainz, in der Stadt, in Spanien, in der Schweiz, im Garten, auf dem Land* |

Note that …
Ich fahre jedes Jahr mit meiner Familie nach Mainz.

… may also look like this:
Jedes Jahr fahre ich mit meiner Familie nach Mainz.

4b Translate the sentences into German. You will need to use some of the expressions in activity 4a.

1 A few days ago I was in Bavaria with friends.
2 At Easter I did a cycle trip with friends along the Thames.
3 Sometimes I go to school by bike.

4c Use the expressions in activities 4a and 4b to write sentences. You will need to provide the verbs and any other information needed to make the sentence make sense. Then translate the sentences into English.

Beispiel: Früher wollte ich mit Freunden in der Türkei wohnen.
(Previously I wanted to live with friends in Turkey.)

Vokabeln

4.1 Germany and customs

4.1 F Hurra! Die Tradition ist da!
➡ *pages 64–65*

der / die	Bekannte (-n)	acquaintance, friend
	berichten	to report
die	Bratwurst (¨e)	(fried) sausage
	bunt	brightly coloured
	feiern	to celebrate
das	Feuerwerk (-e)	firework(display)
der	Frühling	spring
das	Gedicht (-e)	poem
der / die	Geliebte (-n)	loved one
das	Gespenst (-er)	ghost
	grillen	to barbecue
	gruselig	spooky
das	Gute	the good thing
das	Herz (-en)	heart
	herzförmig	heart-shaped
die	Hexe (-n)	witch
der	Karton	cardboard, cardboard box
	kindisch	childish
	kitschig	cheesy
	kleben	to stick
	komisch	funny, comical, strange, odd
das	Kostüm (-e)	costume
der	Kürbis (-se)	pumpkin
die	Laterne (-n)	lantern
der	Nachbar (-n)	neighbour
der	Plüschbär (-en)	teddy bear
die	Praline (-n)	chocolate (in a box of chocolates)
das	Straßenfest (-e)	street party
der	Streich (-e)	trick
der	Valentinstag (-e)	Valentine's Day
	sich verkleiden	to put on fancy dress, to dress up, to disguise oneself
der	Zauberer (–)	magician

4.1 H Bräuche braucht das Land
➡ *pages 66–67*

	abkühlen	to cool
der	Aschermittwoch	Ash Wednesday
der	Bär (-en)	bear
das	Blei	lead
der	Brauch (¨e)	custom, tradition
	brennen	to burn
	deuten	to interpret
	duftend	sweet-smelling
die	Einschränkung (-en)	restriction
	erhitzen	to heat
	erstarren	to set
der	Fink (-en)	finch
	flüssig	fluid, liquid
	gehören zu (+ dative)	to belong (to)
	gießen	to pour
	giftig	poisonous
die	Kälte	cold
der	Karfreitag	Good Friday
die	Kerze (-n)	candle
das	Königreich (-e)	kingdom
der	Löffel (–)	spoon
der	Löwe (-n)	lion
	merkwürdig	remarkable
der	Ostersonntag	Easter Sunday
der	Papagei (-en)	parrot
das	Rätsel (–)	puzzle
der / die	Reisende (-n)	traveller
die	Sammlung (-en)	collection
das	Schloss (¨er)	castle, palace
	schmelzen	to melt
die	Schüssel (-n)	bowl
	sonnenreich	sun-drenched
	unterschiedlich	different, varied
	verwöhnt	spoilt (e.g. child)
der	Volkstrauertag	Remembrance Day
	vorhersagen	to predict
	sich wünschen	to wish for
das	Zinn	tin, pewter

4.2 Festivals in Germany and German-speaking countries

4.2 F Das muss gefeiert werden!
➡ *pages 68–69*

	bekommen	to get, to receive
	besonders	especially
	böse	naughty, evil, angry
der	Fasching	*another word for* carnival
die	Fastenzeit	period of fasting, Lent
die	Fastnacht	*another word for* carnival
die	*Feier*	celebration
die	Festlichkeit (-en)	celebration
das	Gebet (-e)	prayer
die	Geister	spirits (pl)
	genau	exact, exactly
die	Glocke (-n)	bell
	heilig	holy
die	Hupe (-n)	horn, klaxon
der	*Karneval*	carnival
der	*Kunde (-n)*	customer (m)
der	*Kundin (-nen)*	customer (f)
das	*Licht (-er)*	light
die	Menge (-n)	crowd
	mitmachen	to join in
die	Moschee (-n)	mosque
	stammen aus	to come from, to date from
	überall	everywhere
der	*Umzug (¨e)*	street procession
	vertreiben	to drive out, to expel
die	*Verwandten*	relatives (pl)
	vorbereiten	to prepare
der	Wagen (–)	float (in a procession)
	wecken	to awaken
	wegtreiben	to drive away
die	*Zeit*	time

4.2 H Feste feiern, wie sie fallen
➡ *pages 70–71*

	abbauen	to take down
	abholen	to pick up, to collect
der	*Abstellraum (¨e)*	store room
	einverstanden	agreed
	erstaunlich	amazing
	festlich	festive
	folgen	to follow
der	Glühwein	mulled wine
der	Handschuh (-e)	glove
der	*Heiligabend*	Christmas Eve
der	*Heiligedreikönigstag*	Epiphany / 6th January
der	König (-e)	king
die	*Krawatte (-n)*	tie
	neugeboren	newborn
die	Ohrringe	earrings (pl)
die	*Pute (-n)*	turkey
	schenken	to give (a gift)
die	Steh-Party	drinks party (literally: standing party)
der	Stern (-e)	star
	übergeben	to present, to hand over
	überraschend	surprising
	gute Vorsätze	resolutions (pl)
die	Weihnachtskarte (-n)	Christmas card
der	*erste Weihnachtstag*	Christmas Day
der	*zweite Weihnachtstag*	Boxing Day
der	Weihrauch	frankincense
der	Wunschzettel (–)	Christmas list, wish list
	zurückgehen auf	to go back to
	zusammenkommen	to get together

Higher – Reading and listening

1 📖 Read this Christmas carol and answer the questions in **English**.

1 In verse 1, how is the lake described? (1 detail) [1 mark]
2 What does the last line of verse 1 encourage us to do, and why? [2 marks]
3 In verse 2, where is it warm? [1 mark]
4 What disappears at this time of year? [1 mark]
5 In verse 3, which day is coming soon? [1 mark]
6 What does the author imagine hearing? [1 mark]

[7 marks]

> *schweigen* – to fall silent
> *verhallen* – to die, to fade away

> Leise rieselt der Schnee,
> Still und starr liegt der See.
> Weihnachtlich glänzet der Wald:
> Freue Dich, Christkind kommt bald
>
> In den Herzen ist's warm,
> Still schweigt Kummer und Harm,
> Sorge des Lebens verhallt:
> Freue Dich, Christkind kommt bald
>
> Bald ist Heilige Nacht,
> Chor der Engel erwacht,
> Horch' nur wie lieblich es schallt:
> Freue Dich, Christkind kommt bald
>
> **Eduard Ebel**

2a 📖 Lies den Artikel und beantworte die Fragen auf **Deutsch**.

Wie essen wir zur Zeit?

A Leider wird es zunehmende Realität, dass wir uns nicht gut ernähren. Die Zahl der verkauften Fertiggerichte steigt, Schnellimbisse schießen wie Pilze aus dem Boden in jeder Stadt und Eltern nehmen sich leider immer weniger Zeit für die Ernährung ihrer Kinder.

B Besonders Kinder aus den Großstädten leiden darunter. Sie verstehen nichts von der Herkunft und Produktion der Lebensmittel. So ist es kein Wunder, wenn Kinder oftmals glauben, dass Milch nur aus der Packung kommt und nicht von der Kuh.

C Das heutige Desinteresse an Nahrung bringt die Gefahr, dass Verbraucher unkritisch einkaufen und essen. Deshalb sehen wir immer mehr sogenannte moderne Zivilisationskrankheiten, wie z.B. Fettleibigkeit.

> *das Fertiggericht* – ready meal
> *der Verbraucher* – consumer
> *die Fettleibigkeit* – obesity

1 Was geschieht in jeder Stadt?
2 Was sollen Eltern besser tun?
3 Was verstehen viele Kinder nicht?
4 Was geschieht, weil Verbraucher unkritisch essen? (2 details)

[5 marks]

> **Strategie**
>
> Don't panic when you come across words you don't immediately recognise. First, try to establish whether it's a word you need to understand to answer one of the questions. If not, move on. If it is, do three things:
>
> 1 Check if the word is provided in the **vocabulary box** below the text.
> 2 Is the word a **near-cognate** and therefore easy to work out? *Realität, Produktion, Desinteresse* and *Zivilisation* are all very like their English equivalents.
> 3 If it's a compound word, look at the **parts** of the word and see if you recognise any of them, e.g. *Lebensmittel: Leben* (to live / life) is coupled with *Mittel* (means / way of doing something / device), so 'the means of living / staying alive' = 'food' or 'groceries'.

2b 📖 Lies den Artikel nochmal und wähle einen passenden Titel für jeden Absatz. Schreib **A**, **B** oder **C**.

1	Wo kommt mein Essen her?
2	Wir werden immer dicker.
3	Schneller essen? Schlechter essen!

[3 marks]

3 📖 Lies die Infos auf der Webseite und sieh dir die Aussagen an. Sind die Aussagen **richtig** (R), **falsch** (F) oder **nicht im Text** (NT)?

die Vorverkaufsstelle – advance ticket office
anfallen – to incur
der Versand – postage

Tickets für Hütte Rockt 9!
Ihr könnt nun hier die „**2-Tage-Spaß-Kombitickets**" kaufen. **Ein Ticket kostet 25€. Das Ticket beinhaltet 2 Tage Festival** (ohne Camping). Zusätzlich zu den 2-Tage-Spaß-Kombitickets könnt ihr nun auch **Tagestickets für Freitag und Samstag** per E-Mail bekommen. Die Kosten sind **17€ pro Ticket.**
Einfach auf das Banner klicken und das Ticket online kaufen oder zu einer der wirklich zahlreichen Vorverkaufsstellen gehen.

Alternativ auch so:
Schreibt eine **Mail** mit der Anzahl Karten die ihr bestellen möchtet, setzt eure Daten ein und ihr bekommt eine **Bestätigungsmail** mit unserer Kontoverbindung **innerhalb von 1-3 Tagen** zurück.
Für den Versand von ein bis vier Tickets fallen 1,50€ an. Für den Versand von fünf oder mehr Tickets fallen aufgrund des erhöhten Gewichts 2,50€ an.

1 Ein 2-Tage-Spaß Kombiticket kostet 25 Euro.
2 Dieses Ticket beinhaltet 2 Tage Festival mit Camping.
3 Das Festival findet im Juli statt.
4 Man kann auch ein Tagesticket für Samstag kaufen.
5 Tickets kann man nur online kaufen.
6 Die Organisation bestätigt Mail-Bestellungen in den folgenden drei Tagen.
7 Wenn man 2 Tickets kauft, kostet es 1,50 Euro, sie zu senden.

[7 marks]

4 🅣 You read the following article on a tourist information website. Translate it into **English**.

Die traditionellen Weihnachtsmärkte öffnen im Advent ihre Tore. Hier gibt es zahlreiche schön geschmückte Stände, wo man alles Festliche bekommen kann – Christbaumschmuck, Kerzen, Glühwein und allerlei andere Weihnachtsspezialitäten. Weihnachtsmärkte gibt es seit dem 14. Jahrhundert. Damals hatten Handwerker und Zuckerbäcker die schöne Idee, ihre Waren auf der Straße zu verkaufen.

[9 marks]

5 🎧 Listen to this podcast about May traditions in Germany and answer the questions in **English**.

1 Which changes are mentioned which happen in May? (2 details)
2 What is the idea behind 'dancing into May'?
3 When is Mother's Day celebrated in Germany?
4 What are the 'Eisheiligen'?
5 What can happen after 15th May?   **[6 marks]**

An important skill to develop is **active listening**. This means that you are not simply hearing words and sounds washing around you, but instead you are engaging in the process and focusing in order to pick up key information. Part of this skill is also learning how to distinguish between essential and non-essential content.

It is worth trying out the tactic of jotting down brief notes while you listen, so that you have something to go on, even after the recording has ended.

Strategie

der Maibaum – maypole
säen – to sow (seeds)
empfindlich – sensitive

6 🎧 Hör dir dieses Gespräch zwischen Peter und Maike an. Beantworte die Fragen auf **Deutsch**.

1 Was will Maike heute Abend tun? (**zwei** Details)
2 Warum?
3 Was hat Peter für Maike gekauft?
4 Was will Peter heute Abend tun?
5 Was für ein Spiel ist es? (**zwei** Details)
6 Will Maike das Spiel sehen?   **[8 marks]**

Foundation test and revise tasks are available in the Foundation book.

Higher – Writing and translation

Either:

1a Du schreibst eine E-Mail an deine deutsche Freundin über sportliche Aktivitäten.

Schreib:

- was für Sport du treibst, and wie oft
- warum Sport für dich wichtig / nicht wichtig ist
- wie du die Sportstunden in der Schule findest
- über eine Sportart, die du in Zukunft probieren möchtest.

Du musst ungefähr **90** Wörter auf **Deutsch** schreiben.
Schreib etwas über alle Punkte der Aufgabe.

[16 marks]

Or:

1b Du schreibst ein Blog über deine Essgewohnheiten.

Schreib:

- warum das Frühstück eine wichtige Mahlzeit ist
- was du heute Morgen zum Frühstück gegessen / getrunken hast
- was und mit wem du in der Schule zu Mittag isst
- etwas über das Essen zu Weihnachten bei dir.

Du musst ungefähr **90** Wörter auf **Deutsch** schreiben.
Schreib etwas über alle Punkte der Aufgabe.

[16 marks]

> **Strategie**
>
> In this activity, it's important to cover **the bullet points**. You should tick them off as you go and check at the end that you've covered what's required. It's also vital to write **at least** the number of words suggested. Don't be tempted to cut your work short, as this will almost certainly have an impact on the detail and development you need to produce a full response.
>
> For this activity, you should aim to write about 90 words in total. This means about 20–25 words per bullet, though you could vary the amount between the bullets. Start now to get an idea of what 20–25 words look like in your handwriting and approximately how many lines those words will cover.

Either:

2a ✏️ Du schreibst eine Rezension über einen Film oder eine Fernsehsundung, den / die du gesehen hast.

Schreib:

- über den Film / die Sendung und seine / ihre Handlung
- was du an dem Film / der Sendung gut / nicht gut gefunden hast.

Du musst ungefähr **150** Wörter auf **Deutsch** schreiben. Schreib etwas über alle Punkte der Aufgabe.

[32 marks]

Or:

2b ✏️ Du schreibst einen Eintrag für ein Internet-Forum über Musik.

Schreib:

- über die Rolle der Musik in deinem Leben
- etwas über das letzte Konzert / Festival, an dem du teilgenommen hast.

Du musst ungefähr **150** Wörter auf **Deutsch** schreiben. Schreib etwas über alle Punkte der Aufgabe.

[32 marks]

> **Strategie**
>
> **Planning your response**
>
> Remember that a bullet point may have more than one aspect, so read bullets carefully before you plan your response.
>
> A rough plan by paragraph will help you to produce your best work, and it's worth dedicating a few minutes to jotting down in German the ideas / vocabulary / useful phrases you want to use. Since you have to write about 150 words, you could write four paragraphs with about 40 words in each. It's up to you to decide though. You may find you have more to say for some points, and should develop your ideas as much as you can.
>
> A plan will also help to keep your response focused and relevant.

3 🔵 Translate the paragraph into German.

> I'm interested in cinema and music, and they are both really important in my life. Music can be exciting as well as relaxing, and I find listening to music calming if I'm stressed. At weekends I often go swimming with friends. I can forget my problems when I'm in the water.

[12 marks]

> *sowohl … als auch … –*
> *… as well as …*
> *beruhigend –* calming

4 🔵 Translate the paragraph into German.

> Do you know that Father Christmas, like Halloween, is an import from America? He is of course a very important character at Christmas time, especially for younger children. They are so excited on Christmas Eve that they can hardly sleep. The next morning they get up early to see which presents Father Christmas has brought.

[12 marks]

> Foundation test and revise tasks are available in the Foundation book.

Higher – Speaking

1 🖸 Role play

Your teacher or partner will play the part of your friend and will speak first.

You should address your friend as *du*.

When you see this – **!** – you will have to respond to something you have not prepared.

When you see this – **?** – you will have to ask a question.

> Du besprichst deine Pläne für Halloween mit deinem Austauschpartner / deiner Austauschpartnerin.
>
> - Halloween Pläne.
> - **!**
> - Süßes oder Saures – Meinung.
> - **?** Aktivitäten zu Halloween.
> - Halloween Essen und Getränke.

[15 marks]

2 🖸 Role play

Your teacher or partner will play the part of the teacher and will speak first.

You should address your friend as *Sie*.

When you see this – **!** – you will have to respond to something you have not prepared.

When you see this – **?** – you will have to ask a question.

> Sie sprechen mit der Englischlehrerin / dem Englischlehrer in der Austauschschule über Fernsehen und Freizeit.
>
> - britische Jugendliche – welche Fernsehsendungen (**zwei** Details).
> - **!**
> - *Coronation Street* – Meinung.
> - **?** *Coronation Street* – warum.
> - Freizeit – zwei andere Aktivitäten.

[15 marks]

Strategie

In many role plays, you will be asked to give your opinion about something (food, music, sport, films, clothes, school subjects, holidays, and so on). Why not start early by developing a list of expressions you can use to fulfil this task fluently and effectively!

You will perhaps immediately think of *ich liebe* to express a positive view, and perhaps *ich hasse* for a negative one, but there are many more interesting ones, which will add to the quality of what you say.

3 Photo card

- Look at the photo during the preparation period.
- Make any notes you wish to on an Additional Answer Sheet.
- Your teacher or partner will then ask you questions about the photo and related to the topic of **Free-time activities**.

Strategie

Make sure you divide your preparation time for the speaking test sensibly between the two tasks. Once you've plotted the role play tasks, think through what you want to convey about the photo card and about the broader topic it represents. Start by looking at all the details of the picture in order to give as full an answer as possible to the first question.

Jot down rough notes in German. For any words and phrases you don't know but want to use, try to think of alternative ways to express the same meaning.

Rewrite your notes in usable form, setting them out in the correct order, and using bullet points as reminders.

Your teacher or partner will ask you the following three questions and then **two more questions** which you have not prepared.

- Was gibt es auf dem Foto?
- Was für Musik hörst du gern?
- Kannst du schon ein Instrument spielen?   **[15 marks]**

4 Photo card

- Look at the photo during the preparation period.
- Make any notes you wish to on an Additional Answer Sheet.
- Your teacher or partner will then ask you questions about the photo and related to the topic of **Customs and festivals**.

die Wiese – meadow
der Korb – basket

Your teacher or partner will ask you the following three questions and then **two more questions** which you have not prepared.

- Was gibt es auf dem Foto?
- Was hast du in den Osterferien gemacht?
- Welches ist dein Lieblingsfest des Jahres?   **[15 marks]**

Foundation test and revise tasks are available in the Foundation book.

2 Local, national, international and global areas of interest

5 Home, town, neighbourhood and region

5.1 F Wo wohnst du?
- Using prepositions to say where things are
- Using grammatical markers

5.1 H Wo wohnst du in der Zukunft?
- Using prepositions that take the dative
- Describing something when you don't know the word

5.2 F Meine Gegend
- Using *können*
- Using drawing to help you communicate

5.2 H In der Stadt
- Making questions with interrogatives
- Breaking down long words to understand them

6 Social issues

6.1 F Freiwilligenarbeit im Ausland
- Using *in* with the accusative or dative
- Ignoring words which are not needed

6.1 H Willkommen im Abenteuer
- Using *wenn* clauses
- Using cognates and near-cognates

6.2 F Damals war ich fit
- Using *als* when talking about the past
- Using the layout to help understanding

6.2 H Lebst du gesund oder ungesund?
- Saying 'must not' and 'don't have to'
- Reading authentic texts

7 Global issues

7.1 F Helft der Umwelt!
- Using the imperative
- Spotting near-cognates when listening

7.1 H Globale Umweltprobleme
- Using the pluperfect tense
- Using grammatical categories

7.2 F Endlich in Sicherheit!
- Using and recognising reflexive pronouns
- Recognising suffixes

7.2 H Armut auf der Straße
- Using reflexive verbs with a direct object
- Looking for words inside other words

8 Travel and tourism

8.1 F Ich suche eine Unterkunft
- Recognising the imperfect tense of irregular verbs
- Using paraphrase

8.1 H Wie war denn der Urlaub?
- Using coordinating and subordinating conjunctions
- Using adjectives to improve your work

8.2 F Eine Stadtbesichtigung
- Choosing dative or accusative after prepositions
- Using the social and cultural context to understand meaning

8.2 H Schöne Reiseziele
- Using relative pronouns and *was*
- Using alternatives to *weil*

Victory with verbs

Use your dictionary

Reflexive verbs are easy to find in the dictionary, if you follow a few easy rules.

Remember reflexive verbs? They're the ones used with an extra particle:
*Ich wasche **mich**.* (I get washed.) *Er rasiert **sich**.* (He has a shave.)

- The infinitive of a reflexive verb has **sich** in front of it, e.g. **sich verletzen**.
- To find verbs like these in the dictionary, look under the first letter of the main part of the verb, e.g. **sich verletzen** is under **V**.
- Watch out! Most reflexive verbs are listed after a form of the verb which is not reflexive. So make sure you find the right entry!

---

verkratzt   **Verlobte**

verkratzt *adjective*
  scratched

der **Verlag** (*plural die* **Verlage**)
  publisher (*company*)

verlangen *verb* (*perfect* **hat verlangt**)
  1 **to ask for, to require**
     Wir verlangten die Rechnung. We asked for the bill.
     Sie werden am Telefon verlangt. You are wanted on the phone.
  2 **to demand**
  3 **to charge**

verlängern *verb* (*perfect* **hat verlängert**)
  1 **to extend**
  2 **to lengthen**
  3 **to renew** (*a passport, driving licence*)

der **Verleih** (*plural die* **Verleihe**)
  1 **renting out, hire**
  2 **rental firm, hire shop**

verleihen *verb*✧ (*imperfect* **verlieh**, *perfect* **hat verliehen**)
  1 **to hire out**
  2 **to lend**
  3 **to award**

verlernen *verb* (*perfect* **hat verlernt**)
  to forget

verletzen *verb* (*perfect* **hat verletzt**)
  1 **to injure**
  2 **to hurt**
  3 **to violate** (*a law*)
  4 **sich verletzen** to hurt yourself

♂**verletzt** *adjective*
  injured

German–English

a
b
c
d

---

1 Read the German sentences and write the infinitive of the reflexive verbs. Then translate the sentences into English.

Beispiel: Wir treffen uns jede Woche.
        infinitive: sich treffen (*to get together*)

1 Ich sorge mich um meine Prüfungen.
2 Abends entspanne ich mich.
3 Erinnerst du dich an mich?
4 Er interessiert sich für Musik.
5 Sie freut sich auf den Urlaub.
6 Wir haben uns vorgestellt.
7 Er irrt sich manchmal.

5.1 F

Wo wohnst du?

1 🅣 Separate the words in the sentences. Then translate the sentences into English.

1 UnserReihenhausistinderStadtmitte.
2 WirwohnenineinemschönenaltenBauernhaus.
3 DieWohnungistineinemgroßenWohnblockamStadtrand.
4 UnserEinfamilienhaushatvierSchlafzimmerundeinenGarten.
5 InunsererStraßesindvieleDoppelhäuser.

2a 🎧 Hör dir die sechs Personen an. Wähl die passenden Bilder.

Listen to the six people. Choose the matching pictures.

| 1 Marcus | 2 Sabine | 3 Tarik | 4 Emma | 5 Jürgen | 6 Mia |

2b 🎧 Listen again and write a few details in English about where each person lives.

3 📖 Read the email. What is in Hannes' room? Write a list in English.

> Mein Name ist Hannes. Ich habe einen Bruder, aber zum Glück habe ich ein eigenes Zimmer. Das finde ich prima! In meinem Zimmer habe ich ein großes Bett mit einer roten Bettdecke und weißen Kopfkissen. Ich habe ein Bücherregal und auch eine Kommode, aber eine Schublade ist kaputt. Auf dem Tisch stehen mein Computer und mein kleiner Fernseher. An der Wand habe ich viele Poster von meiner Lieblingsfußballmannschaft, Bayern München. Zwischen dem Tisch und der Tür ist ein Kleiderschrank. Meine Mutter sagt, mein Zimmer ist sehr unordentlich, weil meine Kleider immer herumliegen.

Using grammatical markers

There will be times when you won't know the meaning of a word, but it may help you to know whether it is a verb, noun, adjective, etc. so you can make an intelligent guess at what it means. For example, in *zum Glück habe ich ein eigenes Zimmer* in activity 3, because *eigenes* is between *ein* and *Zimmer*, it must be an adjective.

Challenge: Working with a partner, each copy a sentence from the reading text and work together to identify the different types of words.

Strategie

4 🅣 Translate the paragraph into English.

> Ich habe ein eigenes Zimmer mit einem Bett, einem Kleiderschrank und einem Tisch. Es gibt auch eine weiße Kommode. An der Wand sind ein Bild und viele Poster. Ich spiele gern Computerspiele in meinem Zimmer.

5 🅣 Translate the paragraph into German.

> We have a detached house in the mountains and it has five bedrooms and two bathrooms. There is a kitchen on the ground floor. The village is always quiet and the neighbours are very nice.

6 🅖 Where is the dog? Write sentences in German.

7 🗩 Gruppenarbeit. Sieh das Foto an und mach Notizen. Stellt euch und beantwortet die Fragen. Wechselt euch ab.

Work in groups. Look at the picture and make notes. Ask and answer the questions. Take turns.

- Was gibt es auf dem Foto?
- Kannst du dein Wohnzimmer beschreiben?
- Wo sind die Möbel in deinem Wohnzimmer?
- Hast du ein eigenes Schlafzimmer?
- Was gibt es in deinem Zimmer?

Grammatik — page 180

Using prepositions to say where things are

Many prepositions are followed by the accusative (showing movement) or the dative (no movement). When talking about where things are situated, these prepositions are used with the dative case. You need to choose the correct word for 'the' depending on the gender of the noun, and whether it is singular or plural:

*an **der** Wand* (f) (on (= against) the wall)

*auf **dem** Tisch* (m) (on (= on top of) the table)

*hinter **dem** Schrank* (m) (behind the cupboard)

*in **dem*** (often shortened to *im*) *Zimmer* (n) (in the room)

*neben **dem** Bett* (n) (next to the bed)

*vor **der** Tür* (f) (in front of the door)

*zwischen **den** Schränken* (pl) (between the cupboards)

Notice that nouns in the dative plural must always end in *-n*.

Also revise putting the verb as second idea. See page 93.

5.1 H

Wo wohnst du in der Zukunft?

Schöne Doppelhaushälfte in ruhiger Lage

22175 Hamburg

Wohnfläche ca. 135 m²
Bezugsfrei ab 01.10.2016
Zimmer: 7
Schlafzimmer: 4
TV / Internet / Telefon

Kosten
Miete: 1.700€

Hausbeschreibung
Dieses Doppelhaus wurde im Jahr 2012 mit Vollkeller gebaut und es gibt dem Hausbewohner mit Familie viel Platz. Der Dachboden des Hauses ist mit besten grauen Dachsteinen gedeckt und die weißen Kunststofffenster sind isolierverglast.
Neben dem Haus sind eine Garage sowie ein Gartenhäuschen. Der hintere Garten ist pflegeleicht und hat einen großen Rasen.

Ausstattung
Durch das relativ junge Baualter hat diese Haushälfte eine hochmoderne Ausstattung. Die Wände und Decken sind verputzt. Das Erdgeschoss hat einen 40 m² großen Wohn- / Essbereich und eine Einbauküche mit allen notwendigen Geräten. Dazu sind in der Küche ein Gasherd, eine Mikrowelle und ein neuer Tiefkühlschrank vorhanden. Im Erdgeschoss gibt es auch eine großzügige Diele und ein Duschbad / Gäste-WC.
Im 1. Stock sind zwei geräumige Schlafzimmer und ein Badezimmer mit Vollbad / Dusche.
Im zweiten Obergeschoss findet man noch zwei Schlafzimmer und ein Arbeitszimmer.
Diese erstklassig ausgestattete Haushälfte eignet sich besonders für eine vier- bis fünfköpfige Familie.

wurde … gebaut – was built
der Kunststoff – plastic
isolierverglast – double-glazed
pflegeleicht – easy to look after
der Rasen – lawn
die Ausstattung – fittings, equipment
verputzt – plastered
der Bereich – area
vorhanden – available

1 Lies die Wohnungsanzeige. Sind die Aussagen richtig (R), falsch (F) oder nicht im Text (NT)?

1 Anfang Oktober ist das Haus bezugsfrei.
2 Das Haus hat keinen Keller.
3 Hinter dem Haus gibt es eine große Garage mit Platz für zwei Autos.
4 Die Küche ist sehr gut ausgestattet.
5 Es gibt eine Dusche unten und eine oben.
6 Das Haus ist ideal für eine Familie mit drei Mitgliedern.

2 🎧 Hör dir Tim und Karla an. Beantworte die Fragen auf Deutsch.

`1 Tim` `2 Karla`

a Wo ist Tims ideales Haus?
b Warum hat es keine Treppe?
c Warum mag er das Haus?
d Was gibt es in der Küche?

e In was für einem Haus wohnt Karla jetzt?
f Was ist der Vorteil vom Badezimmer?
g Was wird sie im Sommer machen, wenn sie auf der Terrasse sitzt?
h Und was wird sie im Winter machen?

3a **G** Complete the sentences with *dem*, *der* or *den*.

1 Wir wohnen gegenüber … Spielplatz.

2 Unser Haus ist nicht weit weg von … Bushaltestelle.

3 Das Dorf liegt in der Nähe von … Bergen.

4 Mein Bruder wird morgen früh zu … Bäckerei gehen.

5 Im September werden wir aus … Haus ausziehen, weil es zu klein ist.

6 Von … Stadtrand fährt man mit … Straßenbahn bis zu … Hauptbahnhof.

3b **G** Read your answers in activity 3a. Which answers can you shorten?

4 **T** Translate the paragraph into English.

> Ich möchte eine Wohnung in einem ruhigen Stadtviertel, vielleicht in einem Mehrfamilienhaus. Meine ideale Wohnung hat eine Einbauküche mit Elektroherd und Mikrowelle. Dazu gibt es drei Schlafzimmer für mich und meine Familie. Obwohl ich eine Wohnung suche, wird das Haus einen Garten haben. Die Miete wird auch nicht teuer sein.

5 **T** Translate the paragraph into German.

> We live in a semi-detached house on the outskirts of town. It is quite small and has two bedrooms, but it is comfortable and there is also a cellar. In the cellar, there is the chest freezer and the washing machine. The house is beautiful and we will stay here.

6 Gruppenarbeit. Seht euch das Bild an und macht Notizen. Stellt euch und beantwortet die Fragen.

- Was gibt es auf dem Foto?
- Wie sieht dein ideales Haus aus? Was für ein Haus ist es?
- Wie viele Stockwerke hat es?
- Welche Zimmer gibt es? Was gibt es in den Zimmern?
- Wie findest du das Haus?
- Was wirst du dort machen?

Mein Haus ist	ein Doppelhaus / eine Villa / ein Einfamilienhaus …	
Es hat	… Stockwerke.	
Insgesamt gibt es	… Zimmer.	
Im Erdgeschoss Im ersten / zweiten Obergeschoss	gibt es	eine Küche / einen Abstellraum / ein Esszimmer … vier Schlafzimmer / zwei Badezimmer …
Im Wohnzimmer In der Waschküche In der Küche	haben wir	zwei Sofas / drei Sessel / einen Breitbildfernseher. eine Waschmaschine / zwei Schränke / einen Tiefkühlschrank.
Ich	mag mein Haus,	weil es so groß / schön / gemütlich ist.
In der Küche Im Wohnzimmer	werde ich	kochen / abwaschen / plaudern / mich entspannen.

Grammatik page 180

Using prepositions that take the dative

These prepositions are always followed by the dative, so always check that you use the correct endings on any definite and indefinite articles which come afterwards. See page 179.

aus	from, out of
bei	at the house of, with
gegenüber	opposite
mit	with, by (transport)
nach	after, to
seit	since, for (a period of time)
von	from, by, of
zu	to

Just as *in dem* is often shortened to *im*, look out for *beim* (*bei dem*), *vom* (*von dem*), *zum* (*zu dem*) and *zur* (*zu der*).

Also revise how to use the future tense. See page 92.

Strategie

Describing something when you don't know the word

If you don't know what a word is, think of a way to explain it in simple terms, e.g. if you don't know *Breitbildfernseher*, say *ein sehr, sehr großer Fernseher*.

Challenge: Practise with a partner. Give a word to describe in German. Finally, look up the German words in a dictionary.

7 Du suchst ein Haus oder eine Wohnung. Beschreib das Haus / die Wohnung.

5.1 Groundwork is available in the Foundation book.

5.2 F Meine Gegend

1 **V** **T** Using the vocabulary list on page 95, solve the anagrams. You can find the answers in or near a town. Then translate the words into English.

Beispiel: **1** Friseur (hairdresser)

1 riFuser
2 tophAkee
3 shaWrunea
4 faneH
5 nadeL
6 grezuKun
7 Fibark
8 lAmep

2a Lies die Texte. Zwei Leute sprechen über die Gegend, wo sie wohnen. Wer erwähnt welches Geschäft?

Read the texts. Two people are talking about the areas where they live. Who mentions which shop?

> Ich wohne in einem Vorort einer Großstadt. In der Gegend ist leider nicht viel los, denn die meisten Geschäfte sind jetzt geschlossen. Es gibt einen kleinen Supermarkt, ein Juweliergeschäft und eine Reinigung, aber sonst nichts. Wenn ich Kleidung kaufe, kann ich mit der S-Bahn in die Stadtmitte fahren. Seit einem Jahr gibt es aber ein neues Einkaufszentrum am Stadtrand. Hier kann man alles unter einem Dach kaufen. Am Wochenende fahre ich normalerweise mit meinen Freunden hin. Manchmal kaufen wir was oder gehen einfach ins Fastfood-Restaurant.

Daniel

> Meine Familie und ich wohnen in einer relativ kleinen Stadt, die ich wunderbar finde, weil wir eine große Auswahl an Geschäften haben. Es gibt eine preiswerte Bäckerei, eine Metzgerei, ein traditionelles Lebensmittelgeschäft und einen tollen Obst- und Gemüseladen. Es gibt sogar auch ein ziemlich großes Kleidergeschäft. In unserer Stadt gibt es keinen Supermarkt, weil die Einwohner keinen wollen. Donnerstags und samstags haben wir auch einen Markt, wo man frische Produkte kaufen kann. Natürlich sind die Preise in dieser Stadt ein bisschen höher, aber das macht nichts.

Tina

A
B
C
D
E

2b Read the texts again and complete the statements.

1 Daniel lives in a …   **a** small town.   **b** suburb.   **c** village.
2 He goes to the city centre by …   **a** underground.   **b** bus.   **c** suburban railway.
3 The shopping centre is …   **a** in the city centre.   **b** on the outskirts.   **c** in another town.
4 At weekends he usually goes to the …   **a** shopping centre.   **b** city centre.   **c** market.
5 Tina's town doesn't have a …   **a** butcher's.   **b** clothes shop.   **c** supermarket.
6 There is a market there … a week.   **a** once   **b** twice   **c** three times
7 When shopping, Tina …   **a** is happy to pay more.   **b** dislikes paying more.   **c** tries to get a reduction.

3a Listen to Karin, David and Martina talking about their towns. For each person write what there is in their towns in English.

3b 🎧 Hör noch einmal zu. Was gibt es <u>nicht</u> in den Städten? Schreib eine Liste auf Deutsch.

Listen again. What can you <u>not</u> find in these towns? Write a list in German.

4 🄖 🅣 Complete the sentences with the correct form of *können*. Then translate the sentences into English.

1 Meine Mutter … frisches Obst und Brot auf dem Markt kaufen.
2 Am Samstag … ich meine Freunde im Fastfood-Restaurant treffen.
3 In den Ferien … wir in den Bergen wandern gehen.
4 Man … im Sportzentrum Tischtennis oder Badminton spielen.
5 … du mich vor dem Rathaus treffen?
6 Mein Vater … das neue Einkaufszentrum nicht leiden.

5 🅣 Translate the paragraph into German.

On Saturdays we travel by bus into town. There is a market and a shopping centre. We can shop here or go to the cinema. Then we eat a hamburger with chips in the restaurant.

6 👄 Rollenspiel. Partnerarbeit. Tauscht die Rollen. Vergesst nicht, viele Adjektive zu benutzen!

Role play. Work with a partner. Swap roles. Don't forget to use lots of adjectives.

Using *können*

Können (can, to be able) is one of six modal verbs. Learn each one as you meet it.

ich kann
du kannst
er / sie / es / man kann
wir können
ihr könnt
sie / Sie können

Modal verbs are normally used with another verb in the infinitive form which goes to the end of the sentence or clause, e.g. *Ich **kann** heute in die Stadtmitte **fahren**.*

Also learn about using adjective endings after 'the' and 'a'. See page 92.

Grammatik page 185

Using drawing to help you communicate

When trying to explain something and you don't know the word you need, it can be useful to sketch what you want to refer to, e.g. a picture of a building, a simple map showing where something is, a smiley / unhappy face to say you like / dislike something.

Strategie

Partner / Partnerin A		Partner / Partnerin B
1	Kannst du deine Stadt beschreiben?	1	Describe your town. Say what it is called and where it is.
2	Was gibt es zu sehen?	2	Say what there is to see there.
3	Und was kann man dort machen? Kann man gut einkaufen?	3	Say what you can do there and if the town is good for shopping.
4	Wie findest du deine Stadt?	4	Say what you think of your town.
5	Was ist deine Meinung über …?	5	Say what you think of … in your town.

Die Stadt heißt …	und sie liegt	an der Küste. an einem See / Fluss.
In der Stadt Im Stadtzentrum Hier	gibt es	eine Disko / ein Sportzentrum / ein Kino / ein Schloss. einen guten Markt / eine schöne Kirche / ein interessantes Museum. kein Schwimmbad / keine Cafés / kein Theater. nicht viel / wenig für Jugendliche.
Man kann		ins Kino / ins Sportzentrum / ins Museum / ins Theater gehen. Fußball / Tennis / Badminton spielen. den schönen Dom / das interessante Denkmal / die alte Stadtmauer sehen. in der Stadtmitte / im neuen Einkaufszentrum einkaufen.
Ich finde Für mich ist Meiner Meinung nach ist	die Stadt	toll / prima / ausgezeichnet / interessant. zu groß / todlangweilig / doof / mies.

In der Stadt

Was hat Berlin zu bieten?

Kurz gesagt, eine ganze Menge! Zum Beispiel gibt es den Kurfürstendamm (auch Ku'damm genannt), die bekannteste Einkaufsmeile Berlins. Als Zentrum der City West zieht diese Straße Touristen *und* Berliner an, denn nirgendwo ist Berlin kosmopolitischer als hier.

Auf der 3,5 Kilometer langen Straße laden Kaufhäuser und Geschäfte zum Einkaufen auf breiten Bürgersteigen ein. Zahlreiche Modeketten und Schmuckgeschäfte, Luxusboutiquen und Kaufhäuser wie Karstadt findet man hier.

Das traditionsreiche Café Kranzler an der Ecke Joachimstaler Straße bietet bei Kaffee und Kuchen Erholung vom hektischen Leben der Hauptstadt.

In der nächsten Straße befindet sich das KaDeWe, das größte Warenhaus auf dem europäischen Kontinent. Neben exklusiven Modemarken kann man hochwertigen Schmuck- und Haushaltswaren kaufen.

Aber wenn die Füße weh tun und man die Nase voll hat? Dann kann man eine der schönen Grünanlagen besuchen, denn in der Nähe liegt der Tiergarten, die größte Grünanlage der Stadt und die grüne Lunge Berlins. Auf dem Stadtplan sieht der Tiergarten wie eine Insel mitten in der Stadt aus. Dort kann man in der Sonne sitzen oder liegen, spazieren gehen, grillen, eine Radtour machen usw.

1 Lies den Text. Beantworte die Fragen auf Deutsch.

1 Wen sieht man auf dem Kurfürstendamm?
2 Wie lange ist diese Straße?
3 Was kann man im Café Kranzler bestellen?
4 Wo ist das KaDeWe?
5 Was für Artikel kann man dort kaufen?
6 Wann kann man in den Tiergarten gehen?
7 Wie sieht der Tiergarten auf einem Stadtplan aus?

Breaking down long words to understand them

When you encounter long words which you have not seen before, break them down into parts that you can recognise:
traditionsreich = traditions + reich (rich in tradition)
Haushaltswaren = Haushalts + waren (household goods)
Bushaltestelle = Bus + halte + stelle (bus + stopping + place = bus stop)

Challenge: Split these words into their component parts and see if you can work out what they mean. Use a dictionary to check your answers: *Buchhandlung, Essecke, Zebrastreifen, Einkaufstasche, Wolkenkratzer.*

Strategie

2a  Hör dir Birgit, Richard und Marlene an. Finde die passenden Bilder. Es gibt zwei Bilder pro Person.

| 1 Birgit | 2 Richard | 3 Marlene |

A

B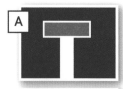

C

D

E

F

2b Listen again and complete the sentences.

		a	b	c
1	Birgit lives in a … part of town.	quiet	busy	clean
2	She has a flat on the … floor.	sixth	seventh	sixteenth
3	At night she can hear noise from …	people in the street.	traffic.	aircraft.
4	Richard thinks where he lives is …	nice.	OK.	unpleasant.
5	He finds going into town …	difficult.	boring.	easy.
6	Marlene prefers travelling by …	bus.	car.	suburban railway.
7	When she goes into town, she gets a …	parking space.	free trip.	discount.

3 **G** These sentences are answers to questions. Write the questions for the details in bold.

Beispiel: **1** Wo wohnst du?

1   Ich wohne **in Hamburg**.
2   Das Geschäft ist **sonntags** geschlossen.
3   **Meine Mutter** wohnt hier.
4   Ich kaufe **eine neue Jacke**.
5   Ich gehe **mit meinen Freunden**.
6   Ich bleibe **15 Minuten**.
7   Ich besuche **meinen Onkel**.
8   Das Wetter ist **sehr schön**.

4 **T** Translate the paragraph into English.

> Meine Familie und ich wohnen am Stadtrand. Unser Reihenhaus befindet sich in einer Sackgasse. Es gefällt mir, hier zu wohnen, aber leider sind die öffentlichen Verkehrsmittel in dieser Gegend schlecht. Es gibt keine Straßenbahn und die Busse fahren nur alle zwei Stunden. Deshalb müssen wir immer mit dem Auto fahren.

5 **T** Translate the paragraph into German.

> My mother works in the town centre opposite the cathedral. We live 10 kilometres away, but she travels by car because there are no trains. The buses go only once an hour. She sets off at 7 o'clock in order to find a parking place. Unfortunately, that is quite expensive.

6 Partnerarbeit. Sprich über deinen Wohnort / dein Stadtviertel. Was ist in der Nähe? Wie sind die öffentlichen Verkehrsmittel? Was sind die Vor- und Nachteile, hier zu wohnen? Dann schreib einen Artikel darüber.

Grammatik — page 190

Making questions with interrogatives

Questions can be formed in German by using interrogative words such as:

Wann?	When?
Warum?	Why?
Wo?	Where?
Wie?	How?
Wie lange?	How long?
Was?	What?
Was für?	What kind of?

You can also make questions using inversion (turning around the subject and verb):

Die Großstadt hat *viele Geschäfte.*
Hat die Großstadt *viele Geschäfte?*

Notice that there is no need for a special word for 'do' or 'does' when asking questions in German.

Some questions are made using interrogative pronouns such as *Wer?* (Who?), *Wen?* (Whom? – accusative) and *Wem?* (Whom? – dative), followed by the verb: **Wer wohnt** in dieser Straße? **Wen kann** man auf dem Ku'Damm sehen?

Also revise more on how to use the verb as second idea. See page 93.

Ich wohne in	einem	(nicht) sehr / ganz / unglaublich	schönen / ruhigen / langweiligen / lebhaften / ausgezeichneten	Stadtteil / Stadtviertel / Dorf.
	einer			Kleinstadt / Marktstadt.
In der Nähe von / Nicht weit von	unserem	Haus / Reihenhaus	befinden sich / sind	der Martkplatz / die Kunstgalerie und … das Spielzeugmuseum / das Denkmal / der Hafen / das Stadtzentrum.
	unserer	Wohnung		
Hier kann man	frisches Obst und Gemüse kaufen / Bilder von … sehen. ins Theater / Kunstmuseum / Kino gehen.			
Ich finde die öffentlichen Verkehrsmittel	hervorragend,	weil	die Busse regelmäßig fahren / die Fahrpreise billig sind.	
	schrecklich,		man zu lange warten muss / sie unzuverlässig sind.	
Es gefällt mir (nicht),	hier zu wohnen,	weil	es (nicht) viel zu tun / sehen gibt.	

5.2 Groundwork is available in the Foundation book.

G # Home, town, neighbourhood and region

1 Rewrite the sentences, starting with the underlined phrases.

1 Es gibt einen Garten <u>hinter dem Haus</u>.
2 Ich habe viele Poster von meiner Lieblingsgruppe <u>in meinem Schlafzimmer</u>.
3 Ich frühstücke <u>morgens</u> in der Küche.
4 Eine Bushaltestelle ist <u>vor unserem Reihenhaus</u>.
5 Ich lese <u>jeden Tag</u> in meinem Zimmer.
6 Vier Schlafzimmer, das Badezimmer und die Toilette sind <u>im 1. Stock</u>.
7 Ein Teddybär sitzt <u>auf dem Stuhl in der Ecke</u>.
8 Es gibt <u>selten</u> Probleme mit unseren Nachbarn.

2 Add the correct ending to the adjectives. Note that sometimes an ending will not be required!

1 Ich wohne in einer schön__ Stadt.
2 Sie ist sehr sauber__.
3 Es gibt das alt__ Rathaus und ein schön__ Denkmal.
4 Jeden Freitag haben wir einen fantastisch__ Markt.
5 Alles ist sehr frisch__.
6 Die historisch__ Kirche sieht wunderschön__ aus.
7 Vom Kirchturm hat man einen wunderbar__ Blick auf die ganz__ Stadt.
8 In der alt__ Stadtmitte haben wir eine sehr gut__ Bücherei und ein toll__ Schreibwarengeschäft.
9 Ich finde unsere Stadt ausgezeichnet__.

The verb as second idea (revision)

The verb should come as the **second idea** in a sentence. Notice that this does not mean that it has to be the second **word** in the sentence.

       Second idea
   Ich   habe   *ein großes Bett im Zimmer.*
Ein Stuhl   steht   *zwischen der Tür und dem Tisch.*
   Es   gibt   *einen Garten hinter dem Haus.*

When the subject is not mentioned first (this is called inversion), the verb must still come as the second idea.

	second idea	subject	
Im Zimmer	*habe*	*ich*	*ein großes Bett.*
Zwischen der Tür und dem Tisch	*steht*	*ein Stuhl.*	
Hinter dem Haus	*gibt*	*es*	*einen Garten.*

Using adjective endings after 'the' and 'a'

When an adjective is used **before** a noun, it must have an ending depending on the case and gender of the noun, and whether the noun is singular or plural.

When the adjective comes after the word 'the' (*der / die / das*, etc.), use the following endings:

	masculine	feminine	neuter	plural
nominative	-e	-e	-e	-en
accusative	-en	-e	-e	-en
genitive	-en	-en	-en	-en
dative	-en	-en	-en	-en

When the adjective comes after 'a' (*ein / eine / ein*, etc.), use these endings:

	masculine	feminine	neuter	plural (no article)
nominative	-er	-e	-es	-e
accusative	-en	-e	-es	-e
genitive	-en	-en	-en	-er
dative	-en	-en	-en	-en

Learn all the endings in yellow above. Then remember that every other ending is *-en*.

Look at these examples:
Der alte Mann wohnt in der kleinen Wohnung. (The old man lives in the small flat.)
Wir haben ein kleines Haus neben einem großen Supermarkt. (We have a small house next to a large supermarket.)
Ich habe neue Trainingsschuhe gekauft. (I bought (some) new trainers.)

For the full tables of endings, refer to page 181.

3 Rewrite the sentences, starting with another word or phrase in the sentence. Make sure that it still makes sense and has the correct word order.

Beispiel: **1** Normalerweise sind die Busse in meiner Stadt sehr pünktlich.

1 Die Busse in meiner Stadt sind normalerweise sehr pünktlich.

2 Es ist im Winter nicht besonders schön, eine halbe Stunde auf einen Bus zu warten.

3 Es gibt eine große Auswahl an Geschäften und Kaufhäusern in der Stadt.

4 Parken ist sonntags in der Stadtmitte gratis.

5 Ich kann den Kirchturm von meinem Schlafzimmerfenster sehen.

6 Die öffentlichen Verkehrsmittel sind glücklicherweise ausgezeichnet.

7 Man kann nachts hier nichts hören.

8 Wir fahren lieber mit der Straßenbahn als mit dem Bus.

Grammatik · page 189

More on the verb as second idea (revision)

Unless it is a question or the verb is being used after a subordinating conjunction (such as *weil*), the verb will be the second idea in the sentence.

subject	second idea	
Ich	kann	natürlich mit dem Auto hinfahren.
Die Geschäfte	sind	schrecklich in unserem Stadtviertel.
Man	kann	den Hafen von unserem Haus nicht sehen.
Meine Freunde und ich	fahren	jeden Samstag in die Stadtmitte.
Es	gibt	außerdem fast nichts für junge Leute.

Instead of starting a sentence with the subject, you can start it with the object of the sentence, an adverb or an expression of time or place. When you do this, the verb and subject must be switched around (inversion) so the verb is still the second idea.

	second idea	subject	
Natürlich	kann	ich	mit dem Auto hinfahren.
In unserem Stadtviertel	sind	die Geschäfte	schrecklich.
Den Hafen	kann	man	von unserem Haus nicht sehen.
Jeden Samstag	fahren	meine Freunde und ich	in die Stadtmitte.
Außerdem	gibt	es	fast nichts für junge Leute.

---

4 Complete the sentences with the correct form of *werden* and the German for the infinitive form of the verb given in brackets.

1 Meine Eltern und ich … in der Küche … (*sit*)

2 Er … eine Wohnung in der Stadtmitte … (*buy*)

3 Wir … nächstes Jahr nach Berlin … (*move*)

4 Ich … ein Doppelhaus … (*rent*)

5 … du im März …? (*move out*)

6 Mein Bruder … heute Abend … (*wash up*)

7 … Sie eine Wohnung in der Nähe …? (*look for*)

8 Nächstes Wochenende … meine Eltern einen neuen Elektroherd … (*buy*)

Grammatik · page 187

Future tense (revision)

To form the future tense, use the present tense of **werden** + infinitive (at the end of the sentence or clause):

*Ich **werde** im Wohnzimmer fernsehen.* (I shall (I'll) watch TV in the living room.)

*Sie **wird** auf der Terrasse sitzen.* (She will (She'll) sit on the patio.)

Notice that there isn't a special way of saying the shortened forms 'I'll', 'you'll', 'he'll', etc. in German.

ich werde	I shall, will
du wirst	you (informal singular) will
er / sie / es wird	he / she / it will
wir werden	we shall, will
ihr werdet	you (informal plural) will
sie / Sie werden	they / you (formal) will

Vokabeln

5.1 Home

5.1 F Wo wohnst du?
➡ *pages 84–85*

	an	on
	auf	on (top of)
die	Bettdecke (-n)	blanket, duvet
das	Bücherregal (-e)	bookshelf
das	Doppelhaus (¨er)	semi-detached house
	eigen	own (adj)
das	Einfamilienhaus (¨er)	detached house
	zum Glück	fortunately
	hinter	behind
das	Hochhaus (¨er)	high-rise block of flats
	kaputt	broken
der	Kleiderschrank (¨e)	wardrobe
das	Kopfkissen (–)	pillow
der	Nachttisch (-e)	bedside cabinet
die	Pflanze (-n)	plant
das	Reihenhaus (¨er)	terraced house
die	Schublade (-n)	drawer
der	Stadtrand (¨er)	outskirts of town
	unordentlich	untidy
	unter	under
	vor	in front of, before, outside
die	Wand (¨e)	wall (inside)
der	Wohnblock (-s)	block of flats
	zwischen	(in) between

5.1 H Wo wohnst du in der Zukunft?
➡ *pages 86–87*

der	Abstellraum (¨e)	store room
der	Aufzug (¨e)	lift
	ausziehen	to move out
die	Badewanne (-n)	bathtub
	sich befinden	to be situated
	besonders	particularly, especially
der	Dachboden (¨en)	attic, loft
der	Dachstein (-e)	roof tile
	dazu	in addition
	decken	to cover

die	Diele (-n)	hallway
	sich eignen	to be suitable
	zum Entspannen	for relaxing
die	Etage (-n)	floor, storey
	gemütlich	cosy, comfortable
	geräumig	roomy, spacious
	hübsch	pretty
die	Insel (-n)	island
der	Kamin (-e)	fireplace
der	Keller (–)	cellar
die	Küste (-n)	coast
die	Lage (-n)	position
die	Klimaanlage (-n)	air conditioning
die	Miete (-n)	rent
	mieten	to rent
die	Mikrowelle (-n)	microwave oven
das	Obergeschoss (-e)	floor, storey
die	Rolltreppe (-n)	escalator
	sowohl … als auch …	both … and …
das	Stockwerk (-e)	storey, floor
die	Terrasse (-n)	terrace, patio
der	Tiefkühlschrank (¨e)	freezer
die	Tiefkühltruhe (-n)	chest freezer
die	Waschküche (-n)	utility room
die	Wohnfläche (-n)	living space, floor area

5.2 Where you live

5.2 F Meine Gegend
➡ *pages 88–89*

die	Ampel (-n)	traffic light
die	Apotheke (-n)	pharmacy
die	Bäckerei (-en)	bakery, baker's shop
	ein bisschen	a little, a bit
das	Dach (¨er)	roof
das	Denkmal (¨er)	monument
der	Einwohner (–)	inhabitant
das	Elektrogeschäft (-e)	shop for electrical goods
die	Fabrik (-en)	factory
der	Friseur (-e)	hairdresser (m)

die	Friseurin (-nen)	hairdresser (f)
die	Fußgängerzone (-n)	pedestrian precinct
die	Gegend (-en)	region, area
das	Geschäft (-e)	business, shop
der	Hafen (¨)	harbour, port
der	Hauptbahnhof (¨e)	main railway station
die	Hauptstadt (¨e)	capital city
das	Juweliergeschäft (-e)	jeweller's shop
das	Kaufhaus (¨er)	department store
das	Kleidergeschäft (-e)	clothes shop
die	Konditorei (-en)	confectioner's
die	Kreuzung (-en)	crossroads
der	Laden (¨)	shop
das	Lebensmittelgeschäft (-e)	grocer's shop
der	Marktplatz (¨e)	marketplace
die	Mauer (-n)	wall (outside)
die	Metzgerei (-en)	butcher's shop
der	Obst- und Gemüseladen (-läden)	greengrocer's shop
	öffentliche Verkehrsmittel	public transport (pl)
der	Parkplatz (¨e)	parking space
der	Preis (-e)	price
	preiswert	cheap, value for money
die	Reinigung (-en)	dry-cleaner's
die	S-Bahn (-en)	suburban (fast) railway
	sogar	even
die	Sparkasse (-n)	(savings) bank
der	Vorort (-e)	suburb
das	Warenhaus (¨er)	department store

5.2 H In der Stadt

➡ pages 90–91

	alle zwei Stunden	every two hours
	anbieten	to offer
	(un)angenehm	(un)pleasant
	anziehen	to attract
	ausgezeichnet	excellent
	bekannt	well-known, famous
der	Bürgersteig (-e)	pavement
die	Bushaltestelle (-n)	bus stop
die	Einbahnstraße (-n)	one-way street
	entfernt	away
die	Erholung (-en)	recovery, revival, relaxation
die	Gegend (-en)	area
	genannt	named, called
	gratis	free of charge
die	Grünanlage (-n)	green area, park
	hochwertig	valuable
das	Industriegebiet (-e)	industrial area
der	Kirchturm (¨e)	church tower, spire
	lebhaft	lively, busy
	eine Menge	a lot of, lots
	mitten in	in the middle of
die	Modekette (-n)	fashion chain
die	Modemarke (-n)	fashion brand
	die Nase voll haben	to be fed up with something
	nirgendwo	nowhere
der	Rabatt (-e)	discount
die	Sackgasse (-n)	cul-de-sac
der	Schmuck	jewellery
die	Sparkasse (-n)	bank
der	Stadtrand (¨er)	outskirts of the town / city
der	Stadtteil (-e)	part of the town
das	Stadtviertel (–)	district, part of the town
	unzuverlässig	unreliable
der	Verkehr	traffic
das	Warenhaus (¨er)	department store
	zahlreich	numerous

6.1 F Freiwilligenarbeit im Ausland

1a 📖📖 Lies die Texte. Was machen diese Jugendlichen bei der Freiwilligenarbeit? Wähle das passende Bild für jede Person.

Read the texts. What are these young people doing in their voluntary work? Choose the appropriate picture for each person.

1 Ich finde das Meer faszinierend, also arbeite ich freiwillig auf den Bahamas. Das Projekt ist eigentlich unter Wasser und ich muss zuerst das Tauchen lernen. Prima! **Miriam**

2 Ich bin Freiwilliger in einem Kindergarten in Marokko. Meine Aufgaben sind Unterrichten, Spielen und Aktivitäten mit Kunst, Sport, Musik und Natur. Es macht mir viel Spaß. **Timo**

3 Ich interessiere mich sehr für Musik und spiele mehrere Instrumente, z.B. Violine und Keyboard. Auf der Insel Sansibar kann ich mit kleinen Kindern arbeiten. Die Arbeit ist sehr interessant. **Jasmin**

6 Ich verbringe zwei Monate im Reptilien-Zentrum in Mexiko. Ich muss aber ein bisschen Spanisch lernen. Hier arbeite ich mit Schlangen, Schildkröten und kleinen Krokodilen. **Anna**

5 Ich bin zurzeit in Ghana und arbeite in einer Grundschule. Der Arbeitstag beginnt um 7 Uhr und endet um 14 Uhr. Ich finde die Kinder in dieser Schule sehr nett. **Jens**

4 Ich arbeite in einem Tierheim am Stadtrand von Kapstadt in Südafrika. Hier gibt es Hunde, Katzen, Pferde und vieles mehr. Ich helfe beim Füttern. **Dirk**

Mexiko · Bahamas · Marokko · Ghana · Sansibar · Südafrika

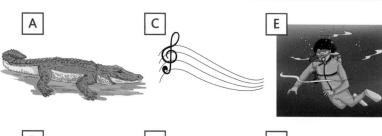

A

C

E

B

D

F

1b 📖📖 Read the texts again and answer the questions in English.

Who …

1 has to learn another language?
2 works on the outskirts of the city?
3 likes the sea?
4 thinks the work is interesting?
5 works in a primary school?
6 teaches a range of subjects?

2a 🎧 Listen to the people talking about their voluntary work. Answer the questions in English.

| 1 Susanna | 2 Robert | 3 Beate | 4 Cem | 5 Daniela |

Who works …

a   in a children's home?

b   in a school?

c   in an old people's home?

d   on an island?

e   with wild animals?

2b 🎧 Hör noch einmal zu. In welchem Land arbeitet jede Person? Schreib das Land auf Deutsch.

Listen again. In which country does each person work? Write the country in German.

3 🄖 Complete the sentences with the correct form of *der* or *ein* in the accusative or dative case.

1   Ich arbeite in ein__ Kinderheim.

2   Jeden Morgen gehen die Kinder in d__ Schule.

3   Meine Freundin arbeitet freiwillig in ein__ Tierpark.

4   Täglich helfe ich der Lehrerin in d__ Klassenzimmer.

5   Ich arbeite sehr gern in ein__ Altenheim.

6   In meiner Freizeit gehe ich gern in d__ Stadt.

7   Wir arbeiten in ein__ Kindergarten.

8   In d__ Mittagspause spiele ich Fußball mit den Kindern.

> **Grammatik** *page 180*
>
> ## Using *in* with the accusative or dative
>
> You will have noticed that *in* can be followed by different words for 'the' and 'a', e.g. *in das (ins)*, *in dem (im)*. This is because *in* is a preposition which can be followed by either the accusative or the dative case and it depends on whether movement is involved.
>
> So when you want to say 'in' meaning 'into', use *in* + accusative. (Remember this little rhyme: Place where <u>to</u> = Akku)
>
> Use *in* + dative when there is <u>no</u> movement. (Place where <u>at</u> = Dat)
>
> Look at these examples:
> *Ich gehe **in das (ins)** Klassenzimmer.* (I go in<u>to</u> the classroom. – movement = accusative)
>
> *Ich arbeite **in dem (im)** Klassenzimmer.* (I work in the classroom. – no movement = dative)
>
> Also learn about the demonstrative adjectives *dieser* and *jeder*. See page 104.

4 🅣 Translate the paragraph into German.

> I am a volunteer in a primary school in Morocco. My working day starts at 8 o'clock and I go into the school. I help the teacher in the classroom. The children are always friendly.

5 🗨 Rollenspiel. Dein Partner / deine Partnerin arbeitet freiwillig im Ausland. Stelle ihm / ihr die folgenden Fragen. Tauscht die Rollen.

Role play. Your partner is doing voluntary work abroad. Ask them the following questions. Swap roles.

Partner / Partnerin A	Partner / Partnerin B
1 Wo arbeitest du?	1 Say where you are working: name of country and the place where you are working.
2 Seit wann arbeitest du dort?	2 Say how long you have been working there.
3 Was machst du jeden Tag?	3 Say what tasks you do in your work every day.
4 Wie findest du die Arbeit?	4 Say what you think of your work and give a reason.

6.1 H   # Willkommen im Abenteuer

1 📖 Read the interview with Horst and his teacher about voluntary work. Answer the questions in English.

Lehrerin:	Hallo, Horst. Wo hast du Freiwilligenarbeit gemacht?
Horst:	Hallo, ich war vor einem Monat auf Borneo in Indonesien. Ich habe sechs Wochen dort verbracht.
Lehrerin:	Und was hast du gemacht?
Horst:	Ich habe am Orang-Utan Projekt teilgenommen. Ich bin ein richtiger Tierfreund und ich hatte die Chance, bei diesem Projekt mitzumachen.
Lehrerin:	Das hört sich faszinierend an. Bitte erzähl weiter.
Horst:	Die Orang-Utans sind gefährdet, weil sie wegen illegaler Abholzung ihren Lebensraum verlieren. Daher gibt es jetzt eine große Fläche im Regenwald, wo diese schönen Tiere in Sicherheit leben können. Viele sind als Waisen aufgewachsen oder haben in Gefangenschaft gelebt. Also müssen sie wieder lernen, in ihrer natürlichen Umgebung zu leben.
Lehrerin:	Und was waren deine Aufgaben?
Horst:	Mit anderen Freiwilligen habe ich gelernt, die gechippten Orang-Utans im Wald zu finden und ihre Gesundheit zu überprüfen. Auch musste ich helfen, Seilbrücken zu bauen. Das Gebiet, wo sie wohnen, kann man nur mit dem Boot erreichen. Es gibt keine Straßen und der Regenwald ist sehr dicht.
Lehrerin:	Und würdest du nach Borneo zurückkehren?
Horst:	Wenn ich das Geld hätte, würde ich das bestimmt machen. Und wenn ich sehr reich wäre, würde ich viel Geld für das Projekt spenden, denn für mich war es ein echtes Abenteuer.

1 For how long did Horst do voluntary work?

2 Why did he want to take part in the work?

3 Why are the orang-utans endangered?

4 Why are some of them having to get used to living in their natural habitat? (2 details)

5 Which tasks did Horst have? (3 details)

6 What makes it difficult to get to where the orang-utans live? (3 details)

7 What would he do if he had a great deal of money?

2a 🇬 Complete the sentences with the correct form of *wäre* or *hätte*. Then finish the sentences appropriately.

1 Wenn ich viel Geld h_____, würde ich …

2 Wenn ich älter w_____, würde ich …

3 Wenn du ein Auto h_____, würden wir …

4 Wenn wir ein größeres Haus h_____, würden wir …

5 Wenn er freundlicher w_____, würde er …

6 Wenn Kirsten eine Katze h_____, würde sie …

2b 🇬 🇹 Translate your sentences in activity 2a into English.

3 🎧 Listen to the three people. Choose the three correct statements.

1 Ayşe volunteered to work in a city.
2 Most people where she was staying worked in factories.
3 She enjoyed working in the the nursery.
4 Hans spent time with disabled children.
5 He was working for the Red Cross.
6 Vanessa was in Ghana three weeks ago.
7 She bought some earrings at the market.

4 🅣 Translate the paragraph into English.

> Wenn ich mehr Zeit hätte, würde ich wieder ehrenamtlich arbeiten. Letztes Jahr habe ich fünf Wochen in einem Kinderheim in Südafrika verbracht. Jeden Tag habe ich im Unterricht den Kindern geholfen und in der Pause mit ihnen gespielt. Ich habe auch ein bisschen unterrichtet. Ich habe dort so viel gelernt.

5 🅣 Translate the paragraph into German.

> I am a real animal lover. Therefore, I would like to work in an animal park in Africa if I had the chance. I spent a week in the summer holidays on a farm in Spain. Every day I worked from 7 o'clock until 5 o'clock, but it was fun.

6 🖊 Stell dir vor, du machst Freiwilligenarbeit irgendwo auf der Welt und du schreibst ein Blog darüber.

- ◆ In welchem Land bist du?
- ◆ Wann bist du angekommen?
- ◆ Wie sind die Einwohner?
- ◆ Was sind deine Aufgaben?
- ◆ Was hast du heute gemacht?
- ◆ Wie gefällt es dir dort?

Zurzeit bin ich	in Ghana / Südafrika / Mexiko / China / Südamerika / Borneo / Kenia.		
	auf Mauritius / Sansibar / Fidji / den Bahamas.		
Ich bin vor	einem Monat / einer Woche / zwei Tagen / drei Wochen	angekommen.	
Die Leute hier sind	sehr arm / freundlich / lieb / dankbar / glücklich / zufrieden.		
Ich arbeite	mit	Kindern / älteren Leuten / Tieren.	
	in einem	Tierpark / Altenheim / Kinderheim / Tierheim.	
Ich helfe den	Kindern / alten Leuten	beim Essen / Lesen / Spielen.	
Ich füttere / betreue die Tiere.			
Heute	Morgen / Nachmittag	habe ich	beim Essen / Spielen (usw.) geholfen. die Tiere gefüttert / betreut. die Gesundheit der Tiere überprüft.
Mir gefällt es hier (nicht), weil ich	die Arbeit / die Einwohner / das Klima /	herausfordernd / mühsam / anspruchsvoll / befriedigend / wunderschön / unangenehm	finde.

6.1 Groundwork is available in the Foundation book.

6.2 F   Damals war ich fit

1 **V** Finde die passenden deutschen und englischen Wörter.

Find the matching German and English words.

geraucht	blöd	probiert	fettleibig	gestorben	schädlich	abnehmen

harmful	stupid	to lose weight	tried	smoked	obese	died

2a 📖 Lies die Absätze über die Lebensstilprobleme dieser Leute und ihrer Verwandten. Dann schreib die Tabelle ab und fülle sie aus.

Read the passages about the lifestyle problems of these people and their relatives. Then copy and complete the grid.

Als ich jünger war ...

Theo
Als ich 11 Jahre alt war, war ich so dick – ich habe täglich eine ganze Menge Kalorien konsumiert: Chips, Schokolade, Pommes, Cola usw. Zum Glück habe ich jetzt abgenommen und bin gesünder. Das ist toll.

Manuela
Leider ist meine Oma vor drei Jahren gestorben. Sie hat jeden Tag ein paar Flaschen Wein getrunken und hat eine Leberkrankheit bekommen. Deswegen will ich keinen Tropfen Alkohol trinken.

Petra
Vor zwei Jahren habe ich viel Sport getrieben und ich war viel gesünder als heute. Jetzt sitze ich lieber vor dem Computer und surfe im Internet. Ich bin eine richtige Stubenhockerin.

Jan
Als er jünger war, hat mein Vater sechs bis acht Zigaretten pro Tag geraucht. Er hat vor einem Jahr aufgehört, weil es für seine Gesundheit so schädlich war. Außerdem findet er Zigaretten heute zu teuer.

Simon
Als ich in der Grundschule war, war ich immer aktiv. Heutzutage esse ich aber zu viele ungesunde Sachen und sehe stundenlang fern. Daher bin ich jetzt fettleibig geworden.

Barbara
Mein älterer Bruder hat vor acht Jahren so gesund gelebt. Er wollte keinen Alkohol trinken und keine Zigaretten rauchen. Heute nimmt er aber Drogen und er ist auch Drogenhändler. Schrecklich!

	Problem?					Wann?	
	Alkohol	Rauchen	Ernährung	Drogen	Faulheit	jetzt	früher
Beispiel: **Theo**			✓				✓

2b 📖 Read the passages again and choose the three correct statements.

1 Jan's father thinks smoking is expensive.
2 Petra enjoys water sports.
3 Simon often watches TV.
4 Manuela's grandmother had lung cancer.
5 Theo has gained a lot of weight now.
6 Barbara dislikes what her brother does.

3 Ⓖ Link the two sentences using *als*. Use the correct word order.

Beispiel: **1** Ich konnte nicht schwimmen, <u>als</u> ich sehr jung <u>war</u>.

1 Ich konnte nicht schwimmen. Ich war sehr jung.
2 Mein Freund hat geraucht. Er war in der Schule.
3 Ich war im Krankenhaus. Ich war 8 Jahre alt.
4 Wir mussten früher ins Bett gehen. Wir waren jünger.
5 Mein Bruder war so gestresst. Er hatte seine Examen.

4 🎧 Listen to the people. What are they doing to improve their health? Match the people with the pictures. Some people can be matched with more than one photo.

| 1 Frau Fischer | 3 Silke | 5 Olivia |
| 2 Herr Schäfer | 4 Kevin | |

5 Ⓣ Translate Theo's comment in activity 2a into English.

6 Ⓣ Translate the paragraph into German.

> When my friend was in primary school, he was not particularly fit or healthy. Now he eats more fruit and vegetables, goes swimming and plays for the football team. I think that is very good.

7 ✏ Stell dir vor, du bist eine prominente Person und du schreibst über deine Gesundheit. Du warst weder gesund noch fit, aber jetzt geht es dir besser. Schreib dein Blog.

Imagine you're a celebrity and you're writing about your health. You used to be neither healthy nor fit, but now you're better. Write your blog.

• Was hast du gemacht, als du jünger warst?
• Wie geht es dir heute?
• Was machst du, um fit zu bleiben?

Grammatik

Using *als* when talking about the past

If you want to say 'when' about things you've done in the past, use *als*. Like the word *weil* (because), *als* makes the verb go to the end of the sentence or clause:
*Ich habe nicht geraucht, **als** ich jünger **war**.* (I didn't smoke when I was younger.)

If the sentence starts with the clause containing *als*, you use inversion in the following clause:
***Als** sie Kopfschmerzen **hatte**, **hat sie** eine Tablette genommen.* (When she had a headache, she took a tablet.)

Don't forget to use the correct word order with modal verbs in the imperfect tense:
*Meine Schwester **musste** zum Arzt **gehen**, **als** sie krank **war**.* (My sister had to go the doctor's when she was ill.)

Also learn how to recognise and understand *um … zu* and verbs that are followed by *zu*. See page 105.

page 184

6.2 H

Lebst du gesund oder ungesund?

1 📖 Read the articles and answer the questions in English.

A Proteste gegen Drogenberatungsstelle

In wenigen Wochen eröffnet in der Nußdorfer Straße am Alsergrund eine Drogenberatungsstelle. Die Anrainer sorgen sich, dass die Drogenszene in die Nachbarschaft kommt, und protestieren gegen das Zentrum.

Am 13. November wird das 126 Quadratmeter große Suchthilfezentrum offiziell eröffnet. Es wird täglich von 9.30 bis 16.30 Uhr zur Verfügung stehen und hier wird man Drogensüchtigen Beratung und Spritzentausch anbieten. Die Anrainer finden dieses Zentrum ungeeignet, weil zahlreiche Schulen und Kindergärten in unmittelbarer Nähe liegen.

B Zehn Tipps für ein gesundes, langes Leben

1. Richtige Ernährung
2. Ausreichend trinken
3. Regelmäßige Bewegung
4. Viel Frischluft und Licht
5. Entspannung für den Ausgleich
6. Genug und regelmäßig schlafen
7. Reges Gehirn-Jogging
8. Genussgifte vermeiden
9. Gesunde Beziehungen
10. Ja zum Leben!

C Betrunkener Autofahrer verursacht Verkehrsunfall

Am Sonntagmorgen kam gegen 3:10 Uhr ein 19-jähriger aus Hühnstetten mit seinem Volvo V40 auf der B417 von der Fahrbahn ab und überschlug sich. Durch den Unfall erlitt der Fahrer schwere Verletzungen und der Rettungsdienst musste ihn medizinisch versorgen. Ein Atemalkoholtest ergab, dass der Fahrer unter der Wirkung von Alkohol stand. Die Polizei nahm ihm den Führerschein ab. Neben Polizei und Rettungsdienst war die Feuerwehr vor Ort.

der Anrainer – resident
ungeeignet – unsuitable
zahlreich – numerous
rege – active
das Genussgift – harmful stimulant
verursachen – to cause
sich überschlagen – to somersault

1   What is going to open shortly?
2   Why are the residents worried about their neighbourhood?
3   What will be offered in the new building? (2 details)
4   Why do the residents think it is unsuitable?
5   What is the most important advice for staying healthy?
6   After having enough to drink, what is the next thing you should you do?
7   What is mentioned on the list before relaxation?
8   What was the cause of the accident?
9   What happened to the driver?
10 What did the police do?

Reading authentic texts

Here are a few tips for dealing with authentic German texts:

• Read through the text **slowly**.

• Don't worry about the words you don't know – pick out those that you **do** know.

• English questions about the text can give you clues about what some of the words mean.

• Try to work out the meanings of words which are similar to those you know already.

• Sometimes an unknown word with a capital letter can be a place name, e.g. *Hühnstetten*.

Challenge: Try each of these tips when you read the texts in activity 1.

Strategie

2 🎧 Listen to the interview with Frau Schröder talking about her son. Complete the sentences in English.

1 When he was younger, Heiko broke his …
2 He started smoking when he was …
3 He wasn't allowed …
4 His mother couldn't …
5 He said his friends …
6 After several months, he was …
7 His girlfriend found him …
8 When he comes out of hospital …

3 🄖 🅣 Translate the sentences into German.

1 I mustn't smoke.
2 He didn't have to take drugs.
3 We don't have to eat chips.
4 He mustn't drink milk.
5 You don't have to drink alcohol.
6 She doesn't have to play on the computer.
7 We weren't allowed to eat eggs.
8 I didn't have to eat so much.

4 🅣 Translate the paragraph into English.

> Als sie jünger war, war meine Schwester magersüchtig. Weil sie geglaubt hat, dass sie dick ist, hat sie wenig gegessen. Manchmal hat sie sich sogar nach einer Mahlzeit erbrochen. Es war furchtbar und wir haben uns große Sorgen gemacht. Sie musste ins Krankenhaus gehen, aber heute geht es ihr viel besser.

Grammatik · page 185

Saying 'must not' and 'don't have to'

Take care when you want to say 'must not' ('mustn't') in German.

- If you mean you are **not allowed to do** something, use the correct form of *dürfen + nicht* or *kein*: *Ich **darf keine** Nüsse essen.* (I mustn't eat nuts.)
- If you mean that you **don't have to do** something (i.e. there is an alternative), use the correct form of *müssen + nicht*: *Ich **muss nicht** fernsehen.* (I don't have to watch TV.)

In the imperfect tense, these examples would be:
*Ich **durfte keine** Nüsse essen.* (I wasn't allowed to eat nuts.)
*Ich **musste nicht** fernsehen.* (I didn't have to watch TV.)

See page 185 for the different forms of *müssen* and *dürfen*. Also do some practice with the imperfect tense. See page 105.

5 🗨 Partnerarbeit. Dein(e) Partner(in) war in der Vergangenheit süchtig, aber jetzt geht es ihm / ihr gut. Stelle ihm / ihr die folgenden Fragen. Dann tauscht die Rollen.

- Was war das Problem?
- Wie lange hast du das gemacht?
- Warum wolltest du aufhören, Zigaretten zu rauchen / Alkohol zu trinken / Drogen zu nehmen / so viel / wenig zu essen?
- Was hast du gemacht, um wieder gesund zu werden?

Als ich jünger war, / In der Vergangenheit	war ich magersüchtig / Drogensüchtige(r) / Alkoholiker(in) / fettleibig. habe ich Drogen genommen / zu viel getrunken / gegessen / geraucht.
Mit vierzehn Jahren habe ich angefangen,	zu rauchen / Alkohol zu trinken / weniger zu essen.
Das habe ich … Jahre lang gemacht.	

Ich wollte damit aufhören, weil	ich krank wurde / war. ich von Drogen / Alkohol / Zigaretten total abhängig war. ich so unglücklch war. ich nicht früh sterben wollte.
Ich war deprimiert / traurig, da	es mir immer schlecht ging. ich keine richtigen Freunde hatte. ich so viel Geld verschwendet habe. ich mich oft einsam gefühlt habe.

Um wieder gesund zu werden,	habe ich	gelernt, richtig zu essen. das Rauchen aufgegeben. Drogen vermieden. eine Entziehungskur gemacht.

🔗 6.2 Groundwork is available in the Foundation book.

G # Social issues

1 Complete the sentences using the German for the word given in brackets. Make sure you use the correct case and gender (or plural form).

1 … Land hat verschiedene Probleme. (*each*)
2 … Projekt ist sehr interessant. (*this*)
3 Ich finde … Tierpark faszinierend. (*every*)
4 … Kinder sind sehr arm. (*these*)
5 Ich mag … Land und … Leute. (*this, these*)

Grammatik page 179

Using *dieser* (this, these) and *jeder* (each, every)

These words have almost the same endings as the definite article (the word for 'the'). As with the definite article, the ending changes depending on case, gender and number of the noun. Notice that there is no plural form for *jeder*. Here are the words you need in the nominative and accusative:

	masculine	feminine	neuter	plural
nominative	dieser	diese	dieses	diese
accusative	diesen	diese	dieses	diese
nominative	jeder	jede	jedes	–
accustive	jeden	jede	jedes	–

Meine Schwester verbringt **jeden** *Tag im Tierpark.* (accusative, masculine)
Dieses *Kind sieht zufrieden aus.* (nominative, neuter)

2 Complete the sentences using the German for the word given in brackets. Make sure you choose the correct case and gender (or plural form).

1 Ich arbeite in … Grundschule. (*this*)
2 Am Ende … Tages war ich so müde. (*of every*)
3 Heute habe ich mit … Kindern gearbeitet. (*these*)
4 In … Land gibt es sehr viele arme Leute. (*this*)
5 Die Eltern … Kinder verbringen viele Stunden bei der Arbeit. (*of these*)
6 Ich habe mit … Kind auf Englisch gesprochen. (*every*)
7 … Kind in … Dorf ist dankbar. (*every, this*)
8 Für … Tiere ist ein sicherer Lebensraum sehr wichtig. (*these*)

Grammatik page 179

Using *dieser* and *jeder* in all the cases

Here are all the words you need:

	masculine	feminine	neuter	plural
nominative	dieser	diese	dieses	diese
accusative	diesen	diese	dieses	diese
genitive	dieses	dieser	dieses	dieser
dative	diesem	dieser	diesem	diesen

	masculine	feminine	neuter	plural
nominative	jeder	jede	jedes	–
accusative	jeden	jede	jedes	–
genitive	jedes	jeder	jedes	–
dative	jedem	jeder	jedem	–

Here are some examples using the genitive and dative:
*Die Einwohner jed***er** *Stadt sind so freundlich.*
(The inhabitants of every town are so friendly.)
*Ich fahre mit dies***em** *alten Bus in die Stadt.*
(I travel into town on this old bus.)

3a Translate the sentences into English.

1   Ich gehe jeden Morgen joggen, um fitter zu werden.
2   Mein Onkel schwimmt regelmäßig, um gesund zu bleiben.
3   Wir essen kleine Portionen, um schlank zu sein.
4   Meine Mutter benutzt Nikotinpflaster, um mit dem Rauchen aufzuhören. (*aufhören* = to stop)

3b Translate the sentences into English.

1   Mein Vater hat beschlossen, keinen Alkohol zu trinken.
2   Ich versuche, jedes Wochenende Fußball zu spielen.
3   Wir haben beschlossen, immer vegetarisch zu essen.
4   Er hofft, zehn Kilo abzunehmen.
5   Ich habe begonnen, früher ins Bett zu gehen.

4a Using the verb tables on pages 192–195 to help you, look again at the article 'Betrunkener Autofahrer verursacht Verkehrsunfall' on page 102. Write down all the verbs in the imperfect tense. Translate the verbs into English.

4b Rewrite the following paragraph in the imperfect tense. Then translate the paragraph into English.

Ich bin Alkoholiker und ich trinke jeden Tag eine Flasche Wodka und mehrere Flaschen Bier. Es geht mir nicht so gut und ich habe Magenschmerzen. Am Tag esse ich nicht viel, denn ich habe nur ein bisschen Geld. Abends gehe ich in die Stadtmitte. In den Mülltonnen finde ich oft ein paar Butterbrote. Dann schlafe ich nachts auf der Straße, was sehr gefährlich ist.

Grammatik page 188

Recognising *um … zu* and verbs that are followed by *zu*

The two little words *um … zu …* mean 'in order to …' and are used with the **infinitive** at the **end of the sentence or clause**.
*Ich gehe jeden Morgen joggen, **um** fit **zu sein**.*
***Um** in Form **zu bleiben**, esse ich immer gesund.*

When this phrase is used with a separable verb in the infinitive, you will find the *zu* part sandwiched between the separable prefix and the verb itself:
*Um ab**zu**nehmen, darf sie kein Fastfood essen.*
(In order to lose weight, she isn't allowed to eat any fast food.)

Some verbs are used with *zu* and then a second verb in the infinitive form at the end of the sentence or clause. These are verbs such as *beginnen* (to begin), *beschließen* (to decide), *hoffen* (to hope) and *versuchen* (to try). Notice that a comma is usually placed after the first verb:
*Ich **hoffe**, Ärztin **zu** werden.* (I hope to become a doctor.)
*Meine Freundin **versucht**, gesünder **zu** essen.* (My friend is trying to eat more healthily.)

Grammatik page 186

Practice with the imperfect tense

You will be quite used to recognising the perfect tense, which is normally used in conversation or informal writing. The **imperfect tense** is used frequently in more formal writing, such as in newspaper articles. You will have seen commonly used examples:
essen → *ich aß* (I ate)
trinken → *ich trank* (I drank)
kommen → *ich kam* (I came)
sein → *ich war* (I was)
haben → *ich hatte* (I had)

Vokabeln

6.1 Charity / voluntary work

6.1 F Freiwilligenarbeit im Ausland
➡ *pages 96–97*

der	Arbeitstag (-e)	working day
	arm	poor
die	Aufgabe (-n)	task, job
	aufräumen	to tidy up
	eigentlich	actually, really
	einfach	simple
	faszinierend	fascinating
	füttern	to feed
die	Grundschule (-n)	primary school
	herkommen	to come from, to originate from
der	Kindergarten (¨)	nursery
das	Kinderheim (-e)	children's home
das	Krokodil (-e)	crocodile
	mehrere	several
die	Natur	nature
der	Ort (-e)	place
die	Schildkröte (-n)	tortoise, turtle
die	Schlange (-n)	snake
	spannend	exciting, thrilling
	spazieren gehen	to go for a walk
	süß	sweet
der	Tierpark (-s)	animal park, zoo
das	Tierheim (-e)	animal shelter
die	Umwelt	environment
der	Unterricht	lessons, teaching
	unterrichten	to teach
	verbringen	to spend (time)
	vorlesen	to read (aloud)
die	Weltkarte (-n)	world map
	zurzeit	at present

6.1 H Willkommen im Abenteuer
➡ *pages 98–99*

die	Abholzung (-en)	deforestation
	anspruchsvoll	demanding
	sich anhören	to sound
	aufwachsen	to grow up
	befriedigend	satisfying
	betreuen	to look after, to supervise
das	Boot (-e)	boat
	dicht	dense
	echt	real, genuine
	ehrenamtlich	voluntary
	erreichen	to reach
das	Feld (-er)	field
die	Fläche (-n)	area
die	Freiwilligenarbeit	voluntary work
	füttern	to feed
das	Gebiet (-e)	region, area
	gechippt	microchipped
	gefährdet	endangered
die	Gefangenschaft	captivity
die	Gesundheit	health
der	Lebensraum (¨e)	habitat, living space
	lieb	kind, lovely
der	Regenwald (¨er)	rainforest
	richtig	real, proper, correct
	(Deutsches) Rotes Kreuz	(German) Red Cross
die	Seilbrücke (-n)	rope bridge
die	Sicherheit	safety, security
	spenden	to donate
der	Teil (-e)	part
der	Tierfreund (-e)	animal lover
	überprüfen	to check, to monitor
die	Umgebung (-en)	surrounding area, environment
die	Waise (-n)	orphan
	wegen	because of
	zurückkehren	to return

6.2 Healthy / unhealthy living

6.2 F Damals war ich fit
➡ *pages 100–101*

	aufgeben	to give up
	aufhören	to stop
	außerdem	besides, furthermore
	daher	**that is why**
	deswegen	therefore, because of that
die	Diät (-en)	diet
die	Faulheit	laziness
	fettleibig	obese
	heutzutage	nowadays
die	Kalorie (-n)	calorie
	konsumieren	to consume
das	Krankenhaus (¨er)	hospital
der	Krebs (-e)	cancer
die	Leber	liver
die	Mannschaft (-en)	team
	schädlich	damaging, harmful
	sparen	to save
	sterben	to die
der	Stubenhocker (–)	couch potato, stay-at-home (m)
die	Stubenhockerin (-nen)	couch potato, stay-at-home (f)
	der Tabak (-e)	tobacco
der	Tropfen (–)	drop
	verbessern	to improve, to get better
	weder … noch …	neither … nor …
	zunehmen	to put on weight, to increase

6.2 H Lebst du gesund oder ungesund?
➡ *pages 102–103*

	abhängig sein von	to be dependent on
	anbieten	to offer
	anstatt	**instead of**
	ausreichend	**sufficient(ly)**
	betrunken	drunk
die	Bewegung (-en)	movement, exercise
	bewusstlos	unconscious
	brechen	to be sick, to break
	darüber hinaus	**furthermore, moreover**
die	Drogenberatungsstelle (-n)	advice centre for drug addicts
die	Entziehungskur (-en)	course of withdrawal treatment, rehab
	sich erbrechen	to be sick
	erleiden	**to suffer**
die	Ernährung (-en)	food, nourishment, nutrition
der/ die	Erwachsene (-n)	adult
	fettleibig	obese
die	Feuerwehr (-en)	fire service
der	Führerschein (-e)	driving licence
das	Gehirn (-e)	brain
der	Magen (¨)	stomach
	magersüchtig	anorexic
der	Rettungsdienst (-e)	emergency service
	riechen	to smell
	schaden	to damage
	… schmerzen haben	to have … ache
	sonst	otherwise, or else
der	Spritzentausch	needle exchange
die	Sucht (¨e)	addiction
die	Überdosis (-dosen)	overdose
der	Vegetarier (–)	vegetarian (n)
	vegetarisch	**vegetarian (adj)**
	zur Verfügung stehen	**to be available**
der	Verkehrsunfall (¨e)	traffic accident
die	Verletzung (-en)	injury
	verschwenden	to waste

Higher – Reading and listening

1 📖 Read the conversation in a German chat room between three teenagers about the places where they live. Copy the grid. Write the **four** correct places in the grid in **English**.

	past	present	future
Example: **Mehmet**	*town centre*	*village*	*Switzerland*
Theresa	block of flats		
Stefan		flat behind station	

[4 marks]

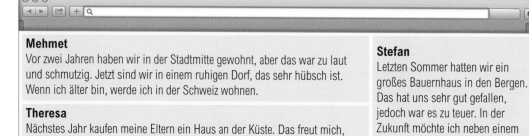

Mehmet
Vor zwei Jahren haben wir in der Stadtmitte gewohnt, aber das war zu laut und schmutzig. Jetzt sind wir in einem ruhigen Dorf, das sehr hübsch ist. Wenn ich älter bin, werde ich in der Schweiz wohnen.

Theresa
Nächstes Jahr kaufen meine Eltern ein Haus an der Küste. Das freut mich, weil ich es hasse, wo wir jetzt wohnen. Es ist in einer Sackgasse und man sieht nur die Nachbarn! Letztes Jahr haben wir in einem Wohnblock gewohnt.

Stefan
Letzten Sommer hatten wir ein großes Bauernhaus in den Bergen. Das hat uns sehr gut gefallen, jedoch war es zu teuer. In der Zukunft möchte ich neben einem Fluss wohnen, aber heute haben wir eine Wohnung hinter dem Bahnhof!

2 📖 Lies diese Geschichte aus dem Märchen *Hänsel und Gretel*, geschrieben von den Brüdern Grimm und sieh dir die Aussagen an. Sind die Aussagen **richtig** (R), **falsch** (F) oder **nicht im Text** (NT)?

Als der Tag anbrach, noch bevor die Sonne aufgegangen war, kam schon die Frau und weckte die beiden Kinder: „Steht auf, ihr Faulenzer, wir wollen in den Wald gehen und Holz holen."

Dann gab sie jedem ein Stückchen Brot und sprach: „Da habt ihr etwas für den Mittag, aber esst es nicht vorher auf, weiter kriegt ihr nichts." Gretel nahm das Brot. Danach machten sie sich alle zusammen auf den Weg in den Wald.

Als sie eine Weile gegangen waren, blieb Hänsel stehen und guckte immer wieder zum Haus zurück. Der Vater sprach: „Hänsel, was guckst du da und bleibst zurück, hab acht und vergiss deine Beine nicht!" – „Ach, Vater," sagte Hänsel, „ich sehe nach meinem weißen Kätzchen. Das sitzt oben auf dem Dach."

1 Die Frau weckte die Kinder, als es noch dunkel war.
2 Sie aßen Brot zum Frühstück.
3 Die Familie ging in den Wald, weil sie kein Holz hatten.
4 Sie wollten später ein Picknick machen.
5 Hänsels Vater wollte nicht stehen bleiben.
6 Hänsel hatte keine Haustiere. **[6 marks]**

3 **T** Your German friend has sent you a text about his new home. Translate the text into **English** for your parents.

> Wir wohnen jetzt in einem gemütlichen Haus am Meer. Mein Vater war letztes Jahr krank und wir sind hierher gekommen, weil er frische Luft braucht. Das Einfamilienhaus ist sehr geräumig und von meinem Zimmerfenster aus kann ich die Segelboote sehen. Wenn es möglich ist, werde ich im Sommer segeln lernen.

[9 marks]

4 You are at your exchange partner's house and his elder brother Timo tells you about the previous evening. Complete the following statements about Timo's evening in **English**. Answer all parts of the question.

1 Timo and his girlfriend had been to see …
2 They had hoped to come home by …
3 The young people had been …
4 A boy was …
5 A girl had …
6 The other young people had decided to …   **[6 marks]**

> **Strategie**
>
> When you are asked to complete sentences, make sure that you are writing in the correct language – check the instruction. When you are listening to the recording, don't expect to hear the exact words or phrases that you need to fill in the gaps. Try to get a real understanding of what has been said. For example, in sentence 1 of activity 4, you need to say that Timo and his girlfriend had been to see a film, but the word 'film' is not mentioned in the recording. However, because Timo says that they have been to the cinema, you can **infer** that they went to see a film.

5 You hear part of a podcast by Franz who lives in a German town. Choose the correct answers.

1 Franz …
   a hates where he lives.
   b enjoys the choice of things to do.
   c thinks his town is boring.

2 He …
   a does not mind the noise.
   b cannot sleep at night.
   c would prefer to live somewhere else.

3 He …
   a never travels by underground.
   b thinks it is cheaper to shop where he lives.
   c prefers shopping in the city centre.

4 In the future, Franz wants to …
   a move abroad.
   b live in a village.
   c continue living here.   **[4 marks]**

6 Hör dir das Interview mit Michelle an, die letzten Monat in Asien war. Beantworte die Fragen auf **Deutsch**.

1 Was ist wichtig für Michelle? Schreib den richtigen Buchstaben.

A	Es ist wichtig, im Ausland Urlaub zu machen.
B	Man soll arbeiten, um Geld zu verdienen.
C	Jugendliche sollen anderen helfen.

2 Wer braucht unsere Hilfe? (**zwei** Details)
3 Was soll man nicht machen?
4 Warum?   **[5 marks]**

Foundation test and revise tasks are available in the Foundation book.

Higher – Writing and translation

Either:

1a ✏️ Dein Freund Max aus Österreich hat dich über deine Gesundheit gefragt. Du schreibst Max eine E-Mail über deine Gesundheit.

Schreib:

- wie gesund du heute bist
- warum du gesund oder nicht gesund bist
- was du letzte Woche gemacht hast, um fit zu bleiben
- was du in der Zukunft machen wirst, um gesund zu bleiben.

Du musst ungefähr **90** Wörter auf **Deutsch** schreiben. Schreib etwas über alle Punkte der Aufgabe.

[16 marks]

Or:

1b ✏️ Deine deutsche Austauschpartnerin kommt zu Besuch und möchte etwas über dein Haus und deinen Wohnort wissen. Du schickst ihr eine E-Mail.

Schreib:

- etwas über deine Stadt / dein Dorf
- warum du gern oder nicht gern da wohnst
- was du gestern in der Gegend gemacht hast
- wo du in der Zukunft wohnen wirst.

Du musst ungefähr **90** Wörter auf **Deutsch** schreiben. Schreib etwas über alle Punkte der Aufgabe.

[16 marks]

Strategie

When you read the bullet points, you **must** be sure which time frame is being used because you need to write about that particular bullet point in the same time frame. Look for clues which indicate which time frame is being used. For the past time frame, you are likely to see a past participle with part of *haben* or *sein*, e.g. *Schreib, was du letzte Woche gemacht hast*., but also look for past time indicators such as *gestern* or *letzte Woche*.

For the future time frame, you might see the future tense with *werden* (will) or conditional forms such as *würde* (would) or *möchte* (would like). Also look for future time indicators such as *in der Zukunft, nächstes Jahr, in zehn Jahren*.

Either:

2a ✏ Du schreibst einen Artikel über deine Freiwilligenarbeit in einer Grundschule für die Schülerzeitung deiner Partnerschule in Deutschland.

Schreib:

- etwas über den Besuch – deine Impressionen und Meinungen
- etwas über dein Leben zu Hause – was ist ähnlich und was ist anders?

Du musst ungefähr **150** Wörter auf **Deutsch** schreiben. Schreib etwas über beide Punkte der Aufgabe.

[32 marks]

Aim to write as accurately as you possibly can, so allow some time to check everything over. Are the items on the checklist correct?

- Verb endings?
- Tenses?
- Cases with articles?
- Adjective endings?
- Noun plurals?
- Word order:
  - T – M – P
  - inversion
  - perfect tense
  - infinitive clauses
  - subordinate clauses

Or:

2b ✏ Du beschreibst dein Traumhaus für einen Wettbewerb in einer deutschen Zeitschrift.

Schreib:

- etwas über das Haus, wo du jetzt wohnst – Vor- und Nachteile
- etwas über dein Traumhaus – Meinungen und Gründe.

Du musst ungefähr **150** Wörter auf **Deutsch** schreiben. Schreib etwas über beide Punkte der Aufgabe.

[32 marks]

3 ⊤ Translate the paragraph into German.

My parents and I live near the coast. It is fantastic here because I like the sea. It is really beautiful when the sun shines. In good weather you can see many ships. I want to stay fit, so I go jogging every morning. Yesterday I also swam two kilometres.

[12 marks]

Translating English into German is a very demanding skill because there is so much to think about: vocabulary, cases, word order, tenses, etc. As you are working out your answer, it is likely that you will keep changing your mind about what you think is correct, so it would be a good idea to write a rough version first. However, do be careful to allow enough time to write your neat version.

4 ⊤ Translate the paragraph into German.

I find my town great because it has very good shopping facilities and a modern sports centre. There is also a theatre and a cinema. We saw a good film there last week. If I had the chance, I would like to live abroad, probably where the weather is warm.

[12 marks]

Foundation test and revise tasks are available in the Foundation book.

Higher – Speaking

1 Role play

Your teacher or partner will play the part of your exchange student and will speak first.

You should address your exchange student as *du*.

When you see this – ! – you will have to respond to something you have not prepared.

When you see this – ? – you will have to ask a question.

> Du sprichst mit deinem deutschen Austauschpartner / deiner deutschen Austauschpartnerin über Häuser.
>
> • Haus / Wohnung – wo.
> • Seit wann da.
> • !
> • Traumhaus (**zwei** Details).
> • ? Ausland gewohnt.

[15 marks]

2 Role play

Your teacher or partner will play the part of your friend and will speak first.

You should address your friend as *du*.

When you see this – ! – you will have to respond to something you have not prepared.

When you see this – ? – you will have to ask a question.

> Du sprichst mit einem Freund / einer Freundin aus der Schweiz über Gesundheit.
>
> • (Nicht) gesund.
> • Fitness: Aktivitäten.
> • !
> • Gesundheit früher.
> • ? Fastfood.

[15 marks]

Strategie

Each role play contains a question for you to ask, so make sure that you learn how to form questions in German. Remember that to form a question in German you just invert the subject and verb. So in this role play, you could ask the question 'Have you lived abroad?' which would be *Hast du im Ausland gewohnt?*

3 Photo card

- Look at the photo during the preparation period.
- Make any notes you wish to on an Additional Answer Sheet.
- Your teacher or partner will then ask you questions about the photo and related to the topic of **Home, town, neighbourhood and region**.

Your teacher or partner will ask you the following three questions and then **two more questions** which you have not prepared.

- Was gibt es auf dem Foto?
- Was findest du besser – ein Haus auf dem Land oder ein Haus in der Stadt? Warum?
- Was hast du gestern in der Gegend gemacht?   **[15 marks]**

4 Photo card

- Look at the photo during the preparation period.
- Make any notes you wish to on an Additional Answer Sheet.
- Your teacher or partner will then ask you questions about the photo and related to the topic of **Social issues**.

Your teacher or partner will ask you the following three questions and then **two more questions** which you have not prepared.

- Was gibt es auf dem Foto?
- Wie findest du Freiwilligenarbeit? Warum?
- Wie hast du letzte Woche in deiner Stadt geholfen?   **[15 marks]**

Strategie

There may be one question which asks you for an opinion with an explanation, so make sure that you are able to give opinions with explanations.

Try to make your answer more interesting by adding adjectives, adverbs, quantifiers (e.g. *ein bisschen*), intensifiers (e.g. *sehr*), etc. You may also need to use more than one tense, so make sure you have learned how to use them and include them whenever you have an opportunity.

Foundation test and revise tasks are available in the Foundation book.

Helft der Umwelt!

1 Ⓥ Was kommt wohin?

What goes where?

1 — Plastik/Metall
2 — Biomüll
3 — Altpapier

a Plastikflaschen   b Zeitungen
c Obst   d Bücher
e Jogurtbecher   f Gemüse
g Verpackungen aus Karton
h Küchenabfall
i Getränkedosen   j Blumen

2a 📖 Lies die Schlagzeilen. Welche Schlagzeile passt zu welchem Foto?

Read the headlines. Which headline matches which photo?

wagen – to dare, to risk
der Sprung – jump, leap

1 **4000 demonstrierten gegen Kohlekraftwerk in Mainz**

Gestern gab es Proteste in der Stadtmitte. Sowohl jüngere als auch ältere Menschen standen vor dem Rathaus und sangen Protestlieder. Sie wollten der Regierung zeigen, dass

2 **Demo gegen Wasserverschmutzung: Elf wagten den Sprung in die Weser**

Zum fünften Mal hat in Münden der „Big Jump", das Schwimmen für eine saubere Weser, stattgefunden.

4 **Forum Lärm und Stadt**

Lärm ist vor allem in Städten und Ballungsräumen eines der größten Umwelt- und Gesundheitsprobleme.

3 **Gewalt in der Innenstadt nimmt zu**

Hannovers Innenstadt ist beliebt und belebt. Doch die Stadtmitte hat ein wachsendes Problem: Seit Jahren steigt die Zahl der Gewalttaten dort extrem an.

5 **EuropäerInnen wollen bessere öffentliche Verkehrsmittel**

Für EU-BürgerInnen sind bessere Verbindungen, eine verlässliche Infrastruktur und billigere Fahrkarten die wichtigsten Anliegen im Verkehrsbereich.

A   B   C   D   E

2b 📖 Lies die Anweisungen. Welche Anweisung passt zu welcher Schlagzeile?

Read the instructions. Which instruction matches which headline?

a Springt in den Fluss!
b Sei ruhig!
c Geben Sie uns mehr Busse und Züge!
d Stoppen Sie die Luftverschmutzung!
e Macht die Stadt sicherer!

3 **G** Complete the sentences with the correct form of the imperative given in brackets.

1   Sandra, … die Heizung herunter! (*drehen*)
2   Frau Demel, bitte … das Licht aus! (*machen*)
3   Katrin und Daniel, … alles! (*recyceln*)
4   Axel, … die Plastikflasche nicht weg! (*werfen*)
5   … Energiesparlampen, Herr Schneider! (*kaufen*)
6   Christof, … morgen mit der Straßenbahn! (*fahren*)

4 🎧 Listen to the people. Which four environmental problems do they mention?

a noise   b violence
c overpopulation
d dangerous roads   e litter
f air pollution   g no public transport

5 **T** Translate the paragraph into German.

Go by tram! It is much quieter and cleaner than the car. It is also more environmentally friendly. Our town has a beautiful pedestrian precinct. Naturally, cars are forbidden there. Therefore, it is very pleasant.

6 🗫 Partnerabeit. Seht euch das Foto an und beantwortet die Fragen. Dann tauscht die Rollen.

Work with a partner. Look at the photo and answer the questions. Then swap roles.

•   Was gibt es auf dem Foto?
•   Ist diese Stadt umweltfreundlich? Warum (nicht)?
•   Gibt es Umweltprobleme in deinem Wohnort?
•   Was hast du neulich für die Umwelt gemacht?

Using the imperative

Grammatik · *page 189*

The imperative is used to tell somebody to do something. There are three different forms of the imperative depending on who you are talking to.

1   If you are talking to one person you know or someone your age or younger, you use the *du* form of the verb, but leave out *du* and take off the ending *-st* (or *-est*) from the verb:
    Du sparst Wasser. → ~~Du sparst~~ *Wasser.* → *Spar Wasser!*
    Notice that an exclamation mark is often used at the end of the imperative sentence.
    If the *du* form of the verb has an *ä* in it, take off the umlaut in the imperative:
    Du fährst mit dem Bus. → *Fahr mit dem Bus!*

2   If you are talking to one or several adults or people you don't know well, you use the *Sie* form of the verb, but place the pronoun *Sie* after the verb:
    Sie sparen Wasser. → *Sparen Sie Wasser!*

3   You also need to be able to understand the *ihr* form of the imperative, which is used for talking to more than one person you know or several people your age. You use the *ihr* form of the verb, but without *ihr*:
    Ihr spart Wasser. → ~~Ihr~~ *spart Wasser.* → *Spart Wasser!*

Also learn how to recognise and understand the pluperfect tense. See page 122.

Spotting near-cognates when listening

Strategie

Always listen out for near-cognates to help you understand. Remember that these are words which sound very similar to English words and have the same meaning:
Europäer (European)
Kohle (coal)
schmutzig (smutty, i.e. dirty)

Sometimes they can help you understand part of the word (and then you might be able to guess the rest!):
*Kau**gummi*** (chewing **gum**)
***Jogurt**becher* (**yogurt** pot)

Challenge: Look at the vocabulary list for this topic and make a list of all the near-cognates you can find. Then take turns with a partner to say a word and the other person has to guess what it means.

Globale Umweltprobleme

Die größten Umweltprobleme

1 Weltbevölkerung wächst
Die Welt ist überbevölkert. Zurzeit sind rund 6 786 610 000 Menschen auf dem Planeten. Pro Jahr kommen etwa 81 Millionen hinzu – ungefähr die Einwohnerzahl Deutschlands.

2 Klimawandel
Im vergangenen Jahrhundert waren die Temperaturen bereits um insgesamt 0,7 Grad gestiegen. Dasselbe galt für den Meeresspiegel: Er stieg seit 1993 um etwa drei Millimeter im Jahr.

3 Artensterben
Auch 40 Prozent aller Arten sind durch die globale Erwärmung vom Aussterben bedroht. Zwölf Prozent aller Vogelarten sind gefährdet. In Europa ist ein Fünftel der Reptilien und nahezu ein Viertel der Amphibien vom Aussterben bedroht.

4 Wasserknappheit
Der Verbrauch steigt, die Qualität sinkt – die Vereinten Nationen warnen seit Jahrzehnten, dass die Wasserknappheit in den Entwicklungsländern zahllose Menschenleben bedroht.

Wie wir Wasser verschwenden:
- Wasserverbrauch zur Erzeugung von Käse: 5000 Liter pro Kilogramm.
- Wasserverbrauch für eine Tasse Kaffee: 140 Liter.
- Für einen Hamburger: 2400 Liter.
- Für ein Ei: 200 Liter.
- Für ein Glas Bier (250 ml): 75 Liter

5 Umweltverschmutzung und Chemikalien
Wir alle verschmutzen die Umwelt, täglich. Spülmittel rauscht den Abfluss hinunter. Düngemittel gelangen ins Grundwasser, die Ölreste nach dem Autowaschen, das Waschmittel für die Waschmaschine. Gifte und Gase von Umweltkatastrophen können Menschen in Sekunden umbringen. Bei einem Chemieunfall im indischen Bhopal waren 2000 Menschen gestorben.

Using grammatical categories

When you are unsure about what a word means, looking at other words in the sentence can give you clues about what type of category it belongs to (noun, plural form of a noun, verb, preposition, etc.). For instance, in *Düngemittel gelangen ins Grundwasser*, the plural form of the verb tells you that *Düngemittel* is a plural noun. Notice in the previous sentence, though, that *Spülmittel* is singular because of the singular ending on *rauscht*.

Challenge: Working with a partner, each copy a sentence from the text and work together to identify the different types of words.

Strategie

der Klimawandel – climate change
die Art – species
die Knappheit – shortage
der Verbrauch – consumption
das Spülmittel – detergent, washing-up liquid
gelangen in – to get into
das Gift – poison
umbringen – to kill

1 Lies den Text und sieh dir die Aussagen an. Sind die Aussagen richtig (R), falsch (F) oder nicht im Text (NT)?

1 Es gibt 81 Millionen Menschen auf der Welt.
2 Im letzten Jahrhundert waren die Temperaturen um 0,7 Grad gestiegen.
3 In Südamerika sind 50 % aller Tierarten gefährdet.
4 Fast 25 % der Amphibien in Europa könnten aussterben.
5 Die Qualität des Wassers steigt.
6 Man braucht 120 Liter Wasser, um ein Glas Wein zu produzieren.
7 Der Wasserverbrauch für ein Liter Bier ist 75 Liter.
8 Man findet gefährliche Chemikalien in jedem Haushalt.

2 Listen to the people talking about environmental problems. Choose the three correct statements.

1 Felix thinks the world would be better if there weren't so many people.
2 Frau Lehmann thinks we should recycle more.
3 Sonja believes that there should be more zoos to protect the animals.
4 Herr Meyer thinks that electric cars wouldn't be more expensive than other cars.
5 Claudia's family grows apples, pears and grapes.
6 Her parents don't approve of using pesticides.

3 **G** **T** Rewrite the sentences in the pluperfect tense. Then translate the sentences into English.

1 Wir haben so viel Wasser verschwendet.
2 Viele Tierarten sind schon ausgestorben.
3 Die Vereinten Nationen haben uns über Wasserknappheit gewarnt.
4 Meine Mutter hat täglich so viele Chemikalien im Haushalt verwendet.
5 Ich habe versucht, mehr Strom zu sparen.
6 Die Weltbevölkerung ist Jahr für Jahr gestiegen.

4 **T** Translate the paragraph into English.

Es gibt so viele Umweltprobleme: Luft-, Wasser- und Bodenverschmutzung, zu viele Menschen, nicht genug Wasser, Artensterben usw. Wenn wir statt fossiler Brennstoffe alternative Energiequellen benutzten und wenn wir den Planeten nicht verschmutzten, hätten wir eine schönere Welt. Es ist wichtig, dass wir an die Zukunft denken.

5 **T** Translate the paragraph into German.

When I went to South America, many bird species had already died out. That was very sad. The rainforest had also become smaller because of deforestation. In the future we must protect the environment. There is too much pollution and we must recycle more: glass, cans, batteries, newspapers, etc.

6 ✎ 🗔 Gruppenarbeit. Was sind deiner Meinung nach die wichtigsten Umweltprobleme? Gib Gründe dafür an. Mach Notizen. Dann halte in deiner Gruppe einen kurzen Vortrag.

Meiner Meinung nach ist		Wasserknappheit Artensterben Verschmutzung die Weltbevölkerung	das größte Umweltproblem.
Es gibt		zu viele Menschen. nicht genug Wasser. zu viele Autos und LKWs.	
Der Mensch	zerstört	die Wälder. den Lebensraum von Tieren / Vögeln. die Ozonschicht.	
	verpestet	die Luft / das Meer / die Flüsse / die Seen.	
Man	verschwendet	zu viel Wasser. zu viele Rohstoffe.	
Wir	verschwenden		
Wir	produzieren	zu viele Gifte / gefährliche Chemikalien. zu viel Kohlendioxid / Schwefeldioxid.	

Grammatik *page 187*

Using the pluperfect tense

The pluperfect tense (called the *Plusquamperfekt* in German) is used to describe something which **had** happened before something else.

To form it, use the **imperfect** tense of **haben** or **sein** + **past participle** at the end of the sentence or clause. (See page 187 for *haben* and *sein* in the imperfect.)
*Viele exotische Vogelarten **hatten** wegen Abholzung ihren Lebensraum **verloren**, bevor wir den Regenwald geschützt haben.* (Many species of exotic birds had lost their habitat because of deforestation, before we protected the rainforest.)
*Es war eine Katastrophe, weil so viele Menschen **gestorben waren**.* (It was a disaster because so many people had died.)

Also learn how to use the conditional and *wenn* clauses. See page 122.

ꙮ

7.1 Groundwork is available in the Foundation book.

7.2 F Endlich in Sicherheit!

1 📖 Read the text and complete the statements.

> **Lina (13) erzählt, wie sie ihre vier Geschwister in Pariang, Südsudan aufzieht**
>
> Ich wache früh auf, wenn es noch dunkel ist und mahle Sorghum für das Frühstück. Dann ziehe ich mich an, wecke meine Geschwister und wir waschen uns und putzen uns die Zähne. Danach gehe ich zur Wasserstelle mit meinem 20-Liter Wasserkanister.
>
> Zwei oder dreimal in der Woche muss ich Feuerholz holen. Das ist weit – das kannst du dir nicht vorstellen. Wenn ich morgens losgehe, komme ich nicht vor dem Abend wieder.
>
> Zum Spielen habe ich keine Zeit. Wir mussten aus unserem Dorf fliehen. Meine Mutter ist vor drei Jahren bei der Geburt meines kleinen Bruders gestorben. Und es gab keine Gesundheitsstation in unserem Dorf. Ich weiß nicht, wo mein Vater ist. Das heißt, ich muss mich um alles kümmern.

1 Lina wakes up …
   a when it gets light.
   b after the others.
   c when it's dark.

2 Before getting dressed, she …
   a cleans her teeth.
   b makes breakfast.
   c washes.

3 Every day she fetches …
   a water.
   b firewood.
   c food.

4 A few years ago, her mother …
   a was in hospital.
   b went missing.
   c died.

> *mahlen* – to grind
> *das Sorghum* – sorghum (a type of grain)

2 🄶 Complete the sentences with the correct reflexive pronoun.

sich	dich	mich	sich
dir	uns	sich	mir

1 Ich wasche … jeden Morgen vor dem Frühstück.
2 Beate kümmert … um die Kinder.
3 Täglich wäscht er … die Haare.
4 Wir fühlen … heute nicht so gut.
5 Zweimal pro Tag putze ich … die Zähne.
6 Ziehst du … um, bevor du ausgehst?
7 Hast du … die Hände gewaschen?
8 Die Kinder ziehen … aus, bevor sie ins Bett gehen.

Using and recognising reflexive pronouns

When talking about washing **something**, we use the verb *waschen*, but when talking about washing **oneself**, it becomes a reflexive verb: *sich waschen*. Depending on who is speaking, the (accusative) reflexive pronoun *sich* changes:
ich wasche **mich** (I wash myself)
du wäschst **dich**
er / sie / es wäscht **sich**
wir waschen **uns**
ihr wascht **euch**
sie / Sie waschen **sich**

Other reflexive verbs include *sich anziehen* (to get dressed = to dress oneself), *sich ausziehen* (to get undressed), *sich umziehen* (to get changed), *sich fühlen* (to feel) and *sich kümmern (um)* (to look after).

When talking about parts of the body, do not use the pronouns *mich, dich, sich*, etc. Instead use the dative reflexive pronouns *mir, dir, sich*:
Ich putze **mir** *die Zähne.* (I clean my teeth.)
Du wäschst **dir** *die Hände.* (You wash your hands.)
Er wäscht **sich** *das Gesicht.* (He washes his face.)
Sie putzt **sich** *die Zähne.* (She cleans her teeth.)

Also learn how to recognise weak masculine nouns. See page 123.

Grammatik *page 183*

Strategie

3 🎧 Hör dir die Berichte von Joseph, Jutta und Paul an und wähle die vier richtigen Aussagen aus.

Listen to the three accounts by Joseph, Jutta and Paul and choose the four correct statements.

1   Die Leute waren nicht freundlich, als Joseph nach Deutschland kam.
2   Joseph ist seit 11 Jahren in Deutschland.
3   Joseph ist nicht glücklich.
4   Jutta hat sich gut mit ihren Eltern verstanden.
5   Jutta lebt seit sechs Monaten auf der Straße.
6   Paul kommt aus Äthiopien.
7   Im Flüchtlingslager leben 45 000 Menschen.
8   Es gibt viel Gewalt im Flüchtlingslager.

Recognising suffixes

Being able to recognise suffixes (a group of letters at the end of a word) can help you to understand what the whole word means. One common suffix is *-los* (-less):

arbeitslos ('work-less' = unemployed)
hilflos ('help-less' = helpless)
obdachlos ('shelter-less' = homeless)

Challenge: Try to work out the meaning of these words: *atemlos, bewusstlos, endlos, humorlos, kostenlos, schlaflos, schmerzlos, sprachlos.*

Check your answers in a dictionary if necessary.

Freunde gewinnen – to make friends
das Flüchtlingslager – refugee camp

4 🅣 Translate the paragraph into English.

Letzten Monat bin ich mit meinen Eltern nach Österreich geflohen. Das Leben ist schwierig, aber unser Nachbar ist nett. Er hat zwei Kinder. Ich habe mit dem Mädchen gesprochen, aber ich kenne den Jungen noch nicht.

5 🅣 Translate the paragraph into German.

I am homeless and spend the day in the pedestrian precinct. It is often very cold. People give me money sometimes, but not much. I don't like sleeping outside because it is quite dangerous.

6 ✏️ Stell dir vor, du bist entweder ein Flüchtling oder du willst nicht mehr zu Hause bleiben. Schreib einen Absatz über deine tägliche Routine.

Imagine either that you are a refugee or don't want to be at home any more. Write a paragraph about your daily routine.

- Um wie viel Uhr wachst du auf?
- Beschreib deine Routine.
- Wie verbringst du den Tag?
- Wie fühlst du dich?

Ich stehe	früh / spät / um 7 Uhr	auf.
Ich wasche	mich (nicht oft).	
	mir (selten) das Gesicht / die Haare / die Hände.	
Ich ziehe mich an. / Ich trage dieselbe Kleidung.		
Ich sitze	auf der Straße / in der Stadtmitte / vor dem Bahnhof / in der Bibliothek / vor dem Rathaus.	
Ich muss	Wasser / Feuerholz	holen / suchen.
	das Frühstück zubereiten / meiner Familie helfen / um Geld betteln.	
Ich bin einsam. Ich habe wenige Freunde / Angst vor Gewalt / der Zukunft.		

7.2 H   Armut auf der Straße

1 📖 Read the story about Ingo and answer the questions in English.

Ohne festen Wohnsitz

Ich heiße Ingo und habe keinen festen Wohnsitz, weil ich seit elf Monaten auf der Straße lebe. Ich bin erst 26 Jahre alt, sehe aber zehn Jahre älter aus, da ich mich selten rasieren oder mich richtig waschen kann. Vor elf Monaten war alles normal, aber mein Leben hat sich seither so verschlechtert.

Wie ist das alles passiert? Sechs Monate früher hatte ich wegen eines Missverständnisses meinen Job verloren. Obwohl ich versucht habe, Arbeit zu finden, habe ich keinen Erfolg gehabt. Meine Freundin und ich haben uns gestritten, weil sie mich nicht unterstützen wollte. Letzten

April hat sie jemand anders gefunden und hat mich aus unserer Wohnung geworfen. Mein Vater konnte mir nicht helfen, denn er war auch pleite und hatte in seiner Wohnung keinen Platz für mich.

Am Anfang war es schwer, obdachlos zu sein, denn ich hatte keine Ahnung, wohin ich gehen sollte. Glücklicherweise ist mir nichts Schlechtes passiert. Nach ein paar Tagen habe ich das Hilfezentrum gefunden, wo ich Informationen über Obdachlosenheime und Suppenküchen bekommen habe.

Hier auf der Straße ist aber etwas Gutes passiert, weil ich jetzt eine neue Freundin habe. Wir hoffen, eines Tages eine Sozialwohnung zu bekommen. Das ist bestimmt kompliziert, aber das würde ohne Zweifel unser Leben verbessern.

1 How long has Ingo been homeless?
2 Why does he look older than he is? (2 details)
3 How has his life changed since he became homeless?
4 How did he lose his job?
5 Why did his former girlfriend throw him out? (2 details)
6 Why couldn't his father help him? (2 details)
7 Why was it hard being homeless at first?
8 What information did the help centre give him? (2 details)
9 How has life now become better for Ingo?
10 What does he hope to do one day?

2 🎧 Hör dir Margit, Christian und Helga an, die über ihr Leben sprechen. Welche vier Aussagen sind richtig?

1 Margit war sehr reich, als sie jünger war.
2 Sie wollte im Ausland wohnen.
3 Ihr Lebensstil hat sich nicht verbessert.
4 Christian trinkt nie Alkohol.
5 Niemand gibt ihm Geld.
6 Ein paar Leute haben keinen Respekt vor ihm.
7 Helga würde lieber in einem Obdachlosenheim schlafen.
8 Sie ist keine Drogensüchtige.
9 Jeden Tag kauft sie sich eine Zeitung.

Looking for words inside other words

Looking for a word inside another word can often help you to work out the meaning. For example, some verbs contain adjectives which give a big clue about the verb's meaning. Here are two from the reading text:

*sich ver**schlechter**n* ('to become **worse**' = to worsen, deteriorate)

*ver**besser**n* ('to make **better**' = to improve)

Challenge: Look for the adjectives contained in these words. Then try to work out what they mean: *bereichern, ermöglichen, ermüden, vergrößern, veröffentlichen, versichern, verstärken*

Check your answers afterwards using a dictionary.

Strategie

3 **G** Complete the sentences with the correct accusative or dative reflexive pronoun.

1 Sie kümmert … um ihre Katze.
2 Hast du … die Füsse gewaschen?
3 Ich wasche … vor dem Frühstück.
4 Hast du … die Zähne geputzt?
5 Meine Verwandten treffen … vielleicht zweimal im Jahr.
6 Seht ihr … den neuen Film an?
7 Wir fühlen … unwohl.
8 Meine Freundin hat … einen neuen Rock gekauft.

4 **T** Translate the paragraph into English.

Ich wohne seit zwei Wochen in diesem relativ neuen Obdachlosenheim am Stadtrand. Hier gefällt es mir nicht so gut, weil hier Alkoholiker, Drogensüchtige und Leute mit verschiedenen Krankheiten sind. Auch sterben jährlich zwei bis drei Menschen im Heim. Trotzdem bin ich dankbar, dass ich im Winter nicht draußen erfrieren werde.

5 **T** Translate the paragraph into German.

Hans has lived on the street for three years. He washes himself in the morning, has a blue rucksack and is always a cheerful person. He sells newspapers and never goes begging. In the future he would like to earn enough money in order to buy himself a flat.

6 Partnerarbeit. Dein(e) Partner(in) ist obdachlos. Stelle ihm / ihr die folgenden Fragen. Dann tauscht die Rollen.

Partner / Partnerin A		Partner / Partnerin B	
1	Wo wohnst du?	1	Say where you live: name of town and the place where you are sleeping.
2	Seit wann bist du obdachlos?	2	Say how long you have been homeless.
3	Was hast du gestern gemacht?	3	Say what you did yesterday.
4	Wie ist deine Morgenroutine?	4	Say what you do when you wake up.
5	Wie findest du dein Leben? Warum?	5	Say what you think of your life and give a reason.

Grammatik *page 183*

Using reflexive verbs with a direct object

Many reflexive verbs are used with **accusative** reflexive pronouns (see page 118), e.g. *Ich wasche **mich**.* (I wash (myself).) *Du kümmerst **dich** um deinen Hund.* (You look after your dog.)

Some verbs are used with **dative** reflexive pronouns because the accusative is used elsewhere in the sentence as a direct object. This usually happens when referring to parts of the body:

dative   accusative

*Ich wasche **mir** das Gesicht.* (literally: I wash to me the face. = I wash my face.)

Here is a summary of the accusative and dative reflexive pronouns:

nominative	accusative	dative
ich	mich	mir
du	dich	dir
er / sie / es	sich	sich
wir	uns	uns
ihr	euch	euch
sie / Sie	sich	sich

There are other verbs which can be used with a dative reflexive pronoun:
kaufen: *Ich kaufe **mir** ein Butterbrot.* (I buy myself a sandwich.)
ansehen: *Wir sehen **uns** einen Film an.* (We are watching a film (for ourselves).)
vorstellen: *Ich stelle **mir** vor, dass sie wenig Geld hat.* (I imagine that she doesn't have much money.)

Also learn about adjective endings after *etwas*, *nichts*, *viel*, *wenig*, *alles*. See page 123.

7.2 Groundwork is available in the Foundation book.

G Global issues

1 Translate the sentences into English.

1. Meine Eltern hatten ein Haus auf dem Land gekauft, bevor wir umgezogen sind.
2. Nachdem ich den Müll getrennt hatte, bin ich zur Schule gegangen.
3. Wir sind mit der Straßenbahn gefahren, weil wir den Bus verpasst hatten.
4. Ich hatte das Licht schon ausgemacht, als meine Mutter ins Zimmer kam.
5. Nachdem wir in der Stadtmitte einkaufen gegangen waren, sind wir nach Hause gekommen.
6. Es gab keine Plastikflaschen im Haus, weil wir sie alle recycelt hatten.

2 Complete the sentences with the correct form of *würde*. Finish the sentences appropriately.

Beispiel: **1** Wenn wir umweltfreundlicher wären, <u>würden</u> wir <u>mehr recyceln</u>.

1. Wenn wir umweltfreundlicher wären, … wir …
2. Wenn wir keine fossilen Brennstoffe mehr hätten, … wir …
3. Wenn wir alle Elektroautos hätten, … die Luft …
4. Wenn wir nicht genug Wasser hätten, … wir …
5. Wenn ich viel Geld hätte, … ich …
6. Wenn du mehr Freizeit hättest, was … du …?
7. Wenn ich Premierminister(in) wäre, … ich …

Grammatik — page 187

The pluperfect tense

The pluperfect tense refers to something which **had happened** before something else:
*Es war kalt, weil wir die Heizung **heruntergedreht hatten**.* (It was cold because we **had turned down** the heating.)

The pluperfect tense is formed by using the <u>imperfect tense of *haben* or *sein*</u> with the **past participle** at the end of the sentence or clause:
*Ich <u>hatte</u> den Müll **getrennt**.*
(I **had separated** the rubbish.)
*Ich <u>war</u> in die Stadt **gefahren**.*
(I **had gone** into town.)

Grammatik — page 188

Using the conditional and *wenn* clauses

Use the conditional when you want to say 'would'. It is formed by using the correct form of *würden* with the infinitive at the end of the sentence or clause (see page 188):
*Ich **würde** ein Elektroauto **kaufen**.* (I would (I'd) buy an electric car.)

The conditional is often used with a *wenn* clause where the verb is in the **subjunctive** form (see page 188). Remember that the verb in the *wenn* clause also goes to the end:
*Wenn ich kein Auto **hätte**, würde ich öfter mit dem Rad fahren.* (If I didn't have a car, I'd go by bike more often.)

Note that *würde* + *haben* and *würde* + *sein* are normally replaced by *wäre* and *hätte*.
*Wenn wir auf dem Land wohnten, **hätten** wir ein größeres Haus.* (If we lived in the country, we would have a larger house.)
*Wenn ich mehr Geld verdiente, **wäre** ich sehr glücklich.* (If I earned more money, I would be very happy.)

3 Find the weak masculine noun in each sentence. Write the noun and which case it is in: nominative or accusative. Then translate the sentences into English.

1 Ich habe den Jungen getroffen, aber nicht seine Schwester.
2 Der Herr hat einen Tisch für zwei Personen reserviert.
3 Man konnte am Strand keinen einzigen Menschen sehen.
4 Wie heißt der Herr? Leider habe ich seinen Namen vergessen.
5 Hier ist ein Apfel für den Jungen.
6 Der Junge und das Mädchen hatten kleine Taschen dabei.

Grammatik | page 178

Recognising weak masculine nouns

There is a special group of masculine nouns called weak nouns which add the ending **-n** or **-en** in the **accusative singular** form. Some examples of weak masculine nouns are:
der Junge (boy), *der Name* (name), *der Mensch* (human being), *der Herr* (gentleman).

Usually, we add *-n* if the noun ends in *-e* and *-en* if it ends in a consonant. But watch out for *Herrn* which is an exception to this rule. *Herr* ends in a consonant, but we only add *-n*.

nominative	accusative
der Junge	den Jungen
der Name	den Namen
der Mensch	den Menschen
der Herr	den Herrn

Make sure that you learn these weak nouns as you meet them.

---

4 Complete the sentences with the German for the phrases given in backets. Choose the correct adjective each time.

gut	interessant	schlecht	schön
~~schrecklich~~	wichtig		

Beispiel: **1** Gestern habe ich **etwas Schreckliches** gesehen.

1 Gestern habe ich … gesehen. (*something awful*)
2 … ist passiert. (*nothing bad*)
3 Er hat … gesehen. (*little (that was) interesting*)
4 Ich habe … gemacht. Es war total langweilig. (*nothing nice*)
5 Es gab … im Fernsehen. (*something important*)
6 Ich habe … über das neue Obdachlosenheim gehört. (*lots of good things*)

Grammatik | page 181

Adjective endings after *etwas, nichts, viel, wenig, alles*

In expressions such as 'something old' or 'nothing new', the adjective becomes a noun in German, so it needs a capital letter. It also needs the ending **-es**. This happens after the words **etwas** (something), **nichts** (nothing), **viel** (a lot of, lots of), and **wenig** (little):
etwas **Gutes** (something good)
nichts **Neues** (nothing new)

However, after **alles** (everything), just add **-e** as well as adding the capital letter:
alles **Gute** (all the best)

When translating these expressions into English, sometimes you will need to add the word 'things' or 'that is':
viel Nützliches (lots of useful things)
wenig Interessantes (little / not much that is interesting)
viel Gutes (many good things)

Vokabeln

7.1 Environment

7.1 F Helft der Umwelt!
➡ *pages 114–115*

der	*Abfall (ˬe)*	rubbish, waste, (litter)
die	*Abgase*	exhaust fumes (pl)
das	*Altpapier*	waste paper
	atmen	to breathe
die	*Bevölkerung (-en)*	population
der	*Biomüll*	organic waste
die	*Dose (-n)*	can
das	*Elektroauto (-s)*	electric car
die	**Energiesparlampe (-n)**	energy-saving bulb
der	*Fahrradweg (-e)*	bicycle track / lane
der	*Flughafen (ˬ)*	airport
die	*Gewalt*	violence
der	*Jogurtbecher (–)*	yogurt pot
der	*Kaugummi (-s)*	chewing gum
die	*Kohle*	coal
das	*Kraftwerk (-e)*	power station
der	*Lärm*	noise
der	*LKW (-s) (Lastkraftwagen)*	HGV, lorry
die	*Luftverschmutzung*	air pollution
	sauber	clean
	schmutzig	dirty
	starten	to take off
die	*Verpackung (-en)*	packaging
die	*Wasserverschmutzung*	water pollution
	wegwerfen	to throw away

7.1 H Globale Umweltprobleme
➡ *pages 116–117*

die	*alternative Energiequelle (-n)*	alternative energy source
	anbauen	to grow (something)
das	*Artensterben*	species extinction
	Auspuffgase	exhaust fumes (pl)
	aussterben	to die out, to become extinct
	bedrohen	to threaten
	bereits	already
der	*Boden (ˬ)*	soil
der	*Brennstoff (-e)*	fuel
die	*Chemikalie (-n)*	chemical
das	*Düngemittel (–)*	fertiliser
	entsetzlich	terrible, awful, appalling
das	*Entwicklungsland (ˬer)*	developing country
die	*Erde*	Earth
	gefährdet	endangered
die	*Hauptverkehrszeit (-en)*	rush hour
	insgesamt	altogether
die	*Katastrophe (-n)*	disaster
der	*Klimawandel*	climate change
das	*Kohlendioxid (-e)*	carbon dioxide
die	*Ozonschicht (-en)*	ozone layer
der	*Rohstoff (-e)*	raw material
das	*Schwefeldioxid (-e)*	sulphur dioxide
	überbevölkert	over-populated
	verpesten	to pollute
	verschmutzen	to pollute
	verschwenden	to waste
	verwenden	to use
	warnen vor	to warn about
die	*Wasserknappheit*	water scarcity
die	*Welt (-en)*	world
die	*Weltbevölkerung (-en)*	world population
	weniger	fewer, less
	wiederverwerten	to recycle

7.2 Poverty / homelessness

7.2 F Endlich in Sicherheit!
➡ *pages 118–119*

die	*Armut*	poverty
	bedrohlich	threatening
	endlich	at last, finally
	erscheinen	to appear, to seem
	fest	fixed, solid
das	*Feuerholz*	firewood
	fliehen	to flee
die	*Flucht (-en)*	escape
der	*Flüchtling (-e)*	refugee
das	*Flüchtlingslager (–)*	refugee camp
	froh	happy, glad, pleased
die	*Geburt (-en)*	birth
	hilflos	helpless
das	*Holz*	wood
	keinen festen Wohnsitz haben	to have no fixed abode
der	*Krieg (-e)*	war
das	*Leben (–)*	life
	losgehen	to set off
	obdachlos	homeless
	rauswerfen	to throw out
	schwierig	difficult
die	*Suppenküche (-n)*	soup kitchen
die	*Tasche (-n)*	bag
	über	over, above, via
	wiederkommen	to come back

7.2 H Armut auf der Straße
➡ *pages 120–121*

	abstinent	teetotal
der	*Albtraum (¨e)*	nightmare
der	*Bart (¨e)*	beard
	bedürftig	needy
	betteln	to beg
die	*Entziehungskur (-en)*	rehab for drug addiction / alcoholism
	erfrieren	to freeze to death
	erst	(at) first, only
die	*Geschäftsfrau (-en)*	businesswoman
	nachts	at night
das	*Obdachlosenheim (-e)*	hostel for homeless people
	pleite	skint, broke
	(sich) rasieren	to shave
der	*Schlafsack (¨e)*	sleeping bag
	streiten	to argue
	unterstützen	to support
	sich verschlechtern	to get worse, to deteriorate
	verschwinden	to disappear
	wahrscheinlich	probably
	(aus …) werfen	to throw out of
	keinen festen Wohnsitz haben	to have no fixed abode
	ohne Zweifel	without doubt

Ich suche eine Unterkunft

1a 📖 Lies die Inserate. Welche Inserate passen zu welchen Fotos?

Read the adverts. Which adverts match with which photos?

1

Pension am Wald

Die ehemalige Jagdhütte liegt direkt am Wald, weit von der Straße entfernt. Sie ist ideal zum Wandern oder Mountainbiken.

Die Hütte hat Platz für maximal sechs Personen: zwei Schlafzimmer mit Doppelbett und eine Schlafcouch im Wohnzimmer.

Die Küche ist komplett eingerichtet. Gäste können die Sauna im Haus und den Grill im Garten kostenfrei benutzen.

die Jagdhütte – hunting lodge
der Stellplatz – pitch (for tent or caravan)
inbegriffen – included

2

Campingplatz am Mittelmeer

Der Campingplatz hat 100 schattige Stellplätze in verschiedenen Größen. Sie können ein privates Badezimmer und einen Stromanschluss mitbuchen.

Inbegriffen im Preis:
- Auto
- Zelt oder Wohnwagen / Camper
- Wasser
- 2 Personen

Weitere Informationen
- Unterkunft geeignet für max. 6 Personen
- Hunde erlaubt

CAMPINGPLATZ FÜR DIE GANZE FAMILIE

3

Perfekt für Familienurlaub: Hotel im Stadtzentrum Salzburg

Hotelausstattung

Ein Restaurant, Kaffee / Tee und kostenlose Zeitungen in der Lobby. Den WLAN-Internetzugang in den öffentlichen Bereichen können Sie kostenlos nutzen.

Zimmerausstattung

Doppelzimmer, Zweibettzimmer und Einzelzimmer sind individuell ausgestattet und bieten Ihnen einen Zimmerservice und einen Haartrockner. Flachbildfernseher, Zimmersafes und Toilettenartikel stehen Ihnen zur Verfügung.

A

B

C

D

E

F

G

H

1b 📖 Lies die Inserate noch einmal. Welche Aussagen passen zu welchem Inserat?

Read the adverts again. Which statements match which advert?

a Wir blieben eine Woche in Salzburg.
b Wir nahmen unseren Hund mit.
c Nur vier Personen schliefen in der Pension.
d Am Mittwoch fuhren wir mit dem Auto ans Mittelmeer.

e Normalerweise aßen wir im Restaurant.
f Ich ging jeden Tag wandern.
g Er las eine Zeitung in der Lobby.
h Wir sahen viele Tiere im Wald.

2 **G** **T** Choose the correct verb in the imperfect tense. Then translate the sentences into English.

1 Unterwegs **schlafen / schliefen** die Kinder im Auto.
2 Wir **kamen / kommen** um 11 Uhr an.
3 Er **nahm / nimmt** den Koffer mit ins Hotel.
4 Ich **liest / las** eine Zeitschrift in der Lobby.
5 Sabine **aß / isst** ein Eis im Schatten.
6 Er **geht / ging** mit seiner Familie ins Restaurant.
7 Wir **bleiben / blieben** acht Tage in Österreich.
8 Er **fuhr / fährt** immer mit dem Zug in Urlaub.

3 🎧 Listen to the two conversations at the hotel reception. Copy and complete the grid in English.

	1 Herr Hoffmann	**2** Frau Schwarz
no. of guests		
room type		
details		
no. of nights		
breakfast (y / n)		
cost		
details of journey		

4 🗨 Partnerarbeit. Du arbeitest in einem Hotel in der Schweiz. Du bist der Rezeptionist / die Rezeptionistin und sprichst mit einem Hotelgast. Stell deinem Partner die folgenden Fragen. Dann tauscht die Rollen.

Work with a partner. You work in a hotel in Switzerland. You are the receptionist and you are talking to a hotel guest. Ask your partner the following questions, then swap roles.

Grammatik   page 186

Recognising the imperfect tense of irregular verbs

One thing that will help you recognise the imperfect tense of irregular (strong) verbs is a change in the vowel. For a list of strong verbs in the imperfect tense, see pages 192–195.

present	imperfect
ich bleibe	*ich blieb*
ich gehe	*ich ging*
ich fahre	*ich fuhr*
ich esse	*ich aß*
ich komme	*ich kam*
ich lese	*ich las*
ich schlafe	*ich schlief*

Look for these endings (no ending for the *ich* and *er / sie / es* forms):

ich sah   *er / sie / es sah*   *ihr saht*
du sahst   *wir sahen*   *sie / Sie sahen*

Also learn how to use the time – manner – place rule in the perfect tense. See page 134.

Using paraphrase

Strategie

If you can't remember how to say a particular word or phrase, try to use alternative expressions which you **do** know. (This is called 'paraphrasing'). For example, if you have forgotten the word for 'without' as in 'without breakfast' (*ohne Frühstück*), you could simply say **kein** *Frühstück* and you will still score the mark.

Challenge: Practise doing this taking turns with a partner. Give them three words in English that they are unlikely to know in German. They must then describe them as accurately as possible. Finally, look up the correct words in a dictionary.

Bitte schön? / Kann ich Ihnen helfen?			
Ich brauche Ich möchte	ein Einzelzimmer / Doppelzimmer / Zweibettzimmer	mit Bad / Dusche / Balkon.	
Für wie viele Nächte? / Wie lange möchten Sie bleiben?			
(Für)	eine Nacht / vier Nächte / eine Woche / zwei Wochen.		
Gibt es	ein Restaurant / einen Aufzug?		
Was kostet	das Zimmer	mit / ohne	Frühstück / Abendessen?
	Halbpension / Vollpension?		
Ich bin Wir sind	mit	dem Auto / Bus / Zug der Fähre	hierher nach …	gefahren. gekommen.
		dem Flugzeug		geflogen.

8.1 H Wie war denn der Urlaub?

1a 📖 Read the reviews and answer the questions in English.

A „Kein schöner Besuch"
★☆☆☆☆

Das war unser erstes Mal in Madrid, aber es war eine Katastrophe.
1. Das Hotel war sehr schwer zu finden – sogar für unseren Taxifahrer, der mehrmals nach dem Weg fragen musste.
2. Als wir endlich angekommen waren, war die Rezeptionistin etwas unhöflich. Es hat lange gedauert, bevor wir auf unser Zimmer gehen konnten.
3. Am schlimmsten war aber das Zimmer: klein, schmutzig und es roch nach Zigaretten. Schade!

B „Ideale Lage, Nickerchen unmöglich!"
★★★☆☆

Mitten in der Stadt ist das Hotel perfekt für sowohl Sightseeing als auch Shopping. Weil der Hauptbahnhof nur fünf Minuten entfernt liegt, ist es auch gut, wenn man einen Ausflug machen will, um die Umgebung zu entdecken. Unser Zimmer war sehr preiswert und wir hatten ein geräumiges, sehr schön ausgestattetes Doppelzimmer. Leider haben meine Frau und ich fast nie geschlafen, weil der Verkehrslärm dies unmöglich machte.

C „Ein tolles Hotel"
★★★★★

Weil sich das Hotel gegenüber vom Kolosseum befindet, war es sehr leicht, die berühmten Sehenswürdigkeiten in Rom zu besichtigen. Wir haben uns auch gefreut, dass unser Zimmer einen Balkon hatte. Obwohl wir im Herbst im Hotel übernachtet haben, war das Wetter noch warm und wir konnten abends auf dem Balkon sitzen. Das Frühstücksbüffet haben wir jeden Morgen richtig genossen, da die Auswahl enorm war. Das Personal hat auch versucht, unseren Aufenthalt perfekt zu machen. Herzlichen Dank!

das Nickerchen – nap

Which review …
1. complained about noise?
2. praised the food?
3. complained about staff?
4. said the hotel was handy for public transport?
5. complained about the hotel's location?
6. praised the hotel's facilities?
7. was positive about the size of the room?
8. complained about the smell in the room?

1b 📖 Read Review C again and answer the questions in English.

1. What was the advantage of the hotel's location?
2. What did the reviewer like about the room?
3. When did they stay at this hotel?
4. What could they do despite the time of year?
5. What was good about breakfast?
6. What did the staff try to do?

2a 🎧 Hör dir diese vier Leute an, die über ihren Urlaub sprechen. Was meinen sie dazu? Ist ihre Meinung positiv (P), negativ (N) oder positiv und negativ (P+N)?

1 Kevin   2 Monika   3 Josef   4 Gisela

2b 🎧 Hör dir die Leute noch einmal an. Beantworte die Fragen auf Deutsch.

1. Wie war das Wetter in Kevins Urlaub? (**zwei** Details)
2. Warum hat Kevin das Hotel ausgezeichnet gefunden?
3. Wie war das Wetter in Monikas Urlaub? (**drei** Details)
4. Wie ging es Monika?
5. Wie hatte Josef eine Ermäßigung für die Fahrkarten bekommen?
6. Was war das Problem während der Reise nach Hause? (**drei** Details)
7. Was war in Giselas Hotel los? (**zwei** Details)
8. Wie hat sich Gisela am letzten Tag gefühlt?

3a **G** Link the sentences using the conjunctions given in brackets.

1   Wir haben in einer Pension übernachtet. Es war billiger. (*denn*)

2   Ich wollte ein größeres Zimmer. Es war unmöglich. (*aber*)

3   Wir können noch einen Tag bleiben. Wir können heute abfahren. (*oder*)

4   Wir waren sehr müde. Wir waren im Hotel angekommen. (*nachdem*)

5   Das Wetter war eigentlich ganz gut. Es war November. (*obwohl*)

6   Ich musste ein Formular ausfüllen. Ich durfte einchecken. (*bevor*)

7   Meine Schwester konnte nicht schlafen. Der Lärm vom Nachtklub war schrecklich. (*da*)

8   Ich habe ein Buch gelesen. Ich habe mich gesonnt. (*während*)

3b **G** Link sentences 4–8 in activity 3a again, starting with the subordinate clause.

4 **T** Translate the paragraph into English.

> Bevor wir das Haus verließen, suchte mein Vater seine Straßenkarte. Schließlich fand er sie, aber weil es ein Problem mit meinem Sicherheitsgurt im Auto gab, fuhren wir erst eine Stunde später ab. Unterwegs zum Hafen hatten wir dann auf der Autobahn eine Panne – unglaublich! Meine Mutter war so sauer!

5 ✏ Du warst gerade im Urlaub. Schreib eine positive oder negative Bewertung über das Hotel / die Pension / den Campingplatz für eine Touristikwebsite.

Grammatik *page 190*

Using coordinating and subordinating conjunctions

You can develop your sentences by using coordinating and subordinating conjunctions.

Coordinating conjunctions *und* (and), *aber* (but), *denn* (because) and *oder* (or) do not affect the word order when they join two clauses together: *Wir sind nach Spanien gefahren,* **aber** *es war ziemlich teuer.*

Subordinating conjunctions include *als* (when + past), *bevor* (before), *nachdem* (after), *da* (since, because), *dass* (that), *wenn* (when, if), *obwohl* (although), *während* (while) and *weil* (because). They make the verb go to the end of the sentence or clause: *Wir sind im Hotel geblieben,* **obwohl** *es laut* **war**. (We stayed in the hotel although it was noisy.)

To add more complexity, you can **start** the sentence with the subordinate clause. When you do this, make sure you invert the subject and verb in the clause that follows:
Obwohl *es laut war,* **sind wir** *im Hotel geblieben.*

Also learn how to use impersonal verbs. See page 134.

Strategie

Using adjectives to improve your work

There are certain words which we tend to use to describe holidays, such as *hervorragend* (outstanding), *ausgezeichnet* (excellent) or *entsetzlich* (appalling). Using words like these can really make what you are saying or writing impressive, so make a point of learning them.

Challenge: Spot all the adjectives used in the reading texts in activity 1a and try to use as many as possible in the writing activity.

Ich war Wir waren	letzte Woche neulich	in einem Hotel / in einer Pension / auf einem Campingplatz.			
Unser Aufenthalt	war	eine Katastrophe, sehr erfolgreich,	da / weil	das Personal so (un)freundlich / hilfsbereit war. das Essen schrecklich / wunderbar war. es keinen Strom / kein Wasser gab.	
				unser Zimmer	(un)bequem nicht groß genug ruhig / laut schmutzig / sauber war.
	hat uns (nicht) gefallen,			der Rezeptionist die Rezeptionistin das Personal	(un)höflich (un)angenehm
Ich werde Ich würde	(nie) wiederkommen. das Hotel / die Pension / den Campingplatz empfehlen.				
Ich freue mich Wir freuen uns	auf meinen / unseren nächsten Besuch.				

8.1 Groundwork is available in the Foundation book.

Regions of Germany

8.2 F — Eine Stadtbesichtigung

Lernziele

- Talking about city breaks
- Choosing dative or accusative after prepositions
- Using the social and cultural context to understand meaning

1 📖 Read the adverts for two city sightseeing trips and then the statements. Are the statements true (T), false (F) or not in the text (NT)?

Münchener Stadtrundfahrten

- Die Tour zeigt kompakt die Sehenswürdigkeiten der Münchener Innenstadt und ist ideal für Besucher mit wenig Zeit.
- Eine Tour dauert 1 Stunde. Wenn Sie ein- und aussteigen, entsprechend länger.
- Ihre Fahrkarte ist den ganzen Tag gültig. Sie können an jeder Haltestelle zu- bzw. aussteigen.
- Achten Sie auf unsere blauen Doppeldeckerbusse.

Höhepunkte
Alte Pinakothek, Neue Pinakothek, Gemäldegalerie, Odeonsplatz, Nationaltheater, Marienplatz, Rathaus, Frauenkirche, Viktualienmarkt und Hofbräuhaus

Täglich Abfahrt
01.04.–31.10.: ab 9.40 Uhr
01.11.–31.03.: ab 10.00 Uhr

Preis bei Buchung vor Ort
Erwachsene ab 15 Jahren: 17€
Kinder von 4 bis 14 Jahren: 10€

Sonderpreis bei Online-Buchung
Erwachsene ab 15 Jahren: 15,50€
Kinder von 4 bis 14 Jahren: 19€

Ring – Vienna's main road which circles the city centre
die Fahrstrecke – route

Vienna Ring Tram

Sehen Sie Wiens herrliche Sehenswürdigkeiten wie Staatsoper, Hofburg, Parlament, Rathaus und vieles mehr.

Wiens schönste Straße, die Ringstraße rund um die Altstadt, können Sie bequem von der Vienna Ring Tram aus kennenlernen – und zwar ganzjährig.

In den Wagons informieren LCD-Bildschirme über die Highlights entlang der Fahrstrecke, dazu gibt es Infos in mehreren Sprachen über Kopfhörer.

Ringrunde-Tickets
1 komplette Fahrt um den Ring, ohne Ausstiegsmöglichkeit, Dauer 25 Minuten

Abfahrt täglich 10–17.30 Uhr zu jeder halben und vollen Stunde

Tipp: Die Vienna Ring Tram ist die einzige Straßenbahnlinie, die eine Runde um die Ringstraße ohne Umsteigen macht.

1 The bus tour is perfect for visitors with little time.
2 You can only get on or off at certain bus stops.
3 Between 1st November and 31st March, the first bus departs at 10 o'clock.
4 Children under 4 years old go free.
5 The fare for a 15-year-old booked online is 9€.
6 The tram operates all year.
7 Headphones for the commentary cost extra.
8 You can get off the tram at any stop.
9 This tram is more expensive than other trams.
10 You can go all the way around the 'ring' on this line without changing.

Using the social and cultural context to understand meaning

Sometimes you can work out the meanings of words by knowing something of the culture of the country. For example, in the passage about Munich, there are places mentioned on the route such as *alte Pinakothek*, *neue Pinakothek* and *Gemäldegalerie* which you may not have seen before. However, because they are in a list of sights in an old city, you might guess that they are buildings of cultural importance. In fact, they are all art galleries.

Challenge: Look at the passages about Munich and Vienna again. Can you guess / work out what *Nationaltheater*, *Viktualienmarkt*, *Staatsoper*, *Hofburg* and *Parlament* mean?

Strategie

2 **G** Complete the sentences with the correct definite article in the accusative (*den*, *die*, *das*) or dative case (*dem*, *der*, *dem*).

1   Man braucht nur eine Fahrkarte für … Bus und für … Straßenbahn.
2   Das neue Restaurant ist gegenüber … Rathaus.
3   Meine Familie und ich saßen um … großen Tisch.
4   Unser Reisebus ist durch … Stadtzentrum gefahren.
5   Vati hat Fotos von … Dom, … Kirche, … Schloss und … Blumen im Park gemacht.

3 🎧 Hör dir die fünf Personen an. Sie sprechen über ihren Urlaub. Dann beantworte die Fragen.

Listen to five people talking about their holidays and answer the questions.

1   Was wissen wir über den Dom in Köln?
2   Wann ist Tanja nach Griechenland gefahren?
3   Warum hatten Tanja und ihre Schwester Angst?
4   An welchem Tag hat Freddy eine Stadtführung gemacht?
5   Wie geht es Barbara?
6   Wann hat Benny das Schloss besichtigt?

4 **T** Translate the paragraph into English.

> Vom Hotel sind wir in die Stadt gefahren. Dort haben wir eine Kirche besichtigt, die sehr alt war. Später haben wir eine Stadtrundfahrt gemacht, aber der Bus, mit dem wir gefahren sind, hat eine Panne gehabt.

5 🗪 Partnerabeit. Seht euch das Foto an und beantwortet die Fragen. Dann tauscht die Rollen.

Work with a partner. Look at the photo. Answer the questions. Then swap roles.

*   Was gibt es auf dem Foto?
*   Was findest du besser – Urlaub in einer Stadt oder am Strand? Warum?
*   Was gibt es für Touristen in deiner Gegend?
*   Was hast du letztes Jahr in den Sommerferien gemacht?

Choosing dative or accusative after prepositions

Grammatik   *page 180*

The prepositions below are **always** followed by the dative, so you will need to check that you use the **correct endings on any definite and indefinite articles** which come afterwards (see page 180).

Think of **MAVS 'N' BAGZ** to help you (or make up your own mnemonic).

*m*it	with, by (transport)
*a*us	from, out of
*v*on	from, by, of
*s*eit	since, for (a period of time)
*n*ach	after, to
*b*ei	at the house of, with
*a*b	from (time)
*g*egenüber	opposite
*z*u	to

Just as *in dem* is often shortened to *im*, look out for *beim* (*bei dem*), *vom* (*von dem*), *zum* (*zu dem*) and *zur* (*zu der*).

The following prepositions are followed by the accusative, so as with the dative prepositons, you must make sure you know all the endings you will need (see page 179). To help you remember the accusative prepositions, think of **FUDGBO**.

*f*ür	for	*g*egen	against
*u*m	around	*b*is	until
*d*urch	through	*o*hne	without

Also learn how to use and recognise relative pronouns. See page 135.

Ich finde Urlaub	in der Stadt	besser, weil ich	gern aktiv bin. mich für Kultur und Geschichte interessiere.
	am Strand		faulenzen / mich sonnen will. gern schwimme / Volleyball spiele.
In meiner Gegend	haben wir gibt es	den Fluss / Fernsehturm / Tierpark / See / die Burg / Stadtmauer. das Schloss / Volksmuseum / Einkaufszentrum. viele Kirchen / Museen / Parks.	
Letztes Jahr In den Ferien	bin ich mit	meiner Familie meinen Eltern / Freunden	nach Italien / Frankreich / Österreich / Deutschland · gefahren. in die Schweiz / die Türkei / die USA · geflogen.

Schöne Reiseziele

Lernziele

Talking about holiday destinations

Using relative pronouns and *was*

Using alternatives to *weil*

1 📖 Read the travel guide and answer the questions in English.

Die Bodenseeregion – Urlaub in Deutschland, Österreich und der Schweiz

Der Bodensee ist eines der beliebtesten Urlaubsziele in Deutschland, das jährlich viele Touristen besuchen. Sein besonderer Reiz liegt in seiner Vielseitigkeit. Kulturfreunde werden in den Städten des Bodensees zahlreiche Sehenswürdigkeiten finden. Sportfans werden das vielseitige Angebot an Wasser- und Landaktivitäten genießen und Liebhaber kulinarischer Genüsse werden sich über die regionalen Spezialitäten des Bodensees freuen.

Am Bodensee liegen viele schöne Städte, deren Besichtigung sich lohnt, sowie einige reizvolle Inseln. Alle bieten Freizeitmöglichkeiten, Sehenswürdigkeiten und Kultur an. Jede dieser Städte ist alleine schon einen mehrwöchigen Aufenthalt wert. Besonders schön sind Konstanz, Friedrichshafen, Ravensburg und St. Gallen.

Hier finden alle etwas, was ihnen Spaß macht: Verliebte Paare können die idyllischen Inseln und romantischen Lokale mit Seeblick genießen. Auf dem See kann man die Dampfer und Segelboote bewundern. Im Sommer können sich Familien mit ihren Kindern in einem der Strandbäder entspannen oder den Bodenseeradweg befahren – es gibt viele Fahrradverleihstationen! Und an Regentagen kann man die verschiedensten Museen, Burgen und Schlösser entdecken.

Auch gibt es viele Ausflugsziele, z.B. das Ravensburger Spieleland oder den Rheinfall Schaffhausen, den größten Wasserfall Europas. Kurz gesagt, ein Besuch in unserer Region ist der Mühe wert!

1 What is Lake Constance's special appeal?
2 Which types of people is it popular with? (3 details)
3 What will people interested in cooking be able to enjoy?
4 What does each town in the area have to offer? (3 details)
5 What can you see on the lake? (2 details)
6 What can families do in good weather? (2 details)
7 What can you visit in bad weather? (3 details)
8 What is the *Rheinfall*?

der Reiz – charm
die Vielseitigkeit – many-sidedness, versatility
der Liebhaber – admirer, lover
sich lohnen – to be worthwhile
wert – worth
kurz gesagt – in a nutshell

2a 🎧 Hör dir dieses Interview an. Welche vier Aussagen sind richtig?

1 Frau Pfeiffer ist gestern Abend in Wien angekommen.
2 Am liebsten frühstückt sie im Hotel.
3 Vom Donauturm aus hat man eine wunderbare Aussicht auf Wien, aber es gibt kein Restaurant.
4 Frau Pfeiffer interessiert sich für die Architektur.
5 Wiener Schnitzel ist ideal für Vegetarier.
6 Grinzing ist ein Dorf, das etwa dreißig Kilometer von Wien entfernt liegt.
7 Man kann sich in Grinzing gut entspannen.
8 Der ideale Urlaubspartner von Frau Pfeiffer ist ihr Ehemann.
9 Nach dem Interview fährt sie wieder nach Hause.

drehbar – revolving
bewundern – to admire
das Kalbfleisch – veal
die Stimmung – atmosphere
locker – loose, relaxed

2b 🎧 Hör das Inteview noch einmal an. Beantworte die Fragen auf Deutsch.

1 Woher ist Frau Pfeiffer gekommen?
2 Wo hat sie übernachtet?
3 Woran hat sie schöne Erinnerungen?
4 Auf wie viel Metern Höhe ist das Restaurant?
5 Was macht sie gern in der Stadt?
6 Was isst man zu Wiener Schnitzel? (**zwei** Details)
7 Wohin fährt sie gern, um sich zu entspannen?
8 Wie lange wird sie in Köln sein?

3 Ⓖ Link the sentences using the correct relative pronoun.

Beispiel: **1** Hier ist ein Prospekt, den ich heute in der Touristeninformation bekommen habe.

1 Hier ist ein Prospekt. Ich habe ihn heute in der Touristeninformation bekommen.
2 Hier sind die Fahrkarten. Ich habe sie gerade gekauft.
3 Der Mann arbeitet am Empfang. Er ist ziemlich unhöflich.
4 Ich musste vierzig Minuten Schlange stehen. Es war so langweilig.
5 Das Andenken war nicht billig. Ich habe es für meine Oma gekauft.
6 Ich habe nichts gesehen. Es hat mich interessiert.

4 Ⓣ Translate the paragraph into English.

> Als ich in Genf war, habe ich in einem Hotel übernachtet, das am See lag. Meiner Meinung nach ist die Stadt eines der schönsten Reiseziele Europas. Obwohl die meisten Leute Französisch sprechen, können sie auch Deutsch verstehen. Sowohl im Winter als auch im Sommer hat die Stadt so viel anzubieten.

5 Ⓣ Translate the paragraph into German.

> When I am in Hamburg, I always like to stay near the harbour. I know a very good hotel which is not too expensive. There is nothing which I don't like to eat. Because Hamburg is on the coast, one eats a lot of fish, but I find that fantastic.

6 ✏️ Schreib ein Blog, in dem du deinen letzten Urlaub beschreibst.

- Wohin bist du gefahren und mit wem?
- Wie war die Fahrt / der Flug? Warum?
- Was konnte man in deinem Urlaubsziel sehen / tun?
- Wie hat dir die Gegend gefallen? Warum?

Grammatik — page 183

Using relative pronouns and *was*

You need to be able to recognise and use relative pronouns in all the cases (see page 183).

Remember that the verb goes to the end of the relative clause and that the relative clause is separated by commas from the rest of the sentence.

If the relative pronoun doesn't refer to a noun or is used after *alles* (everything), *etwas* (something), *vieles* (much) or *nichts* (nothing), use *was*. The verb will still go to the end of the relative clause:
*Wir mussten einen Zuschlag zahlen, **was** ich sehr unfair gefunden **habe**.* (We had to pay a supplement, which (i.e. the act of paying a supplement) I found very unfair.)
*Alles, **was** wir gesehen **haben**, war sehr interessant.* (Everything (which / that) we saw was very interesting.)

Also learn about using more complex question words. See page 135.

Strategie

Using alternatives to *weil*

Being able to use *weil* correctly is important, but it is just as important to be able to use a variety of other vocabulary and structures to give explanations and express opinions. This will make your writing and speaking much more interesting. So do use *weil*, but **not** all the time. Keep reminding yourself to use *da* (which makes the verb go to the end of the clause) or *denn* (which doesn't affect the word order).

Challenge: See if you can write down three opinions about your holidays together with explanations. For each opinion, write the explanation in three ways, using a different word for 'because' each time.

8.2 Groundwork is available in the Foundation book.

G # Travel and tourism

1 Write the sentences in the correct order.

Beispiel: **1** Im Oktober bin ich mit dem Auto nach Polen gefahren.

1 bin ich – nach Polen – gefahren – mit dem Auto – Im Oktober

2 am Flughafen – Er ist – angekommen – um 7 Uhr

3 nach Griechenland – sind – In den Sommerferien – wir – geflogen

4 geflogen – Ich bin – nach Düsseldorf – vorgestern

5 sind – meine Freunde und ich – Letztes Jahr – nach Irland – gefahren – mit der Fähre

6 in die Stadt – mit der Straßenbahn – bin ich – gefahren – Heute früh

2 Complete the sentences so they match the English translation given in brackets.

1 … heute Nachmittag. (*It's snowing this afternoon.*)

2 … ist kalt. (*He is cold.*)

3 Wie geht es …? (*How is she?*)

4 … viele Probleme in diesem Hotel. (*There are lots of problems in this hotel.*)

5 Heute früh … (*It's raining this morning.*)

6 … in München. (*We like it in Munich.*)

7 Es tut … leid. (*They are sorry.*)

8 Ist es … warm? (*Are you warm?*– familiar singular)

Grammatik — *page 190*

Using the time – manner – place rule in the perfect tense

You must use the time – manner – place rule in all the tenses, so remember to mention first **when** (time) you did something, then **how** (manner) you did something and finally **where** (place) you did something:

time	manner	place

Wir sind <u>gestern</u> <u>mit dem Zug</u> <u>nach Bern</u> gefahren. (We went to Berne by train yesterday.)

Grammatik — *page 188*

Using impersonal verbs

Some verbs are never used with the personal pronouns *ich*, *du*, etc. and are used only with *es*, e.g. weather expressions:
Es regnet. (It's raining.) *Es donnert.* (It's thundering.)
Es blitzt. (It's lightning.) *Es friert.* (It's freezing.)
Es hagelt. (It's hailing.) *Es schneit.* (It's snowing.)

With some other impersonal verbs, we don't translate *es* as 'it'. Instead it has different meanings. For example, you have already met *es gibt* (there is / there are) which is used with the accusative case:
Es gibt einen Campingplatz am Stadtrand. (There is a campsite on the edge of town.)
Es gibt viele Touristen in unserem Hotel. (There are lot of tourists in our hotel.)

Another example is *es geht,* used with dative personal pronouns (for a list of dative pronouns, see page 183):
*Wie geht es **dir**?* (How are you?)
*Es geht **mir** gut. / **Mir** geht's gut.* (I am well.)

Learn the following expressions which are also used with dative pronouns:
Es tut mir leid. (I am sorry.)
Es gefällt mir in Hamburg. (I like it in Hamburg.)
Mir ist kalt / warm / übel. (I am cold / warm / sick.)

3a Link the sentences using a relative pronoun. Make sure that you use the correct word order and punctuation.

Beispiel: **1** Der Mann, der in der Pension arbeitet, heißt Herr Neumann.

1 Der Mann heißt Herr Neumann. Er arbeitet in der Pension.
2 Das Haus ist sehr schön. Es liegt in der Stadt.
3 Ich habe einen Freund. Er heißt Max.
4 Der Campingplatz ist toll. Er liegt am Stadtrand.
5 Seine Freundin hat ein Auto. Es ist sehr alt.
6 Wir haben Souvenirs gekauft. Sie waren ganz billig.
7 Er hat einen Fotoapparat verloren. Er war neu.

3b Read the sentences and identify which cases have been used with the relative pronouns. Write N (nominative), A (accusative), G (genitive) or D (dative). Then translate the sentences into English.

1 Die Reisetasche, die ich gestern verloren habe, war nicht teuer.
2 Das ist der Wohnwagen, den mein Vater im Sommer gekauft hat.
3 Das ist das Hotel, dessen Zimmer schmutzig sind.
4 Die Taxifahrerin, mit der wir letzte Woche gefahren sind, war nett.
5 Der Tunnel, durch den wir gefahren sind, ist ein Kilometer lang.

4a Complete the sentences with the correct question word from the *Grammatik* box. Then translate the sentences into English.

1 … kommt dieser Zug?
2 … sind Sie unzufrieden?
3 … fliegt er morgen?
4 … willst du das wissen?
5 … bekommst du dein Geld?
6 … fährst du in den Sommerferien?

4b Complete the sentences with the correct form of *wer*. Then translate the sentences into English.

1 … hast du gestern besucht?
2 … hat er das Geld gegeben?
3 … Fotoapparat ist das?
4 … hat mein Handy benutzt?
5 … hast du eine E-Mail geschickt?
6 … hast du gefragt?

Using and recognising relative pronouns

Grammatik page 183

Relative pronouns are 'who(m)', 'whose', 'which' and 'that' and they introduce a **relative clause**. They are used to refer back to someone, something or somewhere mentioned earlier, e.g. The <u>man</u> **who** lives next door is polite.

Relative pronouns in German often have the same form as the definite article (*der, die, das*). They have to **agree** with the noun they refer to and be in the correct case. Notice that the verb in a relative clause goes to the end and the relative clause is separated by commas:
*Der Mann, **der** nebenan **wohnt**, ist höflich.*
*Die Frau, **die** hier **arbeitet**, kommt aus der Schweiz.*
*Das Hotel, **das** neben dem Dom **liegt**, ist sehr teuer.*
*Die Kinder, **die** draußen **spielen**, heißen Anna und Thomas.*

Also look out for relative clauses being used after prepositions:
*Das Flugzeug, **mit dem** wir geflogen **waren**, war ganz alt.* (The plane we had flown on (literally 'with which we had flown') was quite old.)

For a complete overview of the relative pronouns in all cases, see page 183.

Using more complex question words

Grammatik page 190

More complex question words include *wohin?* (where to?), *woher?* (where from?), *womit?* (with what?) and *wozu?* (what for? / why?):
Wohin gehst du? (Where are you going (to)?)
Woher kommst du? (Where do you come from?)
Womit schreibst du? (What are you writing with? Literally: With what are you writing?)
Wozu brauchst du ein neues Rad? (What do you need a new bike for? Answer with *um … zu …*, e.g. *Um mit dem Rad zur Schule zu fahren*.)
Also learn the different forms of *wer* (who):

nominative	*wer?*	(who?)
accusative	*wen?*	(whom?)
genitive	*wessen?*	(whose?)
dative	*wem?*	(to whom?)

Vokabeln

8.1 Holidays and travel

8.1 F Ich suche eine Unterkunft
➡ *pages 126–127*

die	*Autobahn (-en)*	motorway
das	*Boot (-e)*	boat
das	*Doppelzimmer (–)*	double room
der	*Eingang (¨e)*	entrance
das	*Einzelzimmer (–)*	single room
	erlaubt	allowed
die	*Fähre (-n)*	ferry
die	*Fahrkarte (-n)*	ticket
der	*Fahrpreis (-e)*	fare
das	*Gleis (-e)*	track, platform
der	*Grillplatz (¨e)*	barbecue area
der	*Haartrockner (–)*	hairdryer
die	*Halbpension*	half board
der	*Koffer (–)*	suitcase
das	*Mittelmeer*	Mediterranean Sea
der	*Passagier (-e)*	passenger
der	*Rezeptionist (-en)*	receptionist (m)
die	*Rezeptionistin (-nen)*	receptionist (f)
der	*Schatten (–)*	shade, shadow
	schattig	shady
der	*Stau (-s)*	traffic jam
die	*Übernachtung (-en)*	overnight stay
die	*Übernachtung mit Frühstück*	B&B
die	*Unterkunft (¨e)*	accommodation
die	*Vollpension*	full board
der	*Wohnwagen (–)*	caravan
das	*Zelt (-e)*	tent
das	*Zweibettzimmer (–)*	twin bedroom

8.1 H Wie war denn der Urlaub?
➡ *pages 128–129*

der	*Ärmelkanal*	(English) Channel
der	*Aufenthalt (-e)*	stay
der	*Ausflug (¨e)*	trip, excursion
	ausfüllen	to fill in
	ausgestattet	equipped
das	*Ausland*	foreign country, abroad
der	*Bahnsteig (-e)*	platform
	besichtigen	to sightsee, to visit, to have a look
	bewerten	to assess, to rate
	einchecken	to check in
	entdecken	to discover
die	*Ermäßigung (-en)*	reduction, discount
das	*Formular (-e)*	form
	funktionieren	to work, to function
	heftig	heavy, severe
der	*Herbst (-e)*	autumn
das	*Nickerchen (–)*	nap
die	*Panne (-n)*	breakdown, puncture, flat tyre
das	*Personal (–)*	staff
	sauer sein	to be cross / annoyed
das	*Schwimmbecken (–)*	swimming pool
die	*Sehenswürdigkeit (-en)*	tourist attraction, sight
der	*Sicherheitsgurt (-e)*	safety belt, seat belt
der	*Speisewagen (–)*	dining car, restaurant car (train)
die	*Touristikwebsite (-s)*	travel website
die	*Überfahrt (-en)*	crossing (sea)
die	*Umgebung (-en)*	the surroundings
	unhöflich	impolite
	verstehen	to understand
	im Voraus	in advance

8.2 Regions of Germany

8.2 F Eine Stadtbesichtigung
➡ *pages 130–131*

die	*Abfahrt (-en)*	departure
	aussteigen	to alight, to get off (bus, tram, train)
der	*Bildschirm (-e)*	screen
die	*Burg (-en)*	castle
	einschlafen	to fall asleep, to go to sleep
	einsteigen	to get in / on
die	*Eintrittskarte (-n)*	admission ticket
	entlang	along
der	*Fahrkartenautomat (-en)*	ticket machine
der	*Fahrkartenschalter (–)*	ticket office
die	*Fahrradvermietung (-en)*	bicycle hire
der	*Fotoapparat (-e)*	camera
	ganzjährig	all year round
	herrlich	marvellous, magnificent, glorious
der	*Kopfhörer (–)*	headphones
die	*Linie (-n)*	line, number (tram, bus)
	München	Munich
der	*Notausgang (¨e)*	emergency exit
die	*Öffnungszeiten*	opening times (pl)
das	*Reisebüro (-s)*	travel agency
die	*Reisetasche (-n)*	travel bag
die	*Rundfahrt (-en)*	tour, round trip
das	*Schließfach (¨er)*	locker
	umsteigen	to change (means of transport)
der	*Wartesaal (-säle)*	waiting room
	wieder	again
	Wien	Vienna

8.2 H Schöne Reiseziele
➡ *pages 132–133*

das	*Andenken (–)*	souvenir, memento
das	*Angebot (-e)*	range, offer
	atemberaubend	breathtaking
	befahren	to drive on, to use
die	*Besichtigung(en)*	visit, tour
	bewundern	to admire
der	*Bodensee*	Lake Constance
der	*Dampfer (–)*	steam boat
der	*Empfang (¨e)*	reception (hotel)
	sich erinnern	to remember
der	*Fahrradverleih (-e)*	bicycle hire
	Genf	Geneva
	locker	casual, relaxed
	sich lohnen	to be worth it
das	*Lokal (-e)*	bar, pub
die	*Mühe (-n)*	trouble
der	*Prospekt (-e)*	brochure, leaflet
das	*Reiseziel (-e)*	destination
der	*Reiz (-e)*	attraction, appeal
	Schlange stehen	to queue
das	*Segelboot (-e)*	sailing boat
der	*Stadtbummel (–)*	stroll through town, window shopping
das	*Strandbad (¨er)*	bathing beach
der	*Strandkorb (¨e)*	wicker beach chair
die	*Touristeninformation*	tourist information office
	wegen Betriebsferien geschlossen	closed because of holiday (firm / shop / attraction) (pl)
der	*Zuschlag (¨e)*	extra charge, supplement

📖🎧 # Higher – Reading and listening

1 📖 Read this advert for Berne. Which **four** statements are correct?

Fahren Sie in die Schweiz? Obwohl die Schweiz ideal zum Skifahren und Wandern ist, vergisst man oft die Hauptstadt. Hier genießen die Einwohner die herrliche Altstadt, den Blick auf die Alpen, Kunst und Kultur und geschmackvolles Essen.

Das Münster ist die höchste Kirche der Schweiz. Es gibt 344 Stufen bis nach oben, aber es lohnt sich, weil es bei heiterem Wetter so schön ist.

Sie werden mehr als 100 alte Brunnen in der Stadt finden. Ein besonders eindrucksvolles Beispiel davon ist der Kindlifresserbrunnen mit einer Figur, die ein kleines Kind frisst.

In der Nähe der Nydeggbrücke befindet sich der Bärengraben, obwohl die Bären, die das Wappentier der Stadt Bern sind, 2009 in einen neuen Park umgezogen sind. Hier leben die Tiere nun auf einem Hang mit Flussblick.

In der Hauptstadt hat Einstein die Relativitätstheorie entdeckt und Bern ist sogar der Geburtsort von Toblerone, der bekannten Schweizer Schokolade.

fressen – to devour
der Bärengraben – bear pit

1 Berne is very popular with tourists.
2 There is plenty to do here.
3 No church in the country is higher than the minster in Berne.
4 The city has nearly 100 fountains.
5 There is a bear pit near one of the fountains.
6 Bears don't live in the bear pit any more.
7 The bears have a park with a view of the mountains.
8 Toblerone chocolate was invented here. **[4 marks]**

2 📖 Lies diesen Auszug aus dem Märchen *Die zwei Brüder*, geschrieben von den Brüdern Grimm und sieh dir die Aussagen an. Sind die Aussagen **richtig** (R), **falsch** (F) oder **nicht im Text** (NT)?

Es waren einmal zwei Brüder, ein reicher und ein armer. Der Reiche ist ein Goldschmied und böse. Der Arme ernährt sich davon, dass er auf einem Bauernhof arbeitet, und ist gut und ehrlich. Der Arme hat zwei Kinder. Sie sind Zwillingsbrüder, die sich so ähnlich wie zwei Tropfen Wasser sind. Die zwei Jungen gehen in des Reichen Haus ab und zu und bekommen von dem Abfall manchmal etwas zu essen. An einem Tag geht der arme Mann in den Wald und sieht einen Vogel, der ganz golden ist. Da hebt er ein Steinchen auf, wirft nach ihm und trifft ihn auch glücklich. Es fällt aber nur eine goldene Feder herunter und der Vogel fliegt weg. Der Mann nimmt die Feder und bringt sie seinem Bruder. Der sieht sie an und spricht: „Es ist eitel Gold", und gibt ihm viel Geld dafür.

aufheben – to pick up
das Steinchen – small stone
die Feder – feather

1 Der reiche Bruder hat einen Bauernhof.
2 Der arme Bruder ist eine nette Person.
3 Die Kinder sind sehr verschieden.
4 Im Haus bekommen die Kinder etwas zu trinken.
5 Der reiche Bruder hat ein Pferd.
6 Der arme Bruder bekommt Geld für die Feder. **[6 marks]**

> **Strategie**
>
> When trying to identify the correct statements in this kind of activity, make sure that you read all the statements very carefully because they are designed to check whether you really understand the text. Also, don't be put off if there are some words which you have never seen before and always look to see if some words have been translated for you, as here. As usual, in an activity where the answer choices are provided, have a guess at choosing the correct one(s) if you are absolutely unsure.

3  Lies dieses Gedicht und beantworte die Fragen auf **Deutsch**.

1 Wie war das Klima im Tropenwald? (**zwei** Details)
2 Was wollten die reichen Leute essen?
3 Welche Tierart stirbt aus?
4 Wie sieht die Zukunft für die reichen Leute aus?   **[5 marks]**

Der Tropenwald

Es war einmal ein Tropenwald
mit Bäumen grün, sehr hoch und alt.
Ganz warm und feucht, er wunderbar
für groß und klein die Heimat war.

Fernab in einem reichen Land
der Appetit auf Steak entstand.
Man brauchte Platz. Wozu ein Wald?
Man schlug das Holz. Ganz kahl war's bald.

Die Sonne scheint, der Affe stirbt.
Der Boden blank jetzt erodiert.
Ein Vogel legt ein letztes Ei.
Das Rind es rülpst, Methan wird frei.

Nun sitzt er da am Teakholztisch,
der reiche Mensch, das Hemd nicht frisch.
Der Schweiß, der läuft, das Asthma plagt.
War das o.k?, er sich nun fragt.

4 **T** Your German friend has sent you an email about the area he has just moved to. Translate the email into **English** for your parents.

Wir sind endlich umgezogen! Unser neues Haus gefällt uns sehr, aber ich muss sagen, dass die Stadt nicht ohne Probleme ist. Zum Besipiel sind wir gestern Abend durch die Stadtmitte gefahren und ich war überrascht, wie viele obdachlose Menschen vor dem Supermarkt geschlafen haben … und bei diesem furchtbaren Wetter.

[9 marks]

5 Your German friend Leon has rung to tell you about some problems on holiday. Answer all the questions in **English**.

1 Where did Leon go for his holiday?
2 What happened during the journey?
3 Why **exactly** could they not stay at the hotel?
4 What had caused the confusion?
5 What was the solution to this problem?   **[5 marks]**

Watch out for **distractors**. These are items of information which may lead you to the wrong answer and they are in the activity to make sure that you really do understand the text or conversation thoroughly.

Strategie

6 You hear your exchange partner having an argument with her brother. Choose the correct answers.

1 Sophie thinks Christoph …
   a is not environmentally friendly.
   b should clean his room.
   c is not getting enough exercise.
2 She also thinks he …
   a wastes water.
   b keeps his room too warm.
   c wastes electricity.
3 Christoph uses public transport …
   a for the sake of the environment.
   b because he has no other transport.
   c because he doesn't have much money.   **[3 marks]**

7 Du hörst zwei Leute im Radio. Sie sprechen über ihr Leben. Beantworten Sie die Fragen auf **Deutsch**.

1 Probleme? (**zwei** Details)   Warum? (**zwei** Details)
2 Probleme? (**zwei** Details)   Warum? (**zwei** Details)   **[4 marks]**

Foundation test and revise tasks are available in the Foundation book.

Higher – Writing and translation

Either:

1a ✎ Deine Freundin Bettina aus Österreich hat dich über die Umwelt in deiner Gegend gefragt. Du schreibst Bettina eine E-Mail über die Umwelt in deiner Gegend.

Schreib:

- warum du die Umwelt wichtig oder unwichtig findest
- was für Probleme es in deiner Stadt gibt
- was deine Familie neulich für die Umwelt gemacht hat
- was du in der Zukunft machen wirst, um die Umwelt zu schützen.

Du musst ungefähr **90** Wörter auf **Deutsch** schreiben. Schreib etwas über alle Punkte der Aufgabe.

[16 marks]

Or:

1b ✎ Du bist mit deiner Familie im Urlaub und schickst deiner deutschen Austauschpartnerin eine E-Mail über deinen Urlaub.

Schreib:

- etwas über den Urlaubsort
- was du gestern in der Gegend gemacht hast
- warum du gern oder nicht gern in Urlaub fährst
- wohin du in der Zukunft fahren möchtest.

Du musst ungefähr **90** Wörter auf **Deutsch** schreiben. Schreib etwas über alle Punkte der Aufgabe.

[16 marks]

> **Strategie**
>
> Having enough ideas to write about is essential. Remember you have to write about **each** of the four bullet points, but don't rush to start writing your answer immediately. Instead, take a few minutes to jot down a few ideas that you can mention for each bullet point, making sure, of course, that they are things which you know how to say in German.
>
> In activity 1a, what happens, though, if there aren't any particular problems in your town (bullet point 2) or perhaps your family hasn't done much for the environment recently (bullet point 3)? What you write doesn't have to be true, so if you know how to write something which is appropriate to answer the question, do use it. Think of all the language practice you have had in lessons when learning the topics – what you have read, listened to, spoken about or written about.

Either:

2a ✏️ Du schreibst einen Artikel über Armut für die Schülerzeitung deiner Partnerschule in Deutschland.

Schreib:

- etwas über die Armut in deiner Gegend – deine Impressionen und Meinung
- etwas über die Unterschiede zwischen den Armen und den Reichen.

Du musst ungefähr **150** Wörter auf **Deutsch** schreiben. Schreib etwas über beide Punkte der Aufgabe.

[32 marks]

Or:

2b ✏️ Du warst gerade mit deiner Schul-Fußballmannschaft in Deutschland und hast drei Tage bei einer Familie verbracht. Schreib eine E-Mail an die Familie.

Schreib:

- etwas über deinen Aufenthalt – Meinungen
- etwas über deine Stadt und die Stadt in Deutschland.

Du musst ungefähr **150** Wörter auf **Deutsch** schreiben. Schreib etwas über beide Punkte der Aufgabe.

[32 marks]

3 🅣 Translate the paragraph into German.

> Last summer my family and I travelled to France, which was rather boring. We had to make the crossing from Dover to Calais by ferry and, unfortunately, the weather in the English Channel was stormy. However, there were no traffic jams later and we arrived in Cannes after 11 hours.

[12 marks]

4 🅣 Translate the paragraph into German.

> I like my town but there are problems with air pollution. We must have more buses and trains. Poverty is the biggest problem for young people who don't have a job. In the future, I would like to live in Switzerland because the people are friendly. It is also clean.

[12 marks]

Strategie

When you are answering this type of question, don't be misled into thinking it is easier because there are fewer bullet points than in previous questions. The reason for having just two bullet points is to give you greater opportunity to write about what you would really like to mention. This is good because it gives you more freedom to express yourself however you wish.

On the other hand, you have to be careful because, although the bullet points provide a basic outline of what you need to write about, they don't give you specific reminders about using a **variety of tenses and including opinions and explanations**. This part is down to you!

Strategie

When you are translating from one language to another, it is very easy to miss out an occasional word. Because you need to ensure that all key messages are conveyed, keep checking as you are writing to see that you have included all the necessary words in your translation. When you have finished, check again to make absolutely certain!

Foundation test and revise tasks are available in the Foundation book.

Higher – Speaking

1 🔊 Role play

Your teacher or partner will play the part of your Austrian exchange partner and will speak first.

You should address your exchange partner as *du*.

When you see this – **!** – you will have to respond to something you have not prepared.

When you see this – **?** – you will have to ask a question.

> Du sprichst mit deinem österreichischen Austauschpartner / deiner österreichischen Austauschpartnerin über die Umwelt.
>
> - Größte Umweltprobleme (**zwei** Details).
> - Für die Umwelt – was gemacht.
> - Umweltverschmutzung in deiner Stadt.
> - **!**
> - **?** Meinung über Elektroautos.

[15 marks]

Strategie

In the role play, you may be required to give an opinion about something. There are many ways of expressing opinions, so make sure that you learn a good selection before the day of the test. For example:

Ich finde das … (I think that is … Literally: 'I find that …')

Meiner Meinung nach ist das … (In my opinion, that is …)

Ich bin der Meinung, dass … (I am of the opinion that …)

Ich glaube, das ist … (I think that is …)

Also learn how to give both positive **and** negative opinions as you won't know what you will need to say. (Remember, though, that it is a role play so what you say does not have to be true!)

Positive opinion words / phrases: *prima / klasse / toll / ausgezeichnet / wichtig / nötig / eine gute Idee / eindrucksvoll*, etc.

Negative opinion words / phrases: *blöd / schrecklich / furchtbar / langweilig / mies / eine Zeitverschwendung / eine schlechte Idee*, etc.

2 🔊 Role play

Your teacher or partner will play the part of the assistant and will speak first.

You should address the assistant as *Sie*.

When you see this – **!** – you will have to respond to something you have not prepared.

When you see this – **?** – you will have to ask a question.

> Du bist in einer Touristeninformation in Zürich in der Schweiz. Du sprichst mit dem Angestellten / der Angestellten.
>
> - Fahrt nach Zürich – wann und wie.
> - Was hier gemacht (**eine** Aktivität).
> - **!**
> - **?** Beste Aussicht auf die Stadt – wo.
> - Hinfahren – an welchem Tag.

[15 marks]

Strategie

In the role play, there may be a question requiring you to use a tense other than the present, so make sure that you are certain about how to form each tense. Look for the prompt on the card which refers to the particular tense. In this role play, the key word is *gemacht* (bullet point 2) which is a past participle, but you may also see references to the past such as *letzte Woche* or *in den letzten Ferien*. For the future tense, look out for words or phrases such as *morgen, in der Zukunft* or *nächstes Jahr*.

3 🔲 Photo card

- Look at the photo during the preparation period.
- Make any notes you wish to on an Additional Answer Sheet.
- Your teacher or partner will then ask you questions about the photo and related to the topic of **Global issues**.

Your teacher or partner will ask you the following three questions and then **two more questions** which you have not prepared.

- Was gibt es auf dem Foto?
- Wie findest du Armut? Warum?
- Was kann man für arme Leute machen?   **[15 marks]**

4 🔲 Photo card

- Look at the photo during the preparation period.
- Make any notes you wish to on an Additional Answer Sheet.
- Your teacher or partner will then ask you questions about the photo and related to the topic of **Travel and tourism**.

Your teacher or partner will ask you the following three questions and then **two more questions** which you have not prepared.

- Was gibt es auf dem Foto?
- Wohin fährst du gern in Urlaub?
- Wie hast du deinen letzten Urlaub verbracht?   **[15 marks]**

Foundation test and revise tasks are available in the Foundation book.

3 Current and future study and employment

9 My studies

9.1 F   Wie ist deine Schule?

- Using the prepositions *seit* and *vor*
- Translating into German when you don't know a word

9.1 H   Welche Schularten gibt es?

- Using infinitive constructions (*um … zu, ohne … zu*)
- Using *du / ihr / Sie* in informal and formal situations

10 Life at school / college

10.1 F   Ein typischer Schultag

- Revising reflexive verbs
- Recognising different ways of saying the time

10.1 H   Aspekte des Schullebens

- Using common subjunctive forms
- Making use of grammatical markers and categories

11 Education post-16

11.1 F   Welcher Beruf oder welches Studium?

- Using *welcher*? (which?)
- Simplifying what you say

11.1 H   Universität oder gleich Karriere?

- Using verbs followed by *zu*
- Listening for different ways of saying the same thing

12 Jobs, career choices and ambitions

12.1 F   Welchen Beruf willst du machen?

- Using a range of subordinating conjunctions
- Recognising the verb in a sentence

12.1 H   Mein idealer Job

- Using the genitive case
- Using *von* + dative instead of the genitive

Small words with more than one meaning

Use your dictionary

Small words – big problems?
Not with your dictionary!

Some English words are used in many different ways. To find the correct German translation, look at the example sentences and then make the necessary grammar changes required by your context:

at her brother's   *bei ihrem Bruder*

I'm at my sister's   *Ich bin bei meiner Schwester.*

(plural die Asylbe...)
He's an asylum seeker. Er ist Asylbewerber.

at *preposition*
1 **in** (+DAT)
  at school in der Schule
  at my office in meinem Büro
  at the supermarket im Supermarkt
2 **an** (+DAT)
  at the station am Bahnhof
  at the bus stop an der Bushaltestelle
3 **bei** (+DAT)
  at the dentist beim Zahnarzt
  at Emma's bei Emma
  at the hairdresser's beim Friseur
  She's at her brother's this evening. Sie ist heute Abend bei ihrem Bruder.
4 **at a party** auf einer Party
5 **at home** zu Hause
6 (*talking about the time*) **um**
  at eight o'clock um acht Uhr
7 **at night** nachts
  at Christmas zu Weihnachten
  at the weekend am Wochenende
8 (*in email addresses*) der **Klammeraffe** (*informal*)
9 **at last** endlich
  She's found a job at last. Sie hat endlich einen Job gefunden.

athlete *noun*
  der **Sportler** (*plural* die **Sportler**), die Sportlerin (plural die Sportlerinnen), der

befestigen
attached *adjective*
  (*emotionally*)
  to be attached to somebody/something an jemandem/etwas (DAT) hängen◇
attachment *noun*
1 (*in a letter*) die **Anlage** (*plural* die **Anlagen**)
2 (*in an email*) der **Anhang** (*plural* die **Anhänge**)
attack *noun*
  der **Angriff** (*plural* die **Angriffe**)
  ► to **attack** *verb*
1 **angreifen**◇ SEP
2 (*mug or raid*) **überfallen**◇
attempt *noun*
  der **Versuch** (*plural* die **Versuche**)
  at the first attempt beim ersten Versuch
  ► to **attempt** *verb*
  to attempt to do something versuchen, etwas zu tun
to **attend** *verb*
  teilnehmen◇ SEP **an** (+DAT)
  to attend a meeting an einer Besprechung teilnehmen
  to attend an evening class einen Abendkurs besuchen
attendance *noun*
  die **Anwesenheit**
attention *noun*

---

1   The correct German expressions

Find the correct German expressions in your dictionary.
Then complete the German sentences.

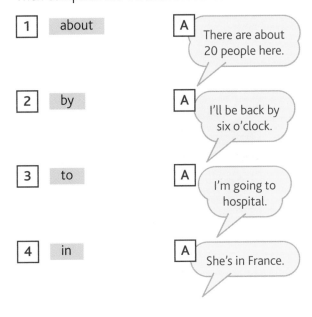
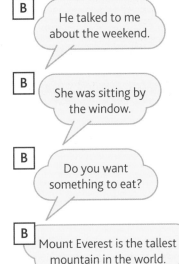

1	about	A	There are about 20 people here.	B	He talked to me about the weekend.
2	by	A	I'll be back by six o'clock.	B	She was sitting by the window.
3	to	A	I'm going to hospital.	B	Do you want something to eat?
4	in	A	She's in France.	B	Mount Everest is the tallest mountain in the world.

1   a   Es gibt ... zwanzig Leute hier.
    b   Er hat mit mir ... das Wochenende geredet.
2   a   Ich bin ... sechs Uhr zurück.
    b   Sie saß ...

3   a   Ich gehe ...
    b   Möchtest du etwas ...?
4   a   Sie ist ...
    b   Der Mount Everest ist der höchste Berg ...

9.1 F Wie ist deine Schule?

1 Ⓥ Räume in einer Schule. Ordne die Wörter in die zwei Kategorien ein.

Places in a school. Sort the words into the two categories.

Kategorie A: Hier haben wir Unterricht.

Kategorie B: Hier machen wir etwas Anderes.

die Turnhalle   das Sprachlabor   der Gang

der Schulhof   die Aula   die Mensa

das Klassenzimmer   das Lehrerzimmer

das Labor   das Sekretariat

2 📖 Lies die Informationen über eine deutsche Schule und sieh dir die Aussagen an. Sind die Aussagen richtig (R), falsch (F) oder nicht im Text (NT)?

Read the information about a German school and look at the statements. Are the statements true (R), false (F) or not in the text (NT)?

Kleist Gymnasium

| Startseite | Unsere Schule | Schüler | Eltern | Lehrer | Kontakt | 🔍 Suchen … |

Herzlich willkommen auf unserer Webseite!

Hallo, mein Name ist Manni. Hier können Sie alles Mögliche über unsere Schule erfahren. Ich gehe seit fünf Jahren auf diese Schule, aber vor drei Jahren hat man sie total umgebaut. Jetzt gibt es viel Neues!

Größe
Es ist ein gemischtes Gymnasium mit fast 1200 Schülern und Schülerinnen. Wir haben ungefähr hundert Lehrer und Lehrerinnen. Vor zehn Jahren gab es nur 800 Schüler. Da mehr Schüler aus dem Ausland in unsere Schule kamen, wurde die alte Schule zu klein. Deswegen gibt es jetzt diesen Neubau.

Gebäude
Am Eingang findet man das Sekretariat. Daneben ist die neue Bibliothek mit Büchern für alle Fächer. Am Ende des Ganges kommt man zur Aula. Hier gibt es manchmal Konzerte, Theatervorführungen oder andere Veranstaltungen. Gegenüber der Aula ist das Lehrerzimmer. Natürlich gibt es auch viele Klassenzimmer und auch Labors für den Unterricht in den Naturwissenschaften. Für den Sprachunterricht haben wir etwas Besonderes: ein Sprachlabor. Wir haben auch eine neue Mensa. Da kann man viel Leckeres zu essen kaufen, wenn man am Nachmittag Schule hat. Draußen gibt es einen ziemlich großen Schulhof. Bei schönem Wetter plaudern wir in der Pause dort.

1 Manni geht seit drei Jahren auf diese Schule.

2 Die Schule ist nur für Jungen.

3 Die meisten Schüler kommen aus einem anderen Land.

4 Das Gymnasium hat moderne Gebäude.

5 In der Aula kann man ab und zu Musik hören.

6 Im Sprachlabor lernt man Naturwissenschaften.

7 Die Schule hat eine Kantine.

8 In der Pause kann man in die Bibliothek gehen.

3 **G** **T** Complete the sentences with *seit* or *vor*. Then translate the sentences into English.

1 Die Schule hat … zwei Stunden angefangen.
2 … fünf Jahren habe ich eine andere Schule besucht.
3 Ich lerne … vier Jahren Deutsch.
4 Man hat diese Schule … hundert Jahren gebaut.
5 Die Schule existiert … 1976.

4a 🎧 Sechs Schüler sprechen über ihre Schule. Verbinde die Leute (1–6) mit den Bildern.

Six pupils are talking about their school. Match the people with the pictures.

Beispiel: 1 B

4b 🎧 Listen again. For each person write one extra detail from their statement in English.

5 **T** Translate the paragraph into English.

Meine Schule ist sehr alt. Es gibt nichts Modernes hier, aber das Gebäude ist schön. Die Lehrer sind nett und nicht zu streng. Viele Lehrer arbeiten seit zehn Jahren hier. Wir haben leider keine Kantine.

6 **T** Translate the sentences into German.

1 My school has 1000 pupils.
2 I have been here for four years.
3 The gym is big and fairly modern.
4 The teachers work in the staffroom.
5 We chat in the yard at break.

7 🗨 Gruppenarbeit. Was gibt es in deiner Schule? Jeder wiederholt den Satz und macht ihn länger.

Work in groups. What is in your school? Everyone repeats the sentence and makes it longer.

Beispiel:
Person 1: In meiner Schule gibt es viele Klassenzimmer.
Person 2: In meiner Schule gibt es viele Klassenzimmer und eine Aula.
Person 3: In meiner Schule gibt es viele Klassenzimmer und eine Aula und …

Grammatik *page 189*

Using the prepositions *seit* and *vor*

Both prepositions are used when talking about how long something has been going on.

Seit means 'since' or 'for':

> Remember that with *seit* you need to use the present tense in German.

Ich wohne seit 2012 hier. (I have been living here since 2012.)

> Remember that *seit* is used with the dative.

Er geht seit einem Jahr in diese Schule. (He has been going to this school for one year.)

The preposition *vor* means 'ago' and is also used with the dative. Unlike in English, it comes before the time:
vor einem Jahr (one year ago)
vor drei Wochen (three weeks ago)
Vor zehn Jahren war meine Schule sehr klein. (Ten years ago my school was very small.)

Also learn about adjective endings after *etwas, nichts, viel, wenig, alles*. See page 154.

Strategie

Translating into German when you don't know a word

If you can't think of a word which you need in German, find a way around it and never leave a blank. For example, if you can't think of the verb 'chat', find an alternative such as 'talk to my friends' (*ich spreche mit meinen Freunden*). If you need to translate 'We have assembly every day.' and don't know the word for 'assembly', you could reword it as something like 'All the pupils come together every day.' (*Alle Schüler kommen jeden Tag zusammen.*)

9.1 H

Welche Schularten gibt es?

Welche Schule ist richtig für dich?

In Deutschland muss ein Kind mindestens neun Jahre zur Schule gehen. Man beginnt die Grundschule mit sechs Jahren. Deutschland hat 16 Bundesländer und in jedem Bundesland ist das Schulsystem anders. Welche Schulen gibt es nach der Grundschule?

Ich gehe auf ein Gymnasium und bin jetzt in der 10. Klasse. Auf dem Gymnasium sollen wir selbstständig lernen. Nächstes Jahr werde ich in die Oberstufe kommen, um Abitur zu machen. Mein Cousin Jonas geht auf ein Internat. Er lebt die ganze Woche in der Schule, ohne am Abend nach Hause zu gehen. Wir sehen uns nur in den Ferien.

Julia

Ich bin auf einer Hauptschule. Auf der Grundschule fand ich Fächer wie Deutsch und Mathe sehr schwer. Hier lernen wir auch praktische Fächer wie Werken oder Hauswirtschaft. Das ist besser, um uns auf die Arbeitswelt vorzubereiten. Am Ende der 9. Klasse werde ich den Hauptschulabschluss bekommen.

Christian

Meine Schule ist eine Gesamtschule. Schüler bekommen entweder den Hauptschulabschluss, den Realschulabschluss (auch mittlere Reife genannt) oder das Abitur. Diese Schule ist auch eine Ganztagsschule. Das heißt, wir bleiben bis 17 Uhr in der Schule. Drei Tage in der Woche haben wir am Nachmittag Unterricht, aber an den anderen Tagen machen wir Sport, Kunst oder Musik.

Osman

1a 📖📖 Lies den Artikel über Schulen. Schreibe eine Liste der Schularten auf, die du im Text findest.

Beispiel: die Grundschule, …

1b 📖📖 Finde drei Wörter im Text für die verschiedenen Schulabschlüsse an deutschen Schulen.

1c 📖📖 Lies den Artikel nochmal. Welche vier Aussagen sind richtig?

1 Die meisten Kinder beginnen die Grundschule, wenn sie vier Jahre alt sind.
2 Das Schulsystem ist in Deutschland überall gleich.
3 Man macht das Abitur am Ende der Oberstufe.
4 Julias Freund geht auf ein Internat.
5 An der Hauptschule lernt man nicht nur Deutsch und Mathe.
6 An der Gesamtschule machen alle Schüler das Abitur.
7 Die mittlere Reife ist ein Schulabschluss.
8 Osman hat nicht an jedem Tag Nachmittagsunterricht.

2 **G** Complete the sentences with *um … zu* or *ohne … zu* and the German for the phrases given in brackets.

1 Wir gehen zur Schule, … (*in order to learn*)
2 Hanna geht ins Bett, … (*without doing her homework*)
3 Schüler gehen in die Oberstufe, … (*in order to get the* Abitur)
4 Man kann nicht Lehrer werden, … (*without studying at university*)

3a 🎧 Julia, Christian und Osman sprechen über ihre Schulen. Wer spricht über …

a Noten?
b Fächer?
c das Personal an der Schule?

3b 🎧 Listen again and answer the questions in English.

1 Who is Frau Schwarz?
2 What does Herr Unger look after?
3 How often do pupils receive a report at Christian's school?
4 How many grades are there for tests?
5 What three things does Osman say about maths?

4 **T** Translate the paragraph into English.

Ich gehe auf eine Gesamtschule im Zentrum der Stadt. Mein Lieblingsfach ist Erdkunde, weil der Lehrer sehr angenehm ist. Ich bekomme meistens gute Noten in den Klassenarbeiten. Letzte Woche habe ich mein Zeugnis bekommen. Glücklicherweise war es nicht schlecht. Mein jüngerer Bruder geht noch in die Grundschule.

5 **T** Translate the paragraph into German.

The head teacher in my school is very strict. We have to get good marks in Maths and English. These subjects are very important. I sometimes find maths difficult. My favourite subject is art. Next year I want to learn Spanish because foreign languages are useful.

6 🗨 Partnerarbeit. Stellt euch und beantwortet diese Fragen über das britische Schulsystem. Dann tauscht die Rollen.

• Auf was für eine Schule gehst du?
• Welche Prüfungen macht ihr dort?
• Welche Noten gibt es?
• Wie oft bekommt ihr Zeugnisse?
• Wie viele Schüler und Lehrer gibt es?
• Wie findest du verschiedene Fächer? Warum?

Grammatik *page 188*

Using infinitive constructions (*um … zu, ohne … zu*)

Use *um … zu* to express 'in order to …'. This construction must be followed by an **infinitive** and should be separated from another clause in the sentence by a **comma**:
*Man braucht das Abitur, **um** an der Uni **zu studieren**.* (You need the Abitur to study at university.)

The construction *ohne … zu* means 'without doing …':
*Er lebt in der Schule, **ohne** am Abend nach Hause **zu gehen**.* (He lives at school without going home in the evening.)

Also learn how to use the correct tense with *seit*. See page 154.

Strategie

Using *du / ihr / Sie* in informal and formal situations

The relationship between teacher and pupil is formal, therefore pupils in Germany always use the *Sie* form when addressing a teacher. A teacher uses *du* to address one pupil and *ihr* to address the whole class. Pupils use *du* and *ihr* when speaking to each other. In German schools teachers might start to address pupils as *Sie* at a certain point, for example in the *10. Klasse* when pupils are turning 16.

Challenge: Think of some questions about school in Germany: three questions using the *du* form to ask a German pupil, and three using the *Sie* form to ask a German teacher.

9.1 Groundwork is available in the Foundation book.

Ein typischer Schultag

1 📖 Die Aussagen beschreiben, was Annika an einem typischen Schultag macht. In welcher Reihenfolge passieren sie?

The statements describe what Annika does on a typical school day. In which order do they happen?

a Ich ziehe mich aus.
b Ich verlasse das Haus.
c Ich stehe auf.
d Ich schlafe ein.

e Ich wache auf.
f Ich spiele in der Mittagspause Schach.
g Ich wasche mich.

h Ich gehe nach Hause.
i Ich ziehe mich an.
j Ich esse ein zweites Frühstück in der Pause.

2a 🎧 Hör dir Jens an. Er beschreibt einen normalen Tag. Was sagt er? Wähl die richtigen Bilder aus.

Listen to Jens describing a normal day. What does he say? Choose the correct pictures.

| A | B | C | D | E | F | G |

2b 🎧 Hör noch mal zu. Schreib die Tabelle ab und füll die Lücken auf Deutsch aus.

Listen again. Copy and complete the grid in German.

Uhrzeit	Was sagt Jens?
a	Ich stehe auf und dusche mich.
7.20	b
c	Der Unterricht beginnt.
d–e	Die erste Pause
12.30–13.30	f
g	Ich ziehe mich um.
15.00	h

Recognising different ways of saying the time

The time 7.15 can be said as *Viertel nach sieben* (quarter past seven) or *sieben Uhr fünfzehn* (seven fifteen). 9.55 could be *fünf vor zehn* (five to ten) or *neun Uhr fünfundfünfzig* (nine fifty-five). Be aware of this in listening tasks. In German the 24-hour clock is often used, so 22.00 could be said as *zweiundzwanzig Uhr*, but also as *zehn Uhr abends*.

Be especially careful when you hear times such as *halb eins* (12.30), which can be confusing for English speakers.

Challenge: Look again at the times in your table in activity 2b. How many different ways can you say these times in German?

3 🇬 🇹 Translate the sentences into German, using the reflexive verb given in brackets.

1 I get undressed at 22.00. (*sich ausziehen*)
2 He shaves at 7.15. (*sich rasieren*)
3 She puts on make-up at 7.30. (*sich schminken*)
4 They got dressed yesterday at 9.00. (*sich anziehen*)
5 We got washed at half past six. (*sich waschen*)

Revising reflexive verbs

Remember that reflexive verbs often have the sense of doing something to yourself. So the verb *waschen* is to wash, but *sich waschen* is to wash oneself (though we would usually say to get washed in English). With reflexive verbs, you need to use the reflexive pronouns *mich, dich, sich, uns, euch, sich* to agree with the subject. Here are some examples:
*Ich dusche **mich**.* (I have a shower.)
*Er zieht **sich** an.* (He gets dressed.)
*Wir putzen **uns** die Zähne.* (We clean our teeth.)

In the perfect tense, the reflexive pronoun goes after *haben*:
Wir haben uns umgezogen. (We got changed.)

Also learn how to use the imperative. See page 154.

4  Read the article and complete the sentences in English.

1 If you leave home at 7.00 in summer you don't need a …

2 Some pupils find it difficult to get up early in winter because it is … and …

3 It is especially hard to concentrate at 8 a.m. when you have a …

4 It is worst for pupils who come to school from further away or …

5 Young people often don't go to sleep before midnight because they …

6 Some scientists want lessons to begin …

Wann sollte morgens der Unterricht beginnen?

Im Sommer geht es ja noch. Wenn man um 7 Uhr das Haus verlässt, braucht man auf dem Weg zur Schule kein Fahrradlicht. Aber in den Herbst- und Wintermonaten ist es kalt und dunkel. Dann wird das frühe Aufstehen für viele Schüler zur Qual. Für die meisten Schüler ist es schwer, sich um 8 Uhr oder noch früher zu konzentrieren, vor allem wenn sie Klassenarbeiten schreiben müssen.

Am schlimmsten ist es für Schüler, die mit dem Schulbus oder von weiter her zum Unterricht kommen. Viele sitzen übermüdet im Unterricht. Vor Mitternacht ist ein Jugendlicher selten müde genug, um zu schlafen. Gleichzeitig brauchen Teenager viel Schlaf. Einige Wissenschaftler wollen deshalb, dass die Schulen erst um 9 oder gar um 10 Uhr mit dem Unterricht beginnen.

zur Qual werden – to become torture
von weiter her – from further away
übermüdet – overtired
der Wissenschaftler – scientist

5 **T** Translate the paragraph into English.

Ich stehe früh auf und gehe zu Fuß zur Schule. Meine Freundin Laura fährt mit dem Fahrrad. In der Pause plaudern wir meistens über Kleider oder Hausaufgaben. Sie ist sehr fleißig und konzentriert sich gut im Unterricht. Ich mag die Schule, obwohl ich manchmal ein bisschen faul bin.

6 Schreib zehn Sätze auf Deutsch über einen typischen Tag. Dann arbeite mit einem Partner / einer Partnerin, um diesen Tag zu beschreiben.

Write ten sentences in German about a typical day. Then work with a partner to describe this day.

Was machst du an einem typischen Tag?		
Ich wache / stehe	um Viertel vor sieben / um sieben Uhr / um halb acht	auf.
Ich ziehe mich		an / um / aus.
Ich	wasche mich / dusche mich / frühstücke / rasiere mich / schminke mich / verlasse das Haus / mache meine Hausaufgaben	um Viertel vor acht. um acht Uhr.
Die Schule beginnt		
Ich schlafe	um zehn Uhr / um halb vier / nach dem Abendessen / um neun Uhr	ein.
Ich gehe		nach Hause / ins Bett.
In der Pause In der Mittagspause Nach der Schule	plaudere ich esse ich ein Brot spiele ich Fußball / Schach	im Schulhof. in der Kantine. mit meinen Freunden.

10.1 H Aspekte des Schullebens

Probleme in der Schule?
Frag Frau Doktor Reiter, unsere Online-Lehrerin

Frage von Paul: Leider habe ich die neunte Klasse nicht geschafft. Eine Fünf in Mathe und auch in Geschichte. Ich werde nicht versetzt. Dieser Notendruck macht mich wahnsinnig! Was soll ich tun?

Antwort: Wenn man auf dem Zeugnis zwei Fünfen hat, fällt man durch. Dann bleibst du sitzen. Du könntest schon vor Beginn des neuen Schuljahres eine Nachprüfung machen. Aber dann müsstest du im Sommer viel lernen. Du hättest in den Ferien keine Zeit dich zu entspannen. Und vielleicht hättest du trotzdem keinen Erfolg. Es wäre besser, das Jahr zu wiederholen. Sei nächstes Jahr fleißiger und passe im Unterricht besser auf.

Frage von Susi: Vor Klausuren habe ich so eine Angst, dass ich am liebsten blau machen würde! Meine Freundin lässt mich von ihr abschreiben. Soll ich das machen?

Antwort: Erstens hilft Schwänzen gar nicht! Das musst du selber wissen. Zweitens solltest du auf keinen Fall von einer anderen Schülerin abschreiben. Der Lehrer würde das bestimmt merken, wenn er die Arbeit korrigiert. Dann müsstet ihr beide erklären, was passiert ist und vielleicht bekommt deine Freundin auch eine Fünf. Das wäre sehr ungerecht, oder? Am besten gehst du am Abend vor der Klassenarbeit früh ins Bett.

Strategie

Making use of grammatical markers and categories

If you come across an unknown word in a text, use your knowledge of grammar to work out what category of word it is. For example, in the reading text, what does *Schwänzen* mean? It has a capital letter, so it's a noun. The *-en* ending suggests it might be a plural noun, but the verb (*hilft*) is singular so the noun must be singular too. The *-en* ending could indicate a verb infinitive which has been made into a noun. In English such nouns will often end in *-ing*. The verb *schwänzen* is 'to play truant', and the noun *Schwänzen* means 'truanting'.

Challenge: Find three more words in the reading text that you don't already know. Can you work out what category of word each one is? Does this help you to understand the meaning?

1 📖 Read the advice and answer the questions in English.

1 Why has Paul failed the year?
2 What does the teacher say you have to do if you fail the year?
3 Give two reasons why the teacher advises against a resit.
4 What advice does the teacher give Paul about next year?
5 What effect do tests have on Susi?
6 Which two things does the teacher advise her against doing?
7 What does the teacher say would be unfair?
8 What should Susi do before a test?

2 **G** **T** There are 10 examples of verbs in the subjunctive in the text in activity 1. Write the sentences and translate them into English.

Grammatik page 188

Using common subjunctive forms

These are the forms of the subjunctive that you will come across most often:

ich könnte	I could
ich sollte	I ought to
ich würde	I would
ich möchte	I would like
ich wäre	I would be
ich hätte	I would have
ich hätte gern	I would like
ich müsste	I would have to

Usually, the first three in this list will be followed by an infinitive at the end of the sentence or clause:
*Wir **könnten** Berlin **besuchen**.*
*Die Schüler **sollten** fleißiger **sein**.*
Also revise the comparative and the superlative. See page 155.

3 🎧 Listen to three German pupils talking about their experiences during a school exchange in England. What did they find positive or negative? Copy and complete the grid in English with as many details as possible.

		positive	negative
1	Annika		
2	Nico		
3	Franziska		

4 🅣 Translate the paragraph into German.

> Last year we went on a school trip to Austria. On one day we visited a school. It was quite different from here. Firstly, there was no uniform. Most pupils wore jeans. I find that much more comfortable than my black trousers. Secondly, they went home earlier at the end of the day.

5 ✒ Schreib ungefähr 150 Wörter über das Thema Schule. Schreib:

- über deine Schule
- über einen typischen Schultag
- über Probleme, die Schüler heutzutage haben
- darüber, ob du lieber in Deutschland oder in Großbritannien zur Schule gehen würdest.

6a 🗪 Partnerarbeit. Sieh dir das Bild an und bereite Antworten zu den Fragen vor. Dann stellt euch und beantwortet die Fragen.

- Was siehst du auf dem Foto?
- Was sind die Vor- und Nachteile einer Schuluniform?
- Welche Regeln sind wichtig an einer Schule?

10.1 Groundwork is available in the Foundation book.

6b 🗪 Erfinde zwei weitere Fragen zu diesem Thema für deinen Partner / deine Partnerin.

G # My studies; Life at school / college

1 Translate the sentences into English.

1 Im Winter muss man sich etwas Warmes anziehen.
2 Heute habe ich nichts Interessantes gelernt.
3 In den Sommerferien will Silke etwas Besonderes machen.
4 An der Schule lernen wir wenig Nützliches.
5 Ich wünsche dir alles Gute zum Geburtstag.
6 In der Kantine gibt es viel Leckeres.
7 Hans wird alles Mögliche tun, um gute Noten zu bekommen.
8 Du solltest nichts Süßes essen, bevor du ins Bett gehst.

2a Would you use the present or imperfect tense to translate these sentences into German?

1 We had been waiting for the teacher for 20 minutes.
2 He has been learning German for six months.
3 Have you been sitting here since break?
4 She had not been listening since the beginning of the lesson.
5 I had been speaking Spanish for a year when I went to Spain.
6 The pupils have been wearing this uniform for 30 years.

2b Translate the sentences in activity 2a into German.

3 Choose the correct command to use in the situations.

Hört zu!   Stehen Sie bitte auf!   Setzt euch!
Wasch dich!   Wiederholen Sie bitte!
Schlaft jetzt!   Machen Sie bitte auf!   Hör zu!
Seid ruhig!   Schreib das noch einmal!

1 You want a teacher to repeat something.
2 A teacher wants the whole class to listen.
3 You tell an adult guest it is time to get up.
4 A parent tells a child to get washed.
5 A teacher asks a pupil to write something again.
6 You ask your friend to listen.
7 A teacher asks a class to be quiet.
8 You want an adult to open a door.
9 Your brother tells you and your friend to go to sleep.
10 A teacher tells a class to sit down.

Grammatik · page 181

Adjective endings after *etwas*, *nichts*, *viel*, *wenig*, *alles*

In expressions such as 'something old' and 'nothing new', the adjective becomes a noun in German. It therefore needs a capital letter. It also has an ending **-es**. This happens after *etwas* (something), *nichts* (nothing), *viel* (much), *wenig* (little):
*etwas **Altes*** (something old), *nichts **Neues*** (nothing new)

After *alles* (everything) the ending is **-e**:
*alles **Mögliche*** (everything possible)

When translating these expressions into English, sometimes you will need to add the word 'things' or 'that is':
viel Nützliches (lots of useful things), *wenig Interessantes* (little / not much that is interesting), *viel Gutes* (many good things)

Grammatik · page 189

Using the correct tense with *seit*

The preposition *seit* means 'since' or 'for'. It takes the dative case. If you want to say 'I have been going to this school for five years.', you use it with the **present tense** because you are still there: *Ich gehe seit fünf Jahren auf diese Schule.* You can also use *seit* with the **imperfect tense** if you want to say what you had done in the past: *Ich ging seit fünf Jahren auf diese Schule, als der neue Direktor ankam.* (I had been going to this school for five years when the new head teacher arrived.)

Grammatik · page 189

The imperative

The imperative is used to give commands or instructions. There are three different forms, depending on who you are talking to.

1 If you are talking to a child or family member, use the *du* form of the verb. But take off the *-st* from the end of the verb and miss out the word *du*: *Warte!*
2 For an adult or adults you don't know very well, use the *Sie* form: *Warten Sie!*
3 If you are talking to more than one child, friend or family member, use the *ihr* form: *Wartet!* This is the form which teachers use a lot when giving instructions in class.

The imperative works in this way for every verb. The only exception is the verb *sein*, which has an irregular imperative form, meaning 'be': *sei* (du form), *seien Sie* (Sie form), *seid* (ihr form): *Sei vorsichtig!* (Be careful!)

4a Rewrite the sentences in the comparative and superlative forms.

1 Mein Minirock ist kurz.
2 Meine Jacke ist modisch.
3 Meine Noten sind gut.
4 Mein Buch war interessant.
5 Ich kann schnell laufen.
6 Ich singe schön.
7 Ich wache früh auf.
8 Am Samstag werde ich spät aufstehen.

4b Translate the sentences into German using the adjective or adverb given in brackets.

1 In my opinion history is important. Maths is more important, but English is the most important subject. (*wichtig*)
2 Markus likes learning French. He prefers learning music, but he likes learning geography most of all. (*gern*)
3 Ilse is young. Fatma is younger. Max is the youngest in the class. (*jung*)
4 I walk to school slowly. My brother walks more slowly than me, but our sister walks most slowly. She is the slowest! (*langsam*)

Grammatik · pages 181 & 182

Revising the comparative and the superlative

When comparing things, you generally just add -*er* to the adjective or adverb:

schön → schön**er**   hässlich → hässlich**er**
früh → früh**er**   spät → spät**er**

Sometimes with one-syllable adjectives, you need to add an umlaut to the vowel:

kurz → k**ü**rz**er**   lang → l**ä**ng**er**

Add -*er* even when the adjective has more than two syllables:

langweilig → langweilig**er**

Exceptions include:

gut → **besser**   hoch → **höher**   gern → **lieber**

Use *als* when comparing two things:
*Die moderne Uniform ist schöner **als** die altmodische Uniform.*
*Mein Bruder singt besser **als** ich.*

To say something is 'biggest', 'best', 'oldest' etc., add -*ste* to the adjective:

schön → schön**ste**
hässlich → hässlich**ste**
früh → früh**ste**

Exceptions include:

gut → **beste**
gern → **liebste**

Don't forget to add the correct adjective endings:
*Wir wohnen im schönst**en** Haus der Straße.*
*Unsere Schule hat die best**en** Lehrer.*

Another way to form the superlative is to add *am … -(e)sten* after a form of *sein*:
schön → **am** schön**sten**
*Das Haus ist **am** schön**sten**.*

This is also the only possible way to form the superlative of adverbs:
*Sie läuft **am** schnell**sten**.*

Sometimes you need to add an -*e* to make the superlative easier to pronounce:
spät → spät**e**ste
alt → am ält**e**sten

Vokabeln

9.1 School and subjects

9.1 F Wie ist deine Schule?
➡ *pages 146–147*

die	Aula (Aulen)	school hall
die	**Bibliothek (-en)**	library
	erfahren	to learn, to find out
der	Gang (¨e)	corridor
das	Gebäude (–)	building
	gemischt	mixed
das	Gymnasium (Gymnasien)	grammar school
das	Labor (-e)	laboratory
das	Lehrerzimmer (–)	staffroom
die	**Mensa (-s)**	dining hall, canteen
der	**Neubau (-ten)**	new build
die	Pause (-n)	break
	plaudern	to chat, to talk
der	Schüler (–)	pupil, school student (m)
die	Schülerin (-nen)	pupil, school student (f)
der	Schulhof (¨e)	school yard, playground
das	Sekretariat (-e)	admin office
das	Sprachlabor (-e)	language lab
der	**Sprachunterricht (-e)**	language lessons
die	**Theatervorführung (-en)**	theatrical performance
die	Turnhalle (-n)	sports hall, gym
	umbauen	to rebuild
die	**Veranstaltung (-en)**	event
die	Versammlung (-en)	assembly
die	Zeitschrift (-en)	magazine

9.1 H Welche Schularten gibt es?
➡ *pages 148–149*

	1 = sehr gut	very good
	2 = gut	good
	3 = befriedigend	satisfactory, fair
	4 = ausreichend	sufficient, pass (just)
	5 = mangelhaft	poor, unsatisfactory, fail
	6 = ungenügend	extremely poor, inadequate
das	Abitur (-e)	German school leaver qualification (A-Level equivalent)
der	**(Schul)abschluss (¨e)**	qualification
das	Abschlusszeugnis (-se)	school leaving certificate
	angenehm	pleasant, agreeable
	bestehen	to pass (an exam / test)
das	**Bundesland (¨er)**	state (of Germany)
der	Direktor (-en)	head teacher (m)
die	Direktorin (-nen)	head teacher (f)
der	Fremdsprachenassistent (-en)	language assistant (m)
die	Fremdsprachenassistentin (-nen)	language assistant (f)
die	Ganztagsschule (-n)	all-day school
die	Gesamtschule (-n)	comprehensive school
	glücklicherweise	fortunately, luckily
die	Hauptschule (-n)	type of secondary school
der	Hausmeister (–)	caretaker (m)
die	Hausmeisterin (-nen)	caretaker (f)
die	Hauswirtschaft (-en)	home economics
der	Internat (-e)	boarding school
die	Klassenarbeit (-en)	test
	mindestens	at least
die	Note (-n)	mark, grade
die	Oberstufe (-n)	sixth form
das	Pflichtfach (¨er)	compulsory subject
die	Prüfung (-en)	exam
die	Realschule (-n)	type of secondary school

die	mittlere Reife	school-leaving certificate usually taken after the sixth year of secondary school
der	Schulleiter (–)	head teacher (m)
die	Schulleiterin (-nen)	head teacher (f)
das	**Schulsystem (-e)**	**school system**
	selbstständig	independent
	vorbereiten	**to prepare**
das	Wahlfach (¨er)	optional subject
(das)	Werken	handicraft
das	Zeugnis (-se)	school report

10.1 Life at school

10.1 F Ein typischer Schultag
➡ *pages 150–151*

	sich anziehen	to get dressed
	aufstehen	to get up, to stand up
das	**Aufstehen**	**getting up**
	aufwachen	to wake up
	sich ausziehen	to get undressed
	bis	until, to
	sich duschen	**to have a shower**
das	**Ereignis (-se)**	**event**
	faul	lazy
	fleißig	hard-working, industrious
	früh	early
	nachsitzen	to have a detention
	sich rasieren	to shave
	sich schminken	to put on make-up
	schwatzen	to chat
	selten	rarely, seldom
	sitzen	to sit
	typisch	typical
der	Umkleideraum (¨e)	changing room
	sich umziehen	to get changed
	verlassen	to leave
	sich waschen	to get washed
	sich die Zähne putzen	**to clean one's teeth**

10.1 H Aspekte des Schullebens
➡ *pages 152–153*

	abschreiben	to copy
die	AG (-s) (Arbeitsgemeinschaft (-en))	extra-curricular activity
	aufpassen	to pay attention
der	Austausch (-e)	exchange
	blau machen	to play truant, to skip school
	durchfallen	to fail (exam / test)
	sich entspannen	to relax
der	Erfolg (-e)	success
	erklären	to explain
	fleißig	hard-working
	gestreift	**striped**
	korrigieren	to correct, to mark
	merken	**to notice**
	mündlich	oral
die	**Nachprüfung (-en)**	**re-sit**
der	Notendruck	pressure to get good marks
die	Regel (-n)	rule
	schaffen	to get, to achieve, to manage
	schwänzen	to play truant, to skip school
	sitzen bleiben	to repeat a school year
	trotzdem	nevertheless, even so
	ungerecht	unfair
	versetzt werden	to be moved up to the next year group
	wahnsinnig	**crazy**
	wiederholen	to repeat

11.1 F

Welcher Beruf oder welches Studium?

1 **V** Für welche Berufe muss man an einer Universität studieren? Welche kann man auf einer Berufsschule lernen? Schreib noch fünf andere in jede Liste.

For which professions do you have to go to university? Which can you learn at a vocational college? Write five more in each list.

Beispiel: **Universität:** der Arzt / die Ärztin, …
Berufsschule: der Bauarbeiter / die Bauarbeiterin, …

2 Listen to the five young people. What do they want to do? Complete the sentences in English.

1 Erika hasn't yet … but she already knows … and …
2 Ralf wants to be a … He does not want to …
3 Ayşe's sister earns …
4 Lutz thinks it might be better …
5 Yasmin thinks she is too young to …

3a **G** Complete the words with the correct letters.

1 Welch__ Frau hast du gesehen?
2 Welch__ Beruf willst du?
3 Welch__ Kleid willst du tragen? Das blaue oder das rote?
4 Mit welch__ Wagen fahren wir? Mit meinem oder mit deinem?
5 Aus welch__ Gründen machst du das? Aus keinen guten Gründen!

3b **T** Translate the sentences in activity 3a into English.

4a **V** Verbinde die Wörter mit den englischen Übersetzungen.

Match the words with the English meanings.

die Berufspraxis   verbringen   pünktlich
geklappt   erfolgreich

successful   to spend time
succeeded / worked   work experience
punctually

Using *welcher?* (which?)

Welcher means 'which'. It is used to ask a question and also in sentences when the question is implied, for example in 'I don't know which job I want.'

As so often in German, the word has **endings**. These are actually the same as the endings you already know for *der / die / das*. For example, in the **nominative** case, the endings are as follows:

masculine	feminine	neuter	plural
welcher	*welche*	*welches*	*welche*

Just watch out for the masculine **accusative** form: *welchen*. You heard examples in the listening activity. This form is used in the question *Welchen Beruf willst du?* (Which job do you want?) Be careful: in English, we can also say 'What job …?' but you can't do that in German.

After *mit* (and other prepositions that take the **dative**) you need *welchem* for masculine and neuter, *welcher* for feminine and *welchen* for plural nouns:
Mit welchem Bus fahre ich? Mit dem grünen Bus da drüben.

Also learn how to use adverbs such as *hoffentlich* and *vielleicht*. See page 166.

Grammatik page 179

4b 📖 Read the text and answer the questions in English.

Erst Sanitäter, dann Medizinstudium

Max wollte immer Medizin studieren, aber als er das Abitur gemacht hat, waren seine Noten nicht gut genug, um sofort einen Studienplatz zu bekommen. Er hat also mit seiner Berufsberaterin gesprochen.

„Es kann ein paar Jahre dauern, bevor du einen Studienplatz bekommst, aber das heißt nicht, dass du aufgeben musst", hat sie gesagt. „Relevante Berufserfahrung ist immer ein Vorteil. Du kannst vielleicht ehrenamtlich in einem Krankenhaus arbeiten, oder als Sanitäter in einem Krankenwagen."

Diesen Vorschlag hat Max sinnvoll gefunden. Er musste zwar zuerst eine Ausbildung machen, aber er war stolz darauf, dass er sie erfolgreich abgeschlossen hat.

Jetzt ist es so weit: Er versucht wieder, an einer Uni zu studieren, und hofft, wegen seiner medizinisch relevanten Berufspraxis diesmal Glück zu haben.

abschließen – to finish
die Ausbildung – training
die Berufspraxis – practical experience
ehrenamtlich – voluntary, unpaid
Glück haben – to be fortunate
der Sanitäter – first-aider (in an ambulance)
sinnvoll – sensible, meaningful
stolz – proud
der Studienplatz – place at university

1 Why did Max not study medicine straight away?
2 Where did he go for advice on what to do?
3 What did Max think of the advice?
4 Did the advice work for Max?
5 How do we know that?

5 🅣 Translate the sentences into German.

1 Which cake do you want?
2 Have you chosen a profession?
3 She is a very successful student.
4 Which job is good for a medical student?
5 I am waiting for a place at university.

6 🗩 Partnerarbeit. Stellt euch und beantwortet die Fragen zur Berufswahl. Dann tauscht die Rollen.

Work with a partner. Ask and answer the questions about career choices. Then swap roles.

Partner / Partnerin A		Partner / Partnerin B	
1	Welchen Beruf möchtest du?	1	Say what job you would like.
2	Was für ein Job ist das?	2	Say what kind of job it is.
3	Wie lernt man diesen Beruf?	3	Say how you learn this job.
4	Was ist gut an diesem Job?	4	Say what is good about this job.
5	Was ist besser nach der Schule? Auf die Uni gehen oder gleich arbeiten? Warum?	5	Say which you think it is better to do after school: university or work. Give reasons.

Simplifying what you say

If you don't know how to say something, one strategy is to make it simpler. If you want to say 'I really enjoyed the party and I'm looking forward to the next one.' you could say *Die Party hat Spaß gemacht. Ich hoffe, die nächste ist auch gut.*

It doesn't show off your German as well as the exact translation (*Die Party hat mir echt gut gefallen und ich freue mich auf die nächste.*), but it definitely gets the message across.

Challenge: Work with a partner and try to find simple ways of saying the following:

When I'd finished work.   I can't make up my mind.   Thank you for inviting me. I thought it was exceptionally good. I got here at ten o'clock.   I hope you are able to visit in the next few days.

Strategie

7 ✏ Schreib deine Antworten auf die Fragen aus Aufgabe 6. Schreib einen Absatz (ungefähr 90 Wörter).

Write your answers to the questions in activity 6. Write a paragraph (approximately 90 words).

11.1 H Universität oder gleich Karriere?

Lernziele

Talking about career choices

Using verbs followed by *zu*

Listening for different ways of saying the same thing

1 📖 Markus hat einen Berufswahl-Test gemacht. Hier ist ein Teil davon. Was wäre ein guter Beruf für Markus?

| Bauarbeiter | Büroangestellter | Lehrer | Koch | LKW-Fahrer | Verkäufer |

Welcher Beruf ist der richtige für mich?

1 Will ich unbedingt machen.
2 Könnte ich mir vorstellen.
3 Kann ich mir teilweise vorstellen.

4 Ist eher nichts für mich.
5 Will ich auf keinen Fall machen.

Ich will ...

im Freien arbeiten.	5	Menüs planen und kochen.	5
an Schulen Schüler unterrichten.	2	in einer Werkstatt Kraftfahrzeuge reparieren.	4
für eine Bibliothek oder Buchhandlung Exemplare bestellen.	1	Blumen zu Sträußen binden.	5
Gäste in einem Hotel oder Restaurant bedienen.	3	ein Büro organisieren.	2
Briefe und Pakete sortieren und zustellen.	5	Waren in einem Lastwagen transportieren.	4
Lebensmittel herstellen (z.B. Backwaren).	4	Menschen etwas lehren.	1
in einem Geschäft Kunden bedienen und über Produkte informieren.	3	einen Artikel für eine Tageszeitung schreiben.	2
Lebensmittel verkaufen.	5	Menschen mit Schmerzen massieren oder behandeln.	5

2 🗨 Partnerarbeit. Mach selbst den Test mit einem Partner / einer Partnerin. Welchen Beruf würdest du deinem Partner / deiner Partnerin empfehlen?

Beispiel: Person 1: Willst du im Freien arbeiten?
Person 2: Könnte ich mir vorstellen.
Person 1: Also eine Zwei. Willst du …

Mach weiter so bis zur letzten Frage. Am Ende:

Person 1: Wenn ich dein Berufsberater wäre, würde ich … empfehlen.

3 🎧 Hör dir die Debatte im Radio an. Zwei Politiker, Herr Thiel und Frau Kekilli, sprechen über die Ausbildungspolitik. Was sagen sie?

Herr Thiel

1 Das Land braucht hochqualifizierte Leute.
2 Alle Leute müssen an der Universität studieren.
3 Eine Ausbildung ist besser als ein Studium.
4 Die Studienzeit ist sehr lang.
5 Die Studienzeit ist zu kurz.
6 Alles kann nicht so bleiben, wie es jetzt ist.

Frau Kekilli

7 Wir teilen eine Meinung, Herr Thiel.
8 Sie haben mich überrascht, Herr Thiel.
9 Ich habe einen Sohn, der das Abitur macht.
10 Mein Sohn will nicht auf eine Universität gehen.

Strategie

Listening for different ways of saying the same thing

The key to tasks like activity 3, which require you to identify the correct German statements, is to listen for different ways of saying the same thing. For example, statements 4 and 5 are both about how long it takes to study at university – and only one can be correct. In the audio, Herr Thiel doesn't use either of these phrases, but he does say how long people are students for, which will lead you to the correct statement.

Challenge: Work with a partner and listen again to the audio for activity 3. Try to note down the different ways in which the speakers say the same things as in the correct statements.

Grammatik *page 188*

4 **G** **T** Write the sentences in the correct order. Then translate the sentences into English.

1 das – versuche – zu – verstehen – Ich
2 Ich – nächstes – kommen – hoffe – wieder – Jahr – zu
3 zu – gehen – ins – Ich – Kino – Lust – habe
4 Fußball – zieht – Er – vor – spielen – zu – es
5 zu – pünktlich – Versuche – kommen
6 habe – zu – USA – in – den – mich – Ich – studieren – entschieden
7 sein – Man – nicht – immer – perfekt – zu – braucht
8 zu – fängt – an – regnen – Es

5 Partnerarbeit. Sieh dir das Foto an und mach Notizen. Beantworte die folgenden Fragen. Dann tauscht die Rollen.

- Was gibt es auf dem Foto?
- Möchtest du als Mechaniker(in) arbeiten? Warum (nicht)?
- Was für eine Person muss man sein, um in einer Werkstatt zu arbeiten?
- Hast du schon Arbeitserfahrung?
- Was ist besser: an der Universität studieren oder eine Lehre machen? Warum?

Using verbs followed by *zu*

Some German verbs are used with *zu* (to) and the infinitive of another verb.
For example: *Ich brauche nur meine Hausaufgaben zu machen.*
These verbs include: *aufhören* (to stop), *beginnen* (to begin), *brauchen* (to need), *sich entscheiden* (to decide), *hoffen* (to hope), *vergessen* (to forget), *versuchen* (to try), *vorziehen* (to prefer).

You heard these examples in the listening:
Wir müssen jetzt beginnen, das anders zu machen.
Sie brauchen nicht so überrascht auszusehen!
Er hofft, auf die Uni zu gehen.
Here are two more examples:
Ich versuche mein Bestes zu tun.
(I'm trying to do my best.)
Er vergisst immer das Licht auszumachen.
(He always forgets to switch the light off.)

As always, the infinitive in German is at the end of the sentence – the word *zu* goes just before it. Notice that when the verb is separable, *zu* goes in between the two parts and it's all written as one word: *auszusehen*.

Also revise using *wäre* and *hätte* in conditional sentences. See page 166.

6 Schreib eine Bewerbung um eine Stelle als Mechaniker(in) oder Verkäufer(in). Schreib, warum du den Job willst und warum du den Job gut machen kannst.

7 **T** Translate the paragraph into German.

University is not for everybody. You do not need to go to university. You can earn money and help people in important jobs, for example as a plumber or a carer. Of course, you need to do an apprenticeship, and then you can begin to work. Try to find a choice of occupation where you can say, I definitely want to do that.

11.1 Groundwork is available in the Foundation book.

12.1 F

Welchen Beruf willst du machen?

1 **V** Wo oder wie übt man diese Berufe aus? Schreib drei Listen: im Freien, man sitzt und man steht.

Where and how do you do these occupations? Make three lists: outside, sitting down and standing up.

Arbeiten in Deutschland

Registrieren:

| Bauarbeiter | Koch | Briefträger | Büroangestellter | Friseurin | Feuerwehrmann |

Eine Arbeit finden

🔍 Suchen …

| Verkäuferin | LKW-Fahrerin | Lehrerin | Krankenpfleger | Tierarzt | Soldatin |

2 📖📖 Read the texts about how two people chose their profession. Choose the five correct statements for each person.

1 Ich bin Max. Ich bin Pfleger von Beruf. Als ich 16 war, habe ich die Schule verlassen. Ich habe zuerst in einer kleinen Fabrik gearbeitet, weil ich mich nicht entscheiden konnte, was ich eigentlich machen will. Nachdem ich drei Monate gearbeitet hatte, ist meine Mutter krank geworden. Dann musste ich sie pflegen. Obwohl ich noch jung war, hat mir das gut gefallen. Ich habe gleich gewusst, dass Pfleger der richtige Beruf für mich ist. Trotz der langen Arbeitstage mag ich immer noch meinen Job.

Max

2 Ich darf mich vorstellen: Ich heiße Cleo und ich bin Klempnerin. Ich habe viele Jobs ausprobiert – Köchin, Kassiererin, sogar Schauspielerin – aber nichts hat mir gefallen. Als eines Tages bei mir der Wasserhahn nicht funktioniert hat, habe ich versucht, ihn selbst zu reparieren. Obwohl ich keine Erfahrung hatte, hatte ich Erfolg. Ich habe dann eine Lehre gemacht und bin jetzt gelernte Klempnerin.

Cleo

Recognising the verb in a sentence

Every sentence has a verb to tell us what is going on, so it is vital to be able to recognise it.

First, you can recognise a verb by looking at the endings, e.g. *ich arbeite*, *sie arbeitet*. Second, in German the verb is always in one of two fixed places in the sentence – the second idea or the last word:
*Am Wochenende **arbeite** ich als Pfleger.* (At the weekend I work as a carer.)
*Du **weißt**, dass ich am Wochenende als Pfleger **arbeite**.* (You know that I work as a carer at the weekend.)

Challenge: Read Cleo's text again. Find all 18 verb forms.

Strategie

a Max is now a carer.
b Max was 15 when he left school.
c He worked part-time in a factory.
d He could not decide what he wanted to do.
e His mother became ill.
f He liked looking after her.
g He won't do this job because of the long hours.
h It is the right job for him.

i Cleo is a cook.
j She wanted to be a singer.
k She has tried many jobs.
l She tried to fix her broken tap.
m She managed to fix the tap.
n She became an apprentice.
o She found the studies difficult.
p She got her qualifications.

Grammatik *page 190*

3a 🌐 Read the texts in activity 2 again. Find and make two lists: *Konjunktion* (the subordinating conjunction) and *Verb* (the verb it sends to the end).

Beispiel: **Konjunktion**   **Verb**
              als   war

3b 🎧🌐 Listen and make two lists, as in activity 3a.

3c 🌐 Link the sentences using the subordinating conjunction given in brackets.

Beispiel: **1** Ich suche einen Job in einem Supermarkt, obwohl ich keine Erfahrung habe.

1 Ich suche einen Job in einem Supermarkt. Ich habe keine Erfahrung. (*obwohl*)
2 Ich weiß nicht. Er ist fertig. (*ob*)
3 Ich habe Paul getroffen. Ich war in der Stadtmitte. (*als*)
4 Ich schlafe ein. Ich sehe fern. (*während*)
5 Ich muss noch lernen. Ich schreibe morgen eine Klassenarbeit. (*bevor*)
6 Kommst du mit? Ich gehe ins Kino. (*wenn*)
7 Ich kann warten. Sie ist fertig. (*bis*)
8 Ich war sehr enttäuscht. Ich hatte die Nachricht bekommen. (*nachdem*)

Using a range of subordinating conjunctions

Remember that words that join together two parts of a sentence (clauses) are called conjunctions. Subordinating conjunctions send the verb to the end of the clause. There is always a comma at the 'junction' of the two clauses:
Ich habe die Schule verlassen, **als** *ich sechzehn war.*
Als *ich sechzehn war, habe ich die Schule verlassen.*

> Of course, when you are listening you can't see the comma! You'll just have to listen carefully in case there is a verb at the end.

Sometimes there will be two verbs at the end of the clause (when using the perfect tense, the future tense or modal verbs, for example):
… , weil ich mich nicht **entscheiden konnte***.*
(… because I **couldn't decide***.)

Here is a range of subordinating conjunctions that you can use to improve your speaking and writing:
als (when – used only when talking about the past), *bevor* (before), *dass* (that), *nachdem* (after), *ob* (whether, if), *obwohl* (although), *seit* (since), *während* (while, whereas), *weil* (because), *wenn* (if, whenever).

Also learn how to recognise prepositions with the genitive case. See page 167.

4 🔤 Translate the sentences into German.

1 I want to be a vet because I like animals.
2 Although I am still young, I have a lot of experience with animals.
3 I will be at university until I am 23.
4 After I have left university, I want to work.
5 I know that I must work hard.

5 💬 Partnerabeit. Seht euch das Foto an und beantwortet die Fragen. Dann tauscht die Rollen.

Work with a partner. Look at the photo and answer the questions. Then swap roles.

- Was gibt es auf dem Foto?
- Möchtest du in einem Büro arbeiten? Warum (nicht)?
- Was ist dein Traumjob? Warum?

6 ✏️ Du schreibst eine E-Mail an deine deutsche Freundin. Schreib ungefähr 50 Wörter über deinen Traumjob, wo du arbeiten möchtest (in einem Büro, im Freien …) und warum.

You are writing an e-mail to your German friend. Write about 50 words about your dream job, where you would like to work (in an office, in the open air …) and why.

12.1 H   Mein idealer Job

1a 🎧 Hör dir Süher an. Sie spricht im Internetradio über ihren Traumjob. Was hat sie beruflich gemacht?

a Kellnerin   c Lehrerin   e Polizistin

b Taxifahrerin   d Büroangestellte   f Verkäuferin

1b 🎧 Hör noch mal zu. Schreib den richtigen Buchstaben!

1 Süher ist jetzt …   a traurig.   b glücklich.   c arm.

2 Ein Job war schrecklich …   a wegen des Chefs.
   b wegen der Arbeitsstunden.   c wegen der Kunden.

3 Ein Job war gut …   a wegen der Kollegen.
   b wegen des Lohns.   c wegen des Chefs.

2 📖 Hier sind ein paar Antworten, die Süher bekommen hat. Lies sie und beantworte die Fragen auf Deutsch.

Frank aus Wuppertal

Traumjob? Irgendeinen Job zu finden ist schon schwer genug. Hundert Bewerbungen haben nichts gebracht.

☆ ✉ ➡

Kirsten aus Ulm

Ja! Meinen Traumjob habe ich gefunden. Der ist wunderbar, und nicht nur wegen des Lohns, sondern auch wegen der netten Kollegen.

☆ ✉ ➡

Andrea aus Köln

Ich habe eine Stelle als Sekretärin statt meines Traumjobs. Ich kann nur hoffen, ich finde bald etwas Anderes.

☆ ✉ ➡

Stephan aus München

Ich wohne noch bei meinen Eltern. Mein Traum ist es, selbstständig zu sein. Zum Glück helfen mir meine Eltern.

☆ ✉ ➡

Imke aus Stuttgart

Während meines Arbeitspraktikums als Verkäuferin habe ich viel gelernt. Jetzt habe ich meinen eigenen Laden eröffnet. Unglaublich!

☆ ✉ ➡

Wer …

1 ist selbstständig?

2 verdient gut und kommt gut mit den anderen aus?

3 hat immer wieder einen Job gesucht, aber ohne Erfolg?

4 bekommt Unterstützung?

5 arbeitet schon, aber nicht im Traumjob?

3a **G** Find the four examples of prepositions followed by the genitive in activity 2.

3b **G** **T** Translate the expressions into German.

1 because of the rain
2 instead of the train
3 outside of the house
4 in spite of the bad weather
5 during the long nights

4 **T** Translate the paragraph into English.

> Ich habe eine Lehre gemacht. Ich wollte Gärtner werden. Ich hatte vorher drei Jahre studiert. Dann wollte ich etwas Geld verdienen und ich hatte eine Gelegenheit, einer Nachbarin mit ihrem Garten zu helfen. Ich bin jetzt selbstständig und ich habe viele Kunden.

5 **T** Translate the paragraph into German.

> When I was 14, I already wanted to be an engineer. In spite of my bad grade in my *Abitur* I studied at university. When I left university, I got a job in a large factory. I like my occupation.

6 Partnerarbeit. Sieh das Foto an. Stellt euch und beantwortet die folgenden Fragen. Dann tauscht die Rollen.

- Was gibt es auf dem Foto?
- Möchtest du Polizist / Polizistin werden? Warum (nicht)?
- Wie muss man sein, um Polizist / Polizistin zu werden?

7 Du hast eine E-Mail von deinem deutschen Freund bekommen. Er fragt, ob du ein Arbeitspraktikum gemacht hast. Schreib ungefähr 150 Wörter über:

- was du in deinem Arbeitspraktikum gemacht hast
- deine Berufspläne.

Using the genitive case

The genitive case is used for two reasons in German:

1 To denote possession

With a name you add the letter **-s**, where we would add an apostrophe and the letter *s* in English: *Andreas Wagen* (Andrea's car).

With other nouns we usually use the word 'of' in English; in German the word for 'the' or 'a' changes and we add **-s** on to the end of the masculine and neuter nouns: *die Farbe des Wagens* (the colour of the car). Feminine nouns do not have an -s at the end: *die Farbe der Katze* (the colour of the cat).

> Look at page 180 to make sure you know all the genitive forms.

2 With certain prepositions

Most prepositions which take the genitive in German have the word 'of' in English: *statt* (instead of), *trotz* (in spite of), *außerhalb* (outside of), *wegen* (because of).

There is one exception: *während* (during): *während des Tages* (during the day), *während der Nacht* (during the night).

These are not just examples of prepositions which take the genitive – they are all the ones you need to know! Also learn about using subordinate clauses to develop your sentences. See page 167.

Using *von* + dative instead of the genitive

It can be difficult to think quickly what the genitive form is when talking about who owns what. There is another way of saying 'of' simply using the German word *von*: *das Auto von der Lehrerin* (the teacher's car), *die Freundin von meinem Bruder* (my brother's girlfriend), *die Farbe von dem Pullover* (the colour of the pullover).

However, to impress when writing you should try to use the genitive.

Challenge: Try saying each of the above phrases using the genitive case. With a partner, make up three more phrases each, using both the genitive and *von* + dative. For example: *die Jeans meines Bruders* and *die Jeans von meinem Bruder*.

Strategie

> 12.1 Groundwork is available in the Foundation book.

G

Education post-16; Jobs, career choices and ambitions

1a Complete the sentences with the correct adverb. Then translate the sentences into English.

> **hoffentlich**   **vielleicht**   **wahrscheinlich**   **sicher**

1 Manfred ist ein Dieb? … nicht. Ich mag ihn.
2 Kommst du mit oder nicht? – … Ich weiß nicht.
3 Kannst du Schach spielen? – Ja, … ! Ich bin Weltmeister!
4 Kommst du am Freitag mit ins Kino? – … nicht. Ich muss meine Hausaufgaben machen.

1b Write the sentences in the correct order, starting with the underlined adverb. Then translate the sentences into English.

1 Wochenende – musst – du – nicht – arbeiten – <u>Hoffentlich</u> – am
2 bleiben – kannst – du – bei – uns – <u>Sicher</u>
3 hat – vergessen – sie <u>Wahrscheinlich</u> – es
4 du – helfen – <u>Vielleicht</u> – mir – kannst

2a Complete the sentences with the correct form of the verbs given in brackets. Remember to use the correct endings. Then translate the sentences into English.

1 Du … dumm, wenn du so was machen würdest. (*wäre*)
2 Wenn er nicht Klempner … , … er gerne als Bauarbeiter arbeiten. (*wäre, würde*)
3 Wenn sie einen Führerschein … , … sie LKW-Fahrerin werden. (*hätte, würde*)
4 Wenn Sie Schauspieler … , … Sie mehr verdienen. (*wäre, würde*)

2b Translate the sentences into German. Look out for 'would be' and 'would have' so you translate the sentences correctly.

1 If I had a CV, I would apply for the job.
2 If I were good at maths, I would be an engineer.
3 He would have a place at university, if he were hard-working.
4 Even if she had no money, she would not work in an office.

Grammatik · page 182

Using adverbs such as *hoffentlich* and *vielleicht*

Remember that an adverb tells you when, where or how something is being done. There is a special group of adverbs which say how likely something is to happen: *hoffentlich* (hopefully / I hope that), *vielleicht* (perhaps), *wahrscheinlich* (probably), *sicher* (certainly / definitely).

These adverbs can come after the verb:
Sie hat wahrscheinlich zu viel zu tun.
(She probably has too much to do.)
Er kann hoffentlich nächste Woche kommen. (He can hopefully / I hope that he can come next week.)
Sie ist sicher sehr krank. (She is definitely very ill.)
Er ist vielleicht zu müde. (Perhaps he is too tired.)

They also work very well at the beginning of a sentence. Remember that the verb has to be the second idea in any sentence:
*Wahrscheinlich **hat** sie zu viel zu tun.*
*Vielleicht **ist** er zu müde.*

Grammatik · page 188

Using *wäre* and *hätte* in conditional sentences (revision)

You already know how to use **wäre** and **hätte** in *wenn* clauses (see page 98):
Wenn ich reich wäre, … (If I were rich, …)
Wenn ich viel Geld hätte, … (If I had a lot of money, …)
The *wenn* clause is then followed by a clause with **würde** (would) and an **infinitive** at the end of the sentence:
*Wenn ich reich wäre, **würde** ich ein großes Haus **kaufen**.*

In this second part of the sentence, *würde + sein* is normally replaced by **wäre**, and *würde + haben* is normally replaced by **hätte**:
*Wenn ich öfter auf deine Rätschläge hörte, **hätte** ich weniger Probleme.* (If I listened to your advice more often, I would have fewer problems.)
These are the forms of the verbs.

ich	wäre / hätte	wir	wären / hätten
du	wärst / hättest	ihr	wäret / hättet
er / sie / es	wäre / hätte	sie / Sie	wären / hätten

3a Thorsten is talking about finding a job. Read the text and make a list of the phrases using the prepositions from the *Grammatik* box.

> Trotz meiner großen Erfahrung in der Restaurantbranche kann ich keinen Job als Koch finden. Während der Suche habe ich gearbeitet, aber statt eines Teilzeitjobs will ich eine Vollzeitbeschäftigung. Wegen der Sorge um einen Job kann ich nicht schlafen. Vielleicht finde ich etwas außerhalb der Stadtmitte in einem Vorort. Das ist auch nicht besser. Wegen der langen Fahrt dorthin muss ich das Auto statt des Busses nehmen.

3b Read the text again and answer the questions in English.

1 Why is it surprising that Thorsten can't find a job?
2 What kind of job has he got now?
3 Why can he not sleep?
4 Where will he now look for a job?
5 What is the problem then?

4a Link the sentences using the word given in brackets. Then write the sentences the other way round, so that the subordinate clause comes first.

1 Ich weiß. Ich bin manchmal dumm. (*dass*)
2 Er hat nie verstanden. Sie hasst ihn. (*warum*)
3 Ich weiß nicht. Ich habe meinen Schlüssel verloren. (*wo*)
4 Sie hasst ihn. Er war nicht sehr höflich zu ihr. (*weil*)
5 Ich habe mit der Schule angefangen. Ich war sechs Jahre alt. (*als*)
6 Er hat ein neues Auto bestellt. Er hat kein Geld. (*obwohl*)

4b Complete the sentences with at least two different subordinate clauses.

> *Beispiel:* Ich will Lehrer werden, <u>weil ich gern mit jungen Leuten arbeite</u>.
> <u>Bevor ich eine Familie habe</u>, will ich Lehrer werden.

1 Er geht gerne in die Schule, …
2 Sie hat früher in einem Geschäft gearbeitet, …
3 Wir wollen sehr viel Geld verdienen, …
4 Ich bleibe hier, …
5 Ich habe als Kellner gearbeitet, …

Grammatik | *page 181*

Recognising prepositions with the genitive case

Während has two meanings: it can mean 'while' (as a conjunction), but it can also mean 'during' (as a preposition). When this is the case, it is followed by a noun, not a verb:
während des Tages (during the day)
Did you notice that it is followed by the genitive (*des*)?

There are a few other prepositions that are used with the genitive. You need to be able to recognise and understand them:
trotz (in spite of), *statt* (instead of), *außerhalb* (outside of), *wegen* (because of)

> Notice that the English translations of these prepositions include the word 'of'.

If an adjective is used after one of these words, it nearly always ends in -*n*:
trotz *des schlechten Wetters* (in spite of the bad weather)
statt *eines großen Geschenks* (instead of a big present)
außerhalb *des normalen Unterrichts* (outside of the normal lessons)
wegen *des starken Regens* (because of the heavy rain)

Grammatik | *page 189*

Using subordinate clauses to develop your sentences

Subordinate clauses are important as longer sentences do not flow as well without them. This is why you should try to use them. (Both those sentences have subordinate clauses, beginning with 'as' and 'why'!)
They can begin with three types of word: **subordinating conjunctions**, **relative pronouns**, and **interrogatives** (question words). Here we'll only be looking at subordinating conjunctions and interrogatives. (For a reminder of how to use relative pronouns, look at page 183.)

Remember that you need a comma before the subordinate clause and the verb goes to the end of the clause.

As you know, it is possible to start a German sentence with the subordinate clause. Remember that the verb in the main clause needs to be the next word after the comma: **Als ich jünger war**, **habe** ich oft Fußball gespielt.

Vokabeln

11.1 University or work?

11.1 F Welcher Beruf oder welches Studium?
➡ *pages 158–159*

das	Alter	age
die	Ausbildung (-en)	(job) training, education
der / die	Azubi (-s) (Auszubildende)	apprentice, trainee
der	Bauarbeiter (–)	construction worker (m)
die	Bauarbeiterin (-nen)	construction worker (f)
die	Berufspraxis (-praxen)	work experience
die	Berufsschule (-n)	vocational training school
die	Bewerbung (-en)	application
	einzig	single, only
	jobben	to (do casual) work
der / die	Jugendliche (-n)	young person
	klappen	to succeed, to work
	langweilig	boring
der	LKW-Fahrer (–)	lorry driver (m)
die	LKW-Fahrerin (-nen)	lorry driver (f)
der	Mindestlohn (¨e)	minimum wage
	nachdenken	to think something over
die	Priorität (-en)	priority
	pünktlich	punctual, on time
der	Studienplatz (¨e)	university place
das	Studium (Studien)	studies
die	Universität (-en)	university
	wirklich	really
	zufällig	by chance

11.1 H Universität oder gleich Karriere?
➡ *pages 160–161*

die	Arbeitserfahrung (–)	experience of work
	Backwaren	baked goods (pl)
	bedienen	to serve
	behandeln	to treat, to handle
der	Berufsberater (–)	careers adviser
die	Buchhandlung (–)	bookshop
der / die	Büroangestellte (-n)	office worker
	eher	rather
(sich)	entscheiden	to decide
das	Exemplar (-e)	example
	auf keinen Fall	under no circumstances
	herstellen	to make, to produce
die	Karriere (-n)	career
der	Klempner (–)	plumber (m)
die	Klempnerin (-nen)	plumber (f)
der	Koch (¨e)	cook (m)
die	Köchin (-nen)	cook (f)
	Lebensmittel	food (pl)
	lehren	to teach
der	Mechaniker (–)	mechanic (m)
die	Mechanikerin (-nen)	mechanic (f)
der	Pfleger (–)	care worker (m)
die	Pflegerin (-nen)	care worker (f)
der	Schmerz (-en)	pain
die	Stelle (-n)	job
der	Strauß (¨e)	bunch of flowers
	teilweise	partly
	theoretisch	theoretically
	unbedingt	definitely
der	Verkäufer (–)	shop assistant (m)
die	Verkäuferin (-nen)	shop assistant (f)
der	Versuch (-e)	attempt
(sich)	vorstellen	to introduce (oneself)
die	Werkstatt (¨en)	garage
	zustellen	to deliver

12.1 Choice of career

12.1 F Welchen Beruf willst du machen?
➡ *pages 162–163*

	ausprobieren	to test, to try out
	ausüben	to practise (a profession)
	(sich um) bewerben	to apply for
der	Briefträger (–)	postman
die	Briefträgerin (-nen)	postwoman
	enttäuscht	disappointed
die	Feuerwehrfrau (-en)	firefighter (f)
der	Feuerwehrmann (¨er)	firefighter (m)
	gedreht	shot (a film)
	gelernt	fully trained
	hochladen	to upload
der	Kassierer (–)	cashier, bank clerk (m)
die	Kassiererin (-nen)	cashier, bank clerk (f)
	pflegen	to care for
	reparieren	to repair
der	Sänger (–)	singer (m)
die	Sängerin (-nen)	singer (f)
der	Soldat (-en)	soldier
die	Soldatin (-nen)	soldier (f)
die	Stimme (-n)	voice
	üben	to practise
das	Vorstellungsgespräch (-e)	job interview
der	Wasserhahn (¨e)	tap

12.1 H Mein idealer Job
➡ *pages 164–165*

das	Arbeitspraktikum (-praktika)	work experience
die	Atempause (-n)	a pause for breath
	eröffnet	opened
der	Gärtner (–)	gardener (m)
die	Gärtnerin (-nen)	gardener (f)
die	Gelegenheit (-en)	opportunity
der	Ingenieur (-e)	engineer (m)
die	Ingenieurin (-nen)	engineer (f)
	lächerlich	ridiculous
der	Lohn (¨e)	wage
	mies	rotten, lousy
der	Radiomoderator (-en)	radio presenter (m)
die	Radiomoderatorin (-nen)	radio presenter (f)
der	Traumjob (-s)	dream job
	unglaublich	unbelievable, incredible
die	Unterstützung (-en)	support, help

Higher – Reading and listening

1 📖 Read this passage about school from the book *Die Welt von gestern* (*Yesterday's World*) by Stefan Zweig. Answer the questions in **English**.

1 At what kind of school did the author spend eight years?
2 What does he tell us about the school day?
3 Which two types of languages did he have to learn?
4 What does he think about the amount he had to learn?
5 What was missing at the school? **[5 marks]**

> Fünf Jahre Volksschule und acht Jahre Gymnasium mussten auf hölzerner Bank durchgesessen werden, täglich fünf bis sechs Stunden, und in der freien Zeit die Schulaufgaben bewältigt und überdies noch, was die ‚allgemeine Bildung' forderte neben der Schule, Französisch, Englisch, Italienisch, die ‚lebendigen' Sprachen neben den klassischen Griechisch und Latein – also fünf Sprachen zu Geometrie und Physik und den übrigen Schulgegenständen. Es war mehr als zuviel und ließ für die körperliche Entwicklung, für Sport und Spaziergänge fast keinen Raum und vor allem nicht für Frohsinn und Vergnügen.

körperlich – physical

2 📖 Verena is a trainee in retail management in Switzerland. She wrote this for a Swiss careers website. Answer the questions in **English**.

> **The setting** – what we call the **context** – of a text is very important when reading. You can use the context to guess the meanings of words. For example, in this text *Gartengeräte* clearly has something to do with gardens, but it does not mean plants, because the word for plants is there, too. So what could it mean? Garden tools? Garden gnomes? What is the most likely **in the context**? The answer is garden tools.
>
> **Strategie**

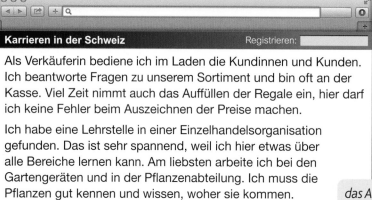

Karrieren in der Schweiz   Registrieren:

Als Verkäuferin bediene ich im Laden die Kundinnen und Kunden. Ich beantworte Fragen zu unserem Sortiment und bin oft an der Kasse. Viel Zeit nimmt auch das Auffüllen der Regale ein, hier darf ich keine Fehler beim Auszeichnen der Preise machen.

Ich habe eine Lehrstelle in einer Einzelhandelsorganisation gefunden. Das ist sehr spannend, weil ich hier etwas über alle Bereiche lernen kann. Am liebsten arbeite ich bei den Gartengeräten und in der Pflanzenabteilung. Ich muss die Pflanzen gut kennen und wissen, woher sie kommen.

Ich bin an einem Tag pro Woche an der Berufsschule.

das Auffüllen – stacking
die Einzelhandelsorganisation – retail business

1 Name **two** things that Verena does in the shop for customers.
2 What takes a lot of time?
3 What is important when writing the prices?
4 What does she think of the work and why? (2 details)
5 What does she like doing best? (2 details)
6 What specialist knowledge does she need? (2 details)
7 How else does she learn about the job? **[11 marks]**

3 🅣 Translate the paragraph into **English**.

> Ich habe mich entschieden, mir einen Teilzeitjob zu suchen. Ich studiere, aber ich brauche Geld. Meine Schwester hat auch gearbeitet, als sie studiert hat. Das war in einer Tierarztpraxis, und das war ein Vorteil für sie, weil sie Erfahrung gesammelt hat. Jetzt ist sie Tierärztin.

[9 marks]

4 Hanna schreibt eine E-Mail über ihren Job mit einer Wohltätigkeitsorganisation. Lies die E-Mail und sieh dir die Aussagen an. Sind die Aussagen **richtig** (R), **falsch** (F) oder **nicht im Text** (NT)?

Mein neuer Job ist wirklich toll. Ich arbeite in einem Team mit anderen Studenten. Ich habe mich darum beworben, weil ich es höchstinteressant finde, für Hilfs- und Umweltschutzorganisationen zu arbeiten. Wir machen Werbung und informieren die Bevölkerung direkt über Ziele und aktuelle Hilfsprojekte. Wir erklären dabei, wie wichtig es ist, solche Organisationen zu unterstützen.

Es gibt so viele Vorteile für mich. Ich habe in Deutschlands größten Städten gearbeitet. Ich habe viele coole neue Leute kennengelernt – Studenten, Hausfrauen, Beamte, die alle den Wunsch haben, ihren Mitmenschen zu helfen.

Und ich verdiene ca. 120€/Tag, mehr als den Mindestlohn für diese wunderbare Gelegenheit, mir meinen Lebenstraum zu erfüllen!

1 Hanna arbeitet gern mit anderen Leuten.
2 Hanna hat diesen Job online gefunden.
3 Sie schreibt Artikel für eine Zeitung.
4 Sie schreibt über die Arbeit der Wohltätigkeitsorganisation.
5 Sie bekommt keine gute Erfahrung von der Arbeit.
6 Sie hat ihren Freund auf der Arbeit kennengelernt.
7 Sie arbeitet zum Mindestlohn.
8 Hanna hat sich immer eine solche Arbeit gewünscht.

[8 marks]

5 Anna is talking about school rules. Answer all parts of the question in **English**.

1 What did she do to annoy the head teacher?
2 What is her opinion about this?
3 Give **one** reason for her opinion.
4 What happened to her brother last week?

[4 marks]

Often you have to get the gist of something, i.e. the overall meaning. For example, you might hear: *Ich habe ein wunderbares Geschenk bekommen!* (I have just got a wonderful present!)

Question: *Wie fühlt sie sich heute?* (How does she feel today?) **Answer:** *glücklich* (happy).

This is also called 'inference' – the drawing out of meaning from details. For example: *Ich wollte gerade das Auto tanken, als ich den Dieb gesehen habe.* (I was just about to put petrol in the car when I saw the thief.)

Question: *Wo war sie, als sie den Dieb sah?* (Where was she when she saw the thief?) **Answer:** *(an der) Tankstelle* (at the petrol station).

Strategie

6 Michael is talking about why he decided to go to university. Answer the questions in **English**.

1 What **two** negative aspects does he mention?
Negative   Aspect 1: …   Aspect 2: …
2 What **two** positive aspects does he mention?
Positive   Aspect 1: …   Aspect 2: …   **[4 marks]**

7 In einem Podcast erklärt Ben, was er an seinem Beruf gut findet und was nicht. Beantworte die Fragen auf **Deutsch**.

1 Was macht er beruflich?
2 Nennen Sie **einen** Nachteil des Berufs.
3 Nennen Sie **einen** Vorteil des Berufs.
4 Was macht Ben gern?   **[4 marks]**

Foundation test and revise tasks are available in the Foundation book.

Higher – Writing and translation

Either:

1a Du schreibst eine E-Mail an deine deutsche Freundin über deine Schule.

Schreib:

* wie du mit den anderen Schülern / Schülerinnen auskommst
* deine Meinung über die Schulregeln
* was du gestern nach der Schule gemacht hast
* was du nächstes Jahr machen wirst.

Du musst ungefähr **90** Wörter auf **Deutsch** schreiben. Schreib etwas über alle Punkte der Aufgabe.

[16 marks]

Strategie

Make sure that you stick to what you are asked to do. If you are not sure that you know all the vocabulary, try to think of different ways of expressing your ideas.

Have a few things ready which you want to make sure you use in your writing. These should be items that show how well you can manipulate the language, such as:

* *obwohl* followed by verb at the end
* any other subordinating conjunction, such as *als, weil, wenn*
* a sentence using the conditional or pluperfect tense
* a comparative such as *besser, schneller, erfolgreicher*
* a superlative, such as *der größte, am liebsten*
* a relative clause, such as *Ich habe einen Job gefunden, der mir gefällt.*
* some phrases using the genitive, such as *während der Woche, wegen des Wetters.*

You might not get them all in, but the more you know, the more you will find you can use with just a bit of imagination.

Or:

1b Du schreibst ein Blog über deinen Traumberuf.

Schreib:

* was dein Traumberuf ist und warum
* wie du deinen Wunsch erfüllen wirst
* was deine Eltern und Freunde darüber denken
* was dir wichtiger ist, viel Geld oder nette Kollegen.

Du musst ungefähr **90** Wörter auf **Deutsch** schreiben. Schreib etwas über alle Punkte der Aufgabe.

[16 marks]

Strategie

Make sure you plan your time. Read the questions carefully before you decide which one to do in each section. You might then find it best to do the one which you find easiest first.

Make sure that you have some time at the end to go back over what you've written.

When checking your work, make sure you cover the following points:

* Have I covered all of the bullet points?
* Have I put all of the verbs in the right place with the right endings?
* Do all the nouns have capital letters?
* Is everything spelt correctly?
* Are the endings after *mit* and other prepositions all correct?
* Have I remembered to put in lots of the little phrases that I learned?
* Have I put in lots of opinions and the reasons for them?
* Have I included the past tense and future tense?
* Have I used plenty of subordinate clauses?
* Is it legible?

Either:

2a 🖊 Du siehst eine Anzeige in der Zeitung. Ein Restaurant sucht einen Kellner / eine Kellnerin. Schreib eine Bewerbung.

Schreib:

• deinen Lebenslauf
• warum du den Job haben willst.

Du musst ungefähr **150** Wörter auf **Deutsch** schreiben. Schreib etwas über beide Punkte der Aufgabe.

[32 marks]

Or:

2b 🖊 Du schreibst einen Eintrag für ein Internet-Forum über deine Berufswahl.

Schreib:

• warum du nicht auf die Uni gehen willst
• warum du eine Lehre machen willst.

Du musst ungefähr **150** Wörter auf **Deutsch** schreiben. Schreib etwas über beide Punkte der Aufgabe.

[32 marks]

3 🅣 Translate the paragraph into German.

> I want to do an English course, because I need a foreign language when I go to university. My careers adviser told me that it is much better if I have that on my CV. When I learnt English in school, I liked it, although I found it terribly difficult. But I will do my best.

[12 marks]

4 🅣 Translate the paragraph into German.

> My employer says that I must do a course in business management. Then he will employ more people and I will be the boss. This is certainly an excellent opportunity for me. If I were the boss, I would have more money. After I left university, I didn't have any money at all.

[12 marks]

Foundation test and revise tasks are available in the Foundation book.

Higher – Speaking

1 ▷ Role play

Your teacher or partner will play the part of your German exchange partner and will speak first.

You should address your exchange partner as *du*.

When you see this – **!** – you will have to respond to something you have not prepared.

When you see this – **?** – you will have to ask a question.

> Du sprichst mit deinem deutschen Austauschpartner / deiner deutschen Austauschpartnerin über deine Schule.
>
> • Deine Klasse.
> • **!**
> • Pflichtfächer.
> • Nach der Schule (**zwei** Details).
> • **?** Lehrer.

[15 marks]

2 ▷ Role play

Your teacher or partner will play the part of your friend and will speak first.

You should address your friend as *du*.

When you see this – **!** – you will have to respond to something you have not prepared.

When you see this – **?** – you will have to ask a question.

> Du sprichst mit einem österreichischen Freund / einer österreichischen Freundin über deinen Berufswunsch.
>
> • Beruf – welchen.
> • **!**
> • Arbeitspraktikum.
> • **?** Geld.
> • Dein Nebenjob.

[15 marks]

3 Photo card

- Look at the photo during the preparation period.
- Make any notes you wish to on an Additional Answer Sheet.
- Your teacher or partner will then ask you questions about the photo and related to the topics of **My studies** and **Life at school / college**.

Your teacher or partner will ask you the following three questions and then **two more questions** which you have not prepared.

- Was gibt es auf dem Foto?
- Was machst du am Computer?
- Welches Schulfach macht dir am meisten Spaß? Warum?

[15 marks]

4 Photo card

- Look at the photo during the preparation period.
- Make any notes you wish to on an Additional Answer Sheet.
- Your teacher or partner will then ask you questions about the photo and related to the topics of **Education post-16** and **Jobs, career choices and ambitions**.

Your teacher or partner will ask you the following three questions and then **two more questions** which you have not prepared.

- Was gibt es auf dem Foto?
- Wo möchtest du arbeiten? Warum?
- Was ist dein Traumberuf?

[15 marks]

> **Strategie**
>
> We often only glance at photos, so one way to prepare is to look at some photos beforehand. Look at each photograph carefully and note everything that you can actually see or that you think about when looking at it. Practise describing people and things, including what they look like, what the people are doing, how large any buildings are, what colour things are and so on. Don't forget to give a few opinions, which you can also have ready, for example: *Das Wetter im Foto ist schlecht. Ich mag schlechtes Wetter nicht.*

> Foundation test and revise tasks are available in the Foundation book.

G Grammatik

Contents

■ Glossary of terms

Adjectives   *die Adjektive*

Words that describe somebody or something:

groß   big   *blau*   blue

Adverbs   *die Adverbien*

Words that describe an action:

*Ich laufe **schnell**.*   I run fast.

Articles (definite   *die Artikel*
and indefinite)

The words 'the' and 'a':

der, die, das   the

ein, eine, ein   a

Cases

They tell you what words are doing in the sentence.

The nominative case is used for the subject:

***Der Junge** spielt Klavier.*

The accusative case is used for the object and after some prepositions:

*Amelie kauft **einen Kuli**.*

*Ich fahre durch **die Stadt**.*

The dative case is used for the indirect object and after some prepositions:

*Ich gebe **dem Kind** einen Apfel.*

*Die Katze ist neben **der Lampe**.*

The genitive case is used to indicate possession:

*Hier ist das Auto **meiner Mutter**.*

Infinitive   *der Infinitiv*

The name of the verb as listed in the dictionary and always ends in *-en*:

spielen   to play

gehen   to go

haben   to have

sein   to be

Nouns   *die Nomen*

Words for somebody or something:

*das **Haus***

*der **Bruder***

*die **Tür***

Susanne

Object   *das Objekt*

A person or thing affected by the verb:

*Ich esse **einen Apfel**.*

*Ich spiele **Tennis**.*

Prepositions   *die Präpositionen*

Words used with nouns to give information about where, when, how, with whom:

mit, aus, nach, zu, in, …

Pronouns   *die Pronomen*

Short words used instead of a noun or name:

ich   I

du   you

er   he / it

sie   she / it

es   it

Singular and plural

Singular refers to just one thing or person:

Hund, Bruder

Plural refers to more than one thing or person:

Hunde, Brüder

Subject   *das Subjekt*

A person or thing 'doing' the verb:

***Martina** lernt Deutsch.*

***Ich** gehe ins Kino.*

***Mein Haus** hat zwei Schlafzimmer.*

Verbs   *die Verben*

They express an action or state:

ich wohne   I live

ich habe   I have

ich bin   I am

ich mag   I like

1   Number and gender

Number

Many words in German change according to whether they are **singular** or **plural**. You use the singular when there is only one of something or someone. You use the plural when there is more than one of something or someone:

das Auto	the car	*die Autos*	the cars
ich wohne	I live	*wir wohnen*	we live

Gender

Many words in German also change according to whether they are **masculine**, **feminine** or **neuter**. This is called grammatical gender. It does not exist in English, but it does in most other languages.

The grammatical gender of something has nothing to do with its sex or gender in real life. For instance, in German, 'table' is masculine but 'girl' is neuter!

Articles

Articles are words like 'the' and 'a', and are usually used with nouns. There are three kinds of article in German: **definite** (the), **indefinite** (a) and **negative** (not a). The **gender** of an article must match the gender of the word(s) it is with. Its **number** must match the number of the word(s) it is with. In the plural, all genders have the same article.

The definite article: *der, die, das, die*

The definite article means 'the'.

masculine	feminine	neuter	plural
der	*die*	*das*	*die*

*Das ist **der** Tisch.*   That is the table.

The indefinite article: *ein, eine, ein*

The indefinite article means 'a' or 'an'. There is no plural because 'a' has no plural!

masculine	feminine	neuter
ein	*eine*	*ein*

*Das ist **ein** Tisch.*   That is a table.

You do not use the indefinite article in German if you are talking about what job someone does or what nationality they are, or for ailments:

Ich bin Lehrerin.	I'm **a** teacher.
Er ist Deutscher.	He's **a** German.
Sie hat Halsschmerzen.	She has **a** sore throat.

The negative article: *kein, keine, kein, keine*

The negative article means 'not a', 'not any' or 'no'.

masculine	feminine	neuter	plural
kein	*keine*	*kein*	*keine*

*Das ist **kein** Tisch.*   That is not a table. /
That isn't a table.

Nouns

A noun is a word used to name something. Nouns are objects or things, but not all nouns are things that can be touched (e.g. laughter). A good test of a noun is whether or not you can put 'the' in front of it (e.g. the book ✓; the have ✗).

All German nouns are either **masculine**, **feminine** or **neuter**, and either **singular** or **plural**. When you see a noun, you can often work out its **gender** or **number** from its **article**.

masculine	feminine	neuter	plural
der Tisch	*die Tasche*	*das Heft*	*die Hefte*

Plurals of nouns

There are different ways of making nouns plural in German, just as in English. Unfortunately, there isn't really a quick rule – you just have to get the feel of them!

- Feminine nouns which end in **-e** usually just add **-n**: *eine Katze – zwei Katz**en***
- Some nouns stay the same in the plural: *ein Hamster – drei Hamster*
- Some nouns (mainly those borrowed from English) just add **-s**, as in English: *ein Auto – zwei Auto**s***
- Some nouns add **-e**: *ein Hund – drei Hund**e***
- Some nouns add **-e**, but also take an umlaut (¨) on the first vowel: *eine Maus – hundert M**ä**use*
- A few nouns add **-er**: *ein Ei – sechs Ei**er***
- Some nouns add **-er** and take an umlaut on the first vowel: *ein Mann – zwei M**ä**nn**er***

Weak nouns

There is a small group of nouns that are called weak nouns. They add an **-(e)n** ending in the accusative, dative and genitive singular and all plural forms. (For cases, see Section 2.)

	singular	plural
nominative	*der Junge*	*die Jungen*
accusative	*den Jungen*	*die Jungen*
genitive	*des Jungen*	*der Jungen*
dative	*dem Jungen*	*den Jungen*

Possessive adjectives

Possessive adjectives are words like 'my', 'your', 'his' and 'her'. Their gender and number must match (or 'agree with') the noun they refer to and their endings change (just like *der*, *ein*, etc.).

Their endings follow the same pattern as *kein* (see page 178).

	masculine	feminine	neuter	plural
my	*mein*	*meine*	*mein*	*meine*
your	*dein*	*deine*	*dein*	*deine*
his	*sein*	*seine*	*sein*	*seine*
her	*ihr*	*ihre*	*ihr*	*ihre*
our	*unser*	*unsere*	*unser*	*unsere*
your	*euer*	*eure*	*euer*	*eure*
their	*ihr*	*ihre*	*ihr*	*ihre*

mein Bruder	my brother
deine Schwester	your sister
sein Vater	his father
ihre Schwestern	her sisters

Demonstrative adjectives and quantifiers

Demonstrative adjectives are words like 'this' or 'that' and quantifiers are words like 'each' or 'every'. You use them in sentences such as these:

Diese Hose ist schön.	These trousers are nice.
Jedes Kind darf mitmachen.	Each child may join in.

masculine	feminine	neuter	plural
dieser Mann	*diese* Frau	*dieses* Kleid	*diese* Röcke
jeder Mann	*jede* Frau	*jedes* Kleid	–

Interrogative adjectives

The interrogative adjective 'which' is used in questions (see also Interrogatives (question words), page 190).

Welcher Pullover ist zu klein? Which pullover is too small?

masculine	feminine	neuter	plural
welcher Mann	*welche* Frau	*welches* Kleid	*welche* Röcke

2 Case

Besides number and gender, German nouns and the words that go with them have a **case**. The way cases work is quite complex, but they tell you certain simple things about the noun.

The nominative

A word is in the nominative if it is the **subject** or 'doer' of an action (and actions include words like 'is').

Der Tisch ist braun.	The table is brown.
Mein Bruder wohnt in London.	My brother lives in London.
Diese Katze ist launisch.	This cat is moody.

	masculine	feminine	neuter	plural
the	*der*	*die*	*das*	*die*
a	*ein*	*eine*	*ein*	–
not a	*kein*	*keine*	*kein*	*keine*
my	*mein*	*meine*	*mein*	*meine*
this	*dieser*	*diese*	*dieses*	*diese*
each	*jeder*	*jede*	*jedes*	–
which	*welcher*	*welche*	*welches*	*welche*

The accusative

For the **object** of most verbs (like *haben* or *es gibt*), and after some **prepositions**, you use the accusative.

Der, ein, mein, etc. are different in the accusative – but only in the masculine form.

Ich habe **einen** *Bruder.*	I have a brother.
Er hat **keinen** *Stuhl.*	He hasn't got a chair.
Es gibt **einen** *Supermarkt.*	There's a supermarket.
Er geht in **den** *Park.*	He goes into the park.

	masculine	feminine	neuter	plural
the	*den*	*die*	*das*	*die*
a	*einen*	*eine*	*ein*	–
not a	*keinen*	*keine*	*kein*	*keine*
my	*meinen*	*meine*	*mein*	*meine*
this	*diesen*	*diese*	*dieses*	*diese*
each	*jeden*	*jede*	*jedes*	–
which	*welchen*	*welche*	*welches*	*welche*

The dative

After some **prepositions** (e.g. *zu*, *mit*) you use the dative. Words like *ein*, *mein*, etc. are different in the dative. You will have to learn them.

mit **dem** *Mann*	with the man
mit **meinem** *Bruder*	with my brother

	masculine	feminine	neuter	plural
the	*dem*	*der*	*dem*	*den*
a	*einem*	*einer*	*einem*	–
not a	*keinem*	*keiner*	*keinem*	*keinen*
my	*meinem*	*meiner*	*meinem*	*meinen*
this	*diesem*	*dieser*	*diesem*	*diesen*
each	*jedem*	*jeder*	*jedem*	–
which	*welchem*	*welcher*	*welchem*	*welchen*

In the plural, an extra **-*(e)n*** is added to the end of the noun.
*Ich komme mit meinen Brüder**n**.* I am coming with my
brothers.
Some prepositions combine with *dem, der, dem* to make
shortened forms (see Section 3).

The genitive

You use the genitive to indicate **possession** (and with
certain **prepositions**). Words like *ein* and *mein* are
different in the genitive. You will have to learn them.
In English, we say 'my brother's room' but in German you
have to say 'the room of my brother'. The 'of my' part is
incorporated into one word – *meines / meiner*.
*Das Zimmer mein**es** Bruder**s** …*
*Das Zimmer mein**er** Schwester …*
*Das Zimmer mein**es** Kind**es** …*
Note the extra **-*(e)s*** on the end of masculine and
neuter nouns.

	masculine	feminine	neuter	plural
the	*des Bruders*	*der Schwester*	*des Kindes*	*der Kinder*
a	*eines Bruders*	*einer Schwester*	*eines Kindes*	–
not a	*keines Bruders*	*keiner Schwester*	*keines Kindes*	*keiner Kinder*
my	*meines Bruders*	*meiner Schwester*	*meines Kindes*	*meiner Kinder*
this	*dieses Bruders*	*dieser Schwester*	*dieses Kindes*	*dieser Kinder*
each	*jedes Bruders*	*jeder Schwester*	*jedes Kindes*	–
which	*welches Bruders*	*welcher Schwester*	*welches Kindes*	*welcher Kinder*

3 Other parts of a German sentence

Prepositions

Prepositions are words that tell you **where** things are (or
their 'position'), for example 'on', 'under', 'by', 'at', 'with'.

Prepositions + dative

These prepositions are always followed by the dative:

ab	from (time)	*nach*	after, to
aus	from, out of	*seit*	since, for (a
bei	at the house of, with		period of time)
gegenüber	opposite	*von*	from, by, of
mit	with, by (transport)	*zu*	to

Shortened forms

zu dem → *zum*		*bei dem* → *beim*
zu der → *zur*		*von dem* → *vom*
zur *Schule*		to school
*gegenüber **dem** Haus*		opposite the house
*bei **ihnen***		at their house

Prepositions + accusative

These prepositions are always followed by the accusative:

bis	until	*gegen*	against
durch	through	*ohne*	without
für	for	*um*	around
*für **meine** Freundin*		for my friend	
*um **die** Ecke*		around the corner	
*ohne **die** Geschenke*		without the gifts	
*durch **den** Tunnel*		through the tunnel	

Prepositions + dative or accusative

Most of the prepositions you have met are sometimes
followed by the dative and sometimes (but not as often)
by the accusative. Here is a list of them with their meaning
when followed by the dative:

an	at, on (vertical)	*über*	over, above
auf	on (horizontal)	*unter*	under, underneath
hinter	behind	*vor*	in front of
in	in	*zwischen*	between
neben	near, next to		
*an **der** Wand*		on the wall	
*auf **einem** Tisch*		on a table	
*in **seiner** Tasche*		in his pocket	
*unter **dem** Bett*		under the bed	

Usually when there is movement involved (e.g. 'into'
rather than 'in'), these same prepositions are followed by
the accusative.

an	up to, over to	*über*	(go) over, across
auf	onto	*unter*	(go) under
hinter	(go) behind	*vor*	(go) in front of
in	into	*zwischen*	(go) between
neben	(go) next to, beside		

Shortened forms

in das → ins	an das → ans
in dem → im	an dem → am
in **die** Schule	into school
ins Schwimmbad	into the swimming pool
auf **den** Tisch	on to the table
Die Katze geht unter **den** Stuhl.	The cat goes under the chair.
Der Hund springt über **die** CDs.	The dog jumps over the CDs.

Prepositions + genitive

These prepositions are always followed by the genitive:

(an)statt	instead of
außerhalb	outside of, excluding
innerhalb	inside of, within
trotz	in spite of
während	during
wegen	because of
wegen **des** Wetters	because of the weather
außerhalb **der** Stadt	outside of the town
während **der** Reise	during the journey

Adjectives

Adjectives are words that describe nouns. When adjectives come **after** the noun, they work just like English adjectives.

Die Blume ist **schön**.	The flower is pretty.
Das Haus ist **rot**.	The house is red.

However, when adjectives come **before** the noun, you have to give them an ending.

Here are the adjective endings for nominative, accusative, dative, genitive and plural nouns after der / die / das / die.

	masculine	feminine	neuter	plural
nominative	der schöne Park	die schöne Stadt	das schöne Haus	die schönen Blumen
accusative	den schönen Park	die schöne Stadt	das schöne Haus	die schönen Blumen
genitive	des schönen Parkes	der schönen Stadt	des schönen Hauses	der schönen Blumen
dative	dem schönen Park	der schönen Stadt	dem schönen Haus	den schönen Blumen

Here are the adjective endings for nominative, accusative, dative and genitive nouns after ein / eine / ein. Note that the genitive and dative adjective endings are all **-en**.

	masculine	feminine	neuter	plural
nominative	ein schöner Park	eine schöne Stadt	ein schönes Haus	schöne Blumen
accusative	einen schönen Park	eine schöne Stadt	ein schönes Haus	schöne Blumen
genitive	eines schönen Parkes	einer schönen Stadt	eines schönen Hauses	schönen Blumen
dative	einem schönen Park	einer schönen Stadt	einem schönen Haus	schönen Blumen

Adjectives as nouns

Adjectives can be used as nouns by giving them a capital letter and adding the correct adjective ending. This is most common when using an adjective of nationality to talk about a person:

deutsch	German
der Deutsche / ein Deutscher	the / a German (m)
die Deutsche / eine Deutsche	the / a German (f)

The noun behaves like an adjective, as if another noun were to follow it.

Adjectives after etwas / nichts, etc.

After the following words, an adjective changes its form: etwas (something), nichts (nothing), viel (much), wenig (little), alles (all).

If you want to say 'something interesting' or 'nothing new', for example, the adjective gains a capital letter (becomes a noun) and you add **-es** to the end of it:

etwas Interessant**es**

nichts Neu**es**

After alles (everything), you just add **-e** to the adjective. You may already be familiar with the form Alles Gute (all the best) at the end of informal cards or letters.

Comparative and superlative adjectives

Comparative

When comparing two things in English, we usually add -er, for example 'quick – quicker'. This applies in German as well.

schnell → schnell**er**

There are some exceptions, however, where an umlaut (¨) is added to the vowel. Some common ones are:

alt → älter   jung → jünger

groß → größer   kalt → kälter

In English, we stop adding -er to longer adjectives and use 'more', e.g. 'more interesting'. In German, though, **-er** is added to all adjectives:

interessant → interessant**er**

To say 'than' when making a comparison, use **als**.

Mein Haus ist größer **als** deine Wohnung.   My house is bigger than your flat.

Superlative

When talking about 'the youngest', 'the quickest', etc., add **-st** to the adjective, plus the usual adjective endings. Add an umlaut if there is one in the comparative form.

Lisa ist das j**üngste** Mädchen.   Lisa is the youngest girl.

To make the superlative adjective into a noun, give the superlative form a capital letter and add the correct adjective ending.

der Jüng**ste**   die Jüng**ste**

das Jüng**ste**   die Jüng**sten**

Max ist **der Jüngste** in der Klasse.   Max is the youngest in the class.

Adverbs

Adverbs are used to qualify the action of the verb.

Der Bus ist **langsam**.   The bus is slow. (adjective)

Ich gehe **langsam** in die Schule.   I walk to school slowly. (adverb)

In English we add -ly to make the adverb, but in German the adjective and adverb forms are the same.

Comparative and superlative adverbs

You form the comparative of adverbs by adding **-er** (and an umlaut for some adverbs). Use **als** to compare.

Ich laufe schnell**er als** mein Bruder.   I run faster than my brother.

For the superlative form, use **am** before the adverb and add **-sten** to the end. (And add an umlaut if there is one in the comparative form.)

Ich laufe **am** schnell**sten**.   I run the fastest.

Adverbs of time and place

immer	always	oft	often
manchmal	sometimes	draußen	outside
selten	rarely	dort	there
nie	never	hier	here
normalerweise	normally		

Adverbs of degree (quantifiers / intensifiers)

Adverbs of degree qualify other adverbs and adjectives.

sehr	very	ein bisschen	a little, a bit
ziemlich	fairly	viel	a lot
zu	too	ganz	quite, rather
fast	almost	ein wenig	a little
Du isst **zu** schnell.		You eat too quickly.	

Interrogative adverbs

Interrogative adverbs are used when asking questions and need to be learnt (see also Interrogatives (question words), page 190).

Wann?	When?	Wie viel?	How much?
Warum?	Why?	Wer?	Who?
Wo?	Where?	Was?	What?
Wie?	How?		

Adverbial phrases

Adverbial phrases give additional information about when, where or how an action takes place. Examples are:

nach dem Essen	after the meal
vor der Schule	before school
jeden Tag	every day
ab und zu	now and again
letzte Woche	last week
nächstes Wochenende	next weekend
so bald wie möglich	as soon as possible

If an adverbial phrase is used at the beginning of a sentence, remember to adjust the word order and to return the verb to its second idea position by swapping around the verb and subject.

Pronouns

Words for 'you'

There are **three** German words for 'you', depending on the number of people and your relationship to them.

du Informal singular – for talking to one young person or friend: Kommst **du** mit?

ihr Informal plural – for talking to more than one young person or friend: Kommt **ihr** mit?

Sie Formal singular or plural – for talking to one or more than one older person or stranger: Kommen **Sie** mit?

Words for 'it'

The German word for 'it' is not always es! It depends on the gender of the noun 'it' refers to. For the nominative case, you use er (m), sie (f) and es (n). So das Buch is es, but die Banane is sie. Don't be put off by the fact that er and sie also mean 'he' and 'she' – it should be clear from the context what the particular meaning is.

*Ich habe einen Apfel. **Er** ist lecker.*
I have an apple. It is delicious.

Subject pronouns

Subject pronouns are words like 'I', 'you', 'he', etc. They are usually used with a verb.

ich	I	*wir*	we
du	you (informal singular)	*ihr*	you (informal plural)
er	he		
sie	she	*Sie*	you (formal singular or plural)
es	it		
man	one, people, you (non-specific)	*sie*	they

The subject pronoun *man* is used when you are not talking about anyone in particular. It is used to say 'one', 'people', 'you', 'they' or 'we'.

***Man** darf nicht rauchen.*	You're not allowed to smoke.
***Man** muss eine Uniform tragen.*	We have to wear a uniform.

Object pronouns

Object pronouns are used to replace the object in a sentence. **Direct objects** are in the **accusative** and **indirect objects** in the **dative**.

	accusative	dative
me	*mich*	*mir*
you (inf sing)	*dich*	*dir*
him / her / it	*ihn / sie / es*	*ihm / ihr / ihm*
us	*uns*	*uns*
you (inf pl)	*euch*	*euch*
them / you (form)	*sie / Sie*	*ihnen / Ihnen*

*Nimmst du Toby mit nach Köln? Ja, ich nehme **ihn** mit nach Köln.* (direct object)

*Gibst du mir bitte ein Eis? Ja, ich gebe **dir** ein Eis.* (indirect object)

Reflexive pronouns

Reflexive pronouns are used with reflexive verbs, which are listed in the infinitive with *sich*, e.g. *sich fühlen, sich waschen, sich treffen*. The reflexive pronoun usually changes as follows:

*ich fühle **mich***	*wir fühlen **uns***
*du fühlst **dich***	*ihr fühlt **euch***
*er / sie / es / man fühlt **sich***	*sie / Sie fühlen **sich***

Some reflexive verbs use *mir* and *dir* etc. (dative reflexive pronouns) instead of *mich* and *dich* etc. (accusative reflexive pronouns).

*Ich wasche **mich**.*	I wash. (lit. I wash myself.)

This is the usual accusative reflexive pronoun.

*Ich putze **mir** die Zähne.*	I brush my teeth. (lit. I clean the teeth to me.)
*Du bürstest **dir** die Haare.*	You brush your hair. (lit. You brush the hair to you.)

These last two examples use dative reflexive pronouns.

Relative pronouns and clauses

Relative pronouns (who, whom, which, that) are used to introduce a relative clause. In German, they vary according to the **gender** and **number** of the word they refer back to, and their **case** depends on their function in the relative clause. The verb in the relative clause goes to the end.

These examples show the nominative form for each gender:

*Das ist mein Bruder, **der** Jürgen heißt.*	This is my brother, who is called Jürgen.
*Ingrid, **die** sehr schön ist, kommt heute.*	Ingrid, who is very beautiful, is coming today.
*Das Meerschweinchen, **das** sehr klein ist, ist schwarz.*	The guinea pig, which is very small, is black.

Relative clauses can also be introduced by question words like 'where' and 'why'.

*Meine Schule hat ein Sprachlabor, **wo** ich Französisch lerne.*	My school has a language lab where I learn French.

Here are the relative pronouns in all the cases.

	masculine	feminine	neuter	plural
nominative	*der*	*die*	*das*	*die*
accusative	*den*	*die*	*das*	*die*
genitive	*dessen*	*deren*	*dessen*	*deren*
dative	*dem*	*der*	*dem*	*denen*

*Das ist der Junge, **den** ich gesehen habe.*	That's the boy (whom) I saw.
*Der Mann, mit **dem** ich gesprochen habe, ist obdachlos.*	The man with whom I spoke is homeless.
*Hier ist die Dame, **deren** Handtasche ich gefunden habe.*	Here is the lady whose handbag I found.

Was can be used as a relative prounoun, meaning 'that' or 'which'. Use it when the relative pronoun doesn't refer to a noun or after *alles, etwas, vieles* or *nichts*.

Ludo ist mitgekommen,
was *echt toll war!*
Alles, **was** *du mir sagst, ist*
interessant.

Ludo came with us, which was really great!
Everything (which / that) you say to me is interesting.

Interrogative pronouns

Words for 'who' and 'whom'

When you're using 'who' in a question, use *wer*.

Wer ist dein Chemielehrer?   Who is your chemistry teacher?

If you're asking 'what kind of' in a question, use *was für*.

Was für einen Hund hast du?   What kind of a dog have you got?

In German, there are two words for 'whom': *wen* and *wem*. Use *wen* after prepositions taking the accusative and *wem* after prepositions taking the dative.

Für **wen** *hatte er das Buch gekauft?*	For whom had he bought the book? (or more commonly you might say 'Who did he buy the book for?')
Mit **wem** *hast du gegessen?*	With whom did you eat? or Who did you eat with?

Words for 'when'

Wenn means 'when', 'if' or 'whenever' and is used to refer to the present, future or a habitual action in the past.

Wenn *ich nach Deutschland fuhr, habe ich immer bei meinem Brieffreund gewohnt.*

When I used to go to Germany, I always stayed with my penfriend.

Als means 'when' and refers to a particular event in the past.

Als *ich in Deutschland war, habe ich bei meinem Brieffreund gewohnt.*

When I was in Germany (one occasion), I stayed with my penfriend.

Wann introduces a 'when' question, in any tense.

Wann *hast du bei deinem Brieffreund gewohnt?*

When did you stay with your penfriend?

4 Verbs

The present tense

Verbs are 'doing words' – they describe actions. You use a **noun** (e.g. *mein Bruder*) or a **pronoun** (*ich, du*, etc.) as the **subject** or doer of the action. For each different person or pronoun, you need to use the correct verb ending.

Regular verbs

In the present tense, regular (or weak) verbs (verbs which follow the usual pattern) have the following endings:

*ich spiel***e**	I play, I'm playing
*du spiel***st***	you play, you're playing
*er spiel***t**	he plays, he's playing
*sie spiel***t**	she plays, she's playing
*es spiel***t**	it plays, it's playing
*man spiel***t**	one plays, one's playing
*wir spiel***en**	we play, we're playing
*ihr spiel***t***	you play, you're playing
*sie spiel***en**	they play, they're playing
*Sie spiel***en***	you play, you're playing

*For *du / ihr / Sie* ('you') see Words for 'you', page 182.

Ich *spiel***e** *Tennis.*	I play tennis.
Mein Onkel *spiel***t** *gern Fußball.*	My uncle likes playing football.
Sie *spiel***en** *Schach.*	They're playing chess.

Other verbs that work like this are:

machen	to do	*kochen*	to cook
kaufen	to buy	*wohnen*	to live (location)

Regular verbs which end in **-ten** (e.g. *antworten* – to answer) add **-est** in the *du* form and **-et** in the *er / sie / es / man* form.

*Warum antwort***est** *du nicht?* Why don't you answer?

Irregular verbs

Irregular (or strong) verbs use the same endings as regular verbs, but there is a difference: the first vowel usually changes in the *du* and *er / sie / es* forms.

laufen (to run, to walk)

ich laufe	*wir laufen*
*du l***äu***fst*	*ihr lauft*
*er / sie / es / man l***äu***ft*	*sie / Sie laufen*

essen (to eat)

ich esse	*wir essen*
du **i***sst*	*ihr esst*
er / sie / es / man **i***sst*	*sie / Sie essen*

Other common verbs in this category are: *fallen, fahren, helfen, schlafen, geben, tragen* and *treffen*.

Some irregular verbs change their vowel sound more radically, such as *lesen* and *sehen*.

lesen (to read)

ich lese	*wir lesen*
*du l***ie***st*	*ihr lest*
*er / sie / es / man l***ie***st*	*sie / Sie lesen*

Haben

Another important irregular verb is *haben* (to have) which drops the *b* in the *du* and *er / sie / es* forms.

ich habe	wir haben
du **hast**	ihr habt
er / sie / es / man **hat**	sie / Sie haben

Sein

The verb *sein* (to be) is totally different and must be learnt!

ich **bin**	wir **sind**
du **bist**	ihr **seid**
er / sie / es / man **ist**	sie / Sie **sind**

Modal verbs

These are verbs like 'will', 'must', 'can' and 'could', and they usually have to be used with another verb, which is in the **infinitive** and goes to the **end** of the sentence.

Usually, the singular forms of modal verbs are different from others because the vowel changes. An exception to this is *sollen* (should, ought to). For all modal verbs there is no **-e** ending for the first person singular.

müssen (must, to have to)	**mögen** (to like)
ich **muss**	ich **mag**
du **musst**	du **magst**
er / sie / es / man **muss**	er / sie / es /man **mag**
wir **müssen**	wir **mögen**
ihr **müsst**	ihr **mögt**
sie / Sie **müssen**	sie / Sie **mögen**

wollen (to want to)	**können** (can, to be able to)
ich **will**	ich **kann**
du **willst**	du **kannst**
er / sie / es / man **will**	er / sie / es / man **kann**
wir **wollen**	wir **können**
ihr **wollt**	ihr **könnt**
sie / Sie **wollen**	sie / Sie **können**

dürfen (may, to be allowed to)	**sollen** (to be supposed to, should)
ich **darf**	ich **soll**
du **darfst**	du **sollst**
er / sie / es / man **darf**	er / sie / es / man **soll**
wir **dürfen**	wir **sollen**
ihr **dürft**	ihr **sollt**
sie / Sie **dürfen**	sie / Sie **sollen**
Ich **will** mein Geld nicht verschwenden.	I don't want to waste my money.
Sie **soll** das Rauchen aufgeben.	She is supposed to give up smoking.

Separable verbs

Some verbs are in **two parts**. They consist of the **normal verb** and a **separable prefix**.

The normal verb goes in the usual place (see Verb as second idea, page 189), but the prefix goes at the end of the sentence. When listed in a dictionary or glossary, the separable prefix is always listed first.

Here is a separable verb, *einkaufen* (to shop), in full:

ich **kaufe ein**	wir **kaufen ein**
du **kaufst ein**	ihr **kauft ein**
er / sie / es / man **kauft ein**	sie / Sie **kaufen ein**
Ich **kaufe** am Montag **ein**.	I go shopping on Monday.
Er **kauft** mit seiner Mutter **ein**.	He goes shopping with his mother.
Sie **kaufen** in Berlin **ein**.	They go shopping in Berlin.

These are some other separable verbs you have met:

abwaschen (ich **wasche ab**)	to wash up
aufräumen (ich **räume auf**)	to tidy up
aufstehen (ich **stehe auf**)	to get up
ausgeben (ich **gebe aus**)	to spend (money)
aufmachen (ich **mache auf**)	to open
ansehen (ich **sehe an**)	to look at
fernsehen (ich **sehe fern**)	to watch TV

Inseparable verbs

Some verbs look like they might have a separable prefix at the front but are in fact inseparable. These include any verbs starting with: be-, emp-, ent-, er-, ge-, miss-, ver- or zer-, e.g. *benutzen* (to use), *empfehlen* (to recommend), *enthalten* (to contain), *erzählen* (to tell), *gewinnen* (to win), *versuchen* (to try), *zerstören* (to destroy).

So these verbs don't split up like separable verbs and are formed in the normal way in the present tense.

The perfect tense

The perfect tense is used to talk about things that happened in the past.

It is made up of two parts: the **auxiliary** (or 'helping' verb) and the **past participle**. The auxiliary verb goes in the usual place (second): it is usually *haben*. The past participle goes at the end of the sentence.

The perfect tense with *haben*

To form the past participle, you take the -en off the infinitive of the verb. Then you (usually) add **ge-** to the beginning of the word and **-t** to the end.

ich **habe gespielt**	I played, I have played
du **hast gemacht**	you did, you have done
er / sie / es / man **hat gekauft**	he / she / it bought, he / she / it has bought

wir **haben gespielt**	we played, we have played
ihr **habt gemacht**	you did, you have done
sie / Sie **haben gekauft**	they / you bought, they / you have bought

Verbs which begin with **ver-** and **be-** and verbs which end in **-ieren** do not add the ge- to the beginning.

Ich **habe versucht**.	I tried.
Ich **habe** Gabi **besucht**.	I visited Gabi.
Hast du dich **amüsiert**?	Did you enjoy yourself?

With separable verbs, the **ge-** goes after the separable prefix.

Ich **habe** in der Stadt **eingekauft**.	I went shopping in town.

Irregular past participles

Some verbs are irregular in the perfect tense. They still make their perfect tense with *haben*, but the past participle is formed differently. You (usually) change the **vowel** in the participle and keep the **-en** from the infinitive on the end:

essen (to eat)	*gegessen*
lesen (to read)	*gelesen*
sehen (to see)	*gesehen*
finden (to find)	*gefunden*
trinken (to drink)	*getrunken*
nehmen (to take)	*genommen*
schreiben (to write)	*geschrieben*
treffen (to meet)	*getroffen*
abwaschen (to wash up)	*abgewaschen*
anfangen (to begin)	*angefangen*
ansehen (to look at)	*angesehen*
fernsehen (to watch TV)	*ferngesehen*

Again, verbs which begin with *be-, emp-, ent-, er-, ge-, miss-, ver-* or *zer-* do not add the ge- to the beginning of the verb.

Ich **habe begonnen**.	I began.
Ich **habe vergessen**.	I forgot.

The perfect tense with *sein*

Another group of verbs form their perfect tense with *sein* (to be). These are usually verbs of movement. As with the other verbs, the auxiliary (*sein*) is in second place and the participle is at the end of the sentence.

Here are the ones you have learnt so far:

fahren → *ich bin gefahren*	I went / drove, I have gone / driven
gehen → *ich bin gegangen*	I went / walked, I have gone / walked
kommen → *ich bin gekommen*	I came, I have come
fliegen → *ich bin geflogen*	I flew, I have flown
fallen → *ich bin gefallen*	I fell, I have fallen
laufen → *ich bin gelaufen*	I ran, I have run

ich **bin gefahren**
du **bist gegangen**
er / sie / es / man **ist gekommen**
wir **sind geflogen**
ihr **seid gefahren**
sie / Sie **sind gekommen**

With separable verbs, the **ge-** goes after the separable prefix.

Ich **bin** um 7 Uhr **aufgestanden**.

The imperfect tense

Regular verbs

The imperfect tense is another way of talking about the past, but is not usually used in speech.

To form the imperfect tense, take the infinitive of the verb, remove the -en and add the endings as follows:

ich spiel**te**	wir spiel**ten**
du spiel**test**	ihr spiel**tet**
er / sie / es / man spiel**te**	sie / Sie spiel**ten**

Irregular verbs

Irregular (strong) verbs have set stems to which the following endings are added. Note that nothing is added in the *ich* and *er / sie / es / man* forms. This example shows the endings for *fahren* (to travel, to drive):

ich fuhr	wir fuhr**en**
du fuh**rst**	ihr fuhr**t**
er / sie / es / man fuhr	sie / Sie fuhr**en**

Some common stems are as follows:

beginnen (to begin)	*begann*
essen (to eat)	*aß*
gehen (to go)	*ging*
lesen (to read)	*las*
sehen (to see)	*sah*
trinken (to drink)	*trank*

Some verbs are mixed verbs and have set stems but add regular endings, e.g. *bringen*.

ich brach**te**	wir brach**ten**
du brach**test**	ihr brach**tet**
er / sie / es / man brach**te**	sie / Sie brach**ten**

Other examples are:

denken (to think)	*dachte*
kennen (to know)	*kannte*

The most common irregular forms used, and ones to learn, are:

sein (to be)

ich **war**

du **warst**

er / sie / es / man **war**

wir **waren**

ihr **wart**

sie / Sie **waren**

haben (to have)

ich **hatte**

du **hattest**

er / sie / es / man **hatte**

wir **hatten**

ihr **hattet**

sie / Sie **hatten**

It's also useful to remember the imperfect tense for *es gibt* (there is / are): *es gab* (there was / were).

Modal verbs

These are the imperfect tense forms for the modal verbs you have encountered.

müssen (must, to have to)

ich **musste**

du **musstest**

er / sie / es / man **musste**

wir **mussten**

ihr **musstet**

sie / Sie **mussten**

mögen (to like)

ich **mochte**

du **mochtest**

er / sie / es / man **mochte**

wir **mochten**

ihr **mochtet**

sie / Sie **mochten**

wollen (to want to)

ich **wollte**

du **wolltest**

er / sie / es / man **wollte**

wir **wollten**

ihr **wolltet**

sie / Sie **wollten**

können (can, to be able to)

ich **konnte**

du **konntest**

er / sie / es / man **konnte**

wir **konnten**

ihr **konntet**

sie / Sie **konnten**

dürfen (may, to be allowed to)

ich **durfte**

du **durftest**

er / sie / es / man **durfte**

wir **durften**

ihr **durftet**

sie / Sie **durften**

sollen (should, ought to)

ich **sollte**

du **solltest**

er / sie / es / man **sollte**

wir **sollten**

ihr **solltet**

sie / Sie **sollten**

The pluperfect tense

The pluperfect tense conveys a moment **further back** in time than the perfect tense and is formed with 'had' in English, e.g. 'By the time I was 16, I had moved house three times.' For verbs which form their perfect tense with *haben*, use the correct form of *haben* in the imperfect tense (*hatte*, etc.) plus the past participle.

ich **hatte gekauft** (I had bought)

du **hattest gekauft**

er / sie / es / man **hatte gekauft**

wir **hatten gekauft**

ihr **hattet gekauft**

sie / Sie **hatten gekauft**

For verbs which form their perfect tense with *sein*, use the correct form of *sein* in the imperfect tense (*war*, etc.) plus the past participle.

ich **war gegangen** (I had gone)

du **warst gegangen**

er / sie / es / man **war gegangen**

wir **waren gegangen**

ihr **wart gegangen**

sie / Sie **waren gegangen**

The future tense

Present tense with future meaning

As in English, the present tense can be used to convey a future meaning if a **future time indicator** is used.

Nächstes Jahr gehe ich auf die Uni.

I'm going to university next year.

Future tense with *werden*

To form the future tense, use the correct present tense form of the verb *werden* plus the infinitive.

Ich **werde** nach Berlin **fahren**.

I will travel to Berlin.*

ich **werde**

du **wirst**

er / sie / es / man **wird**

wir **werden**

ihr **werdet**

sie / Sie **werden**

*Remember that *ich will* doesn't mean 'I will', but 'I want to'.

The conditional tense

The conditional tense (strictly speaking, the conditional 'mood') uses 'would' and is used to talk about actions that are dependent on certain conditions being fulfilled. The easiest way of translating 'would like' into German is to use the following forms of *mögen*: *möchte / möchtest / möchten* (would like) with the infinitive of the second verb at the end of the sentence or clause.

Ich **möchte heiraten** und Kinder **haben**.

I'd like to get married and have children.

To form the standard conditional tense, use *ich würde, du würdest, er / sie / es / man würde, wir würden*, etc., plus the infinitive.

*Was **würdest** du mit einem Lottogewinn **machen**?*	What would you do with a lottery win?
*Ich **würde** um die Welt **fahren**.*	I would travel around the world.

The conditional (*würde* + infinitive) is often used with a *wenn* clause.

Wenn ich reich wäre, <u>würde</u> ich ein Flugzeug <u>kaufen</u>.

Note that <u>würde haben</u> und <u>würde sein</u> are normally replaced by **wäre** und **hätte**.

Wenn ich reich wäre, <u>würde</u> ich ein Flugzeug <u>haben</u>. →

*Wenn ich reich wäre, **hätte** ich ein Flugzeug.*

Wenn ich reich wäre, <u>würde</u> ich glücklich <u>sein</u>. →

*Wenn ich reich wäre, **wäre** ich glücklich.*

Wäre und **hätte** are known as **imperfect subjunctive** forms.

The verb in the *wenn* clause is also the imperfect subjunctive.

*Wenn ich reich **wäre**, …*

The most common imperfect subjunctive forms you'll come across are

wäre (would be), **hätte** (would have), **könnte** (could), **würde** (would), **möchte** (would like), **sollte** (ought to – This form is the same as the imperfect of *sollen*!).

You do not need to learn about subjunctive forms in detail at this stage, but you may want to find out more about them as you progress in your studies.

Infinitive constructions

Um … zu, ohne … zu, anstatt … zu

To say 'in order to', you use the construction *um … zu* plus the infinitive at the end of the clause. Note the comma before *um*.

*Ich treibe Sport, **um** gesund **zu** bleiben.*	I do sport in order to stay healthy.

Ohne … zu (without doing something) and *anstatt … zu* (instead of doing something) work in a similar way.

*Ich werde nach Amerika fliegen, **ohne** viel Geld aus**zu**geben.*	I will fly to America without spending a lot of money.*
*Ich werde in den Osterferien Ski fahren, **anstatt** auf meine Prüfungen **zu** lernen.*	I will go skiing in the Easter holidays instead of studying for my exams.

*Note that with separable verbs such as *ausgeben*, *zu* goes after the prefix.

Zu + infinitive

After modal verbs, you do not need *zu* (*Ich will mit dem Bus **fahren**.*), but after some verbs, the use of *zu* is required. Here are some of them:

beginnen	to begin
beschließen	to decide
helfen	to help
hoffen	to hope
vergessen	to forget
versuchen	to try
vorhaben	to intend
*Ich **versuche**, Energie **zu** sparen.*	I'm trying to save energy.

Impersonal verbs

Some verbs are 'impersonal', which means they do not have a subject like *ich* or *du*. They are used with the impersonal subject *es* (it).

If you want to say 'there is' or 'there are', you use *es gibt* with the accusative case.

Es gibt einen Supermarkt.	There is a supermarket.

If you want to say 'there is no' or 'there are no', use *es gibt* + *kein(e)(n)* + accusative case.

Es gibt kein Schwimmbad.	There is no swimming pool.

Other examples of impersonal verbs are:

Es tut mir leid.	I'm sorry.
Es geht.	It's OK.
Wie geht es dir?	How are you?
Mir geht's gut.	I'm well.
Es tut weh.	It hurts.

Nicht

Nicht means 'not' and it usually comes after the verb.

*Ich bin **nicht** doof.*	I am not stupid.

However, when there is an object in the sentence, *nicht* comes after the object.

*Lena mag Englisch **nicht**.*	Lena doesn't like English.

(Don't forget that you use *kein* to say 'not a'. See page 178.)

Other negatives

nie(mals)	never
*Ich gehe **nie** in die Stadt.*	I never go into town.
nicht mehr	no longer
*Er lernt **nicht mehr** Italienisch.*	He's no longer learning Italian.

niemand — no one

Er hat **niemanden** bei — He saw no one at her house /
ihr gesehen. — accompanying her.

And *niemand*'s opposite, *jemand* (meaning someone), is
also a good one to know.

Jemand ist in diesem — Someone has been in
Zimmer gewesen. — this room.

Gern

When you want to say that you 'like doing' something,
you use **gern**. It comes after the verb.

Ich gehe **gern** einkaufen. — I like going shopping.

When you want to say that you 'don't like' doing
something, you use **nicht gern**.

Ich gehe **nicht gern** einkaufen. — I don't like going shopping.

Giving instructions (the imperative)

When you give someone instructions (e.g. 'Turn right!') you
use a particular form of the verb called the **imperative**.

- With teachers or adults you don't know very well, use
  the *Sie* form. The verb goes first, with *Sie* after.

  Sie machen das Licht aus. **Machen Sie** das Licht aus!
  → Turn the light out!

- With one friend or family member, use the *du* form
  without the **-st** ending. Put the verb first and omit *du*.

  Du **machst** das Licht aus. **Mach** das Licht aus!
  → Turn the light out!

- With more than one friend or family member, use the
  ihr form without the pronoun *ihr*.

  Ihr **macht** das Licht aus. **Macht** das Licht aus!
  → Turn the light out!

Seit *with the present tense*

Seit means 'since' and is usually used with the present
tense in German.

Ich bin **seit** 9 Uhr hier. — I've been here since 9 o'clock.

It is also used to mean 'for', again with the present tense.

Ich lerne **seit** vier Jahren — I have been learning German
Deutsch. — for four years.

(Note that *seit* takes the dative, which is why *Jahren* has an
-n at the end.)

Seit *with the imperfect tense*

You can also use *seit* with the imperfect tense in German
to imply the pluperfect ('had done') tense.

Ich **wohnte seit** vier Jahren — I'd been living in Munich for
in München, als meine Tante — four years when my aunt
starb. — died.

Seit der Hochzeit **war** er — He'd been very happy since
sehr froh. — the wedding.

5   Word order

Basic word order

Here is the basic word order in a German sentence:

subject	verb	rest of the sentence
Ich	spiele	Gitarre.
Lukas	geht	in die Stadt.

Verb as second idea

In German, the verb is always in second place in a
sentence or clause. It's not always the second word,
because you can't separate a phrase like *in meinem
Zimmer*, but the verb must be the second idea or concept
in the sentence.

1	2	3	4
[Ich]	[**treibe**]	[manchmal]	[Sport].

1	2	3	4
[Manchmal]	[**treibe**]	[ich]	[Sport].

Changing a sentence so that the first idea is no longer the
subject is called using **inversion**.

Subordinate clauses

A subordinate clause is dependent on a main clause and
does not make sense on its own, e.g. *weil es 11 Uhr ist*
(because it is 11 o'clock).

- The conjunctions *weil*, *dass*, *da*, *obwohl*, *als* and *wenn*
  send the verb to the end of the subordinate clause
  which they introduce.

  Ich kann nicht gut — I can't sleep well because
  schlafen, **weil** ich — I'm afraid.
  Angst **habe**.

  Ich weiß, **dass** er — I know that he's homeless.
  obdachlos **ist**.

  Er ist dick, **da** er viel **isst**. — He is fat, as he eats a lot.

  Ich will eine Karriere — I want to have a career
  haben, **obwohl** meine — even though my parents
  Eltern reich **sind**. — are rich.

  Er sah fern, **als** seine Mutti — He was watching TV when
  wieder nach Hause **kam**. — his mum came back home.

  Ich gehe zum Strand, — I go to the beach when the
  wenn die Sonne **scheint**. — sun shines.

- If two verbs appear in a subordinate clause, the **finite
  verb** (not the infinitive or past participle) is sent to the
  end of the clause. The finite verb is often an auxiliary
  verb (*haben*, *sein*) or a modal verb (e.g. *können*, *müssen*).

  Ich kann im Meer schwimmen. → Ich gehe gern zum
  Strand, **weil** ich im Meer schwimmen **kann**.

  Ich bin im Meer geschwommen. → Der Urlaub war toll,
  weil ich im Meer geschwommen **bin**.

- If a sentence begins with the subordinate clause, the verbs meet in the middle, separated by a comma.

Wenn die Sonne **scheint, gehe** ich zum Strand.	When the sun shines, I go to the beach.

- Other subordinate clauses are introduced by *damit*, *sodass*, *ob* and *als*.

Ich schreibe schnell, **damit** ich bald fertig **bin**.	I'm writing fast, so that (in order that) I finish quickly.
Ich esse viel Obst, **sodass** ich gesund **bleibe**.	I eat lots of fruit, so that (as a result) I stay healthy.
Ich weiß nicht, **ob** er **kommt**.	I don't know whether he is coming.
Als das Wetter gut **war**, **bin** ich zum Strand gegangen.	When the weather was good, I went to the beach.

Time – manner – place

When you mention when (time), how (manner) and where (place) you do something, you give the time first, then the manner and then the place.

	Time	Manner	Place
Ich fahre	[am Wochenende]	[mit dem Auto]	[nach Paris].

	Manner	Place
Er fährt	[mit dem Zug]	[nach Berlin].

Conjunctions

Conjunctions are words that join together sentences (or clauses, which are parts of sentences).

Coordinating conjunctions

Common conjunctions are *und* (and), *oder* (or) and *aber* (but). They do not affect the word order in a sentence.

Er hat kein Geld. Er kann die Sprache nicht verstehen. → Er hat kein Geld **und** er kann die Sprache nicht verstehen.	He has no money. He can't understand the language. → He has no money and he can't understand the language.
Ich kenne ein paar Leute. Wir sind keine richtigen Freunde. → Ich kenne ein paar Leute, **aber** wir sind keine richtigen Freunde.*	I know a few people. We aren't really friends. → I know a few people but we aren't really friends.

*When using *aber* or *denn*, put a comma before it.

You might like to use some of the following, less common, coordinating conjunctions in your work:

denn	because
Ich mag ihn, **denn** er ist klug.	I like him because he's clever.*
sondern	but (only used after a negative)
Er hat **nicht** drei, **sondern** vier Katzen.	He doesn't have three but four cats.*

*Both *denn* and *sondern* need a comma before them.

Subordinating conjunctions

Some conjunctions including *weil, dass, da, obwohl, als* and *wenn* send the verb in the clause they introduce right to the end (see Subordinate clauses, page 189).

6 Asking questions

Verb first

You can ask questions by putting the verb first in the sentence.

Du hörst Musik. → **Hörst du** Musik?	You are listening to music. → Are you listening to music?
Birgit ist sportlich. → **Ist Birgit** sportlich?	Birgit is sporty. → Is Birgit sporty?

Interrogatives (question words)

You can ask a question by starting with a question word or interrogative. Most German question words start with *w*.

Wer?	Who?	*Wie lange?*	How long?
Wann?	When?	*Wo?*	Where?
Was?	What?	*Wohin?*	Where to?
Welche(r / s)?	Which?	*Woher?*	Where from?
Wie?	How?	*Womit?*	What with?
Warum?	Why?	*Wozu?*	What for? / Why?
Wie viel(e)?	How much / many?		

Most of these are pronouns or adverbs (see Interrogative adverbs, page 182) and are immediately followed by a verb.

Wer kommt mit?	Who's coming with us?
Wann kommt sie?	When is she coming?
Wohin fahren wir?	Where are we going (to)?

Welche(r / s) and *wie viel(e)* can be used as adjectives and followed by a noun (see Interrogative adjectives, page 179).

Wie viel Taschengeld bekommst du?	How much pocket money do you get?

7 Numbers and time

Numbers

Cardinal numbers

1 *eins*	16 *sechzehn*	80 *achtzig*
2 *zwei*	17 *siebzehn*	90 *neunzig*
3 *drei*	18 *achtzehn*	100 *hundert*
4 *vier*	19 *neunzehn*	35 *fünfunddreißig*
5 *fünf*	20 *zwanzig*	45 *fünfundvierzig*
6 *sechs*	21 *einundzwanzig*	55 *fünfundfünfzig*
7 *sieben*	22 *zweiundzwanzig*	65 *fünfundsechzig*
8 *acht*	23 *dreiundzwanzig*	75 *fünfundsiebzig*
9 *neun*	24 *vierundzwanzig*	85 *fünfundachtzig*
10 *zehn*	25 *fünfundzwanzig*	95 *fünfundneunzig*
11 *elf*	30 *dreißig*	200 *zweihundert*
12 *zwölf*	40 *vierzig*	305 *dreihundertfünf*
13 *dreizehn*	50 *fünfzig*	411 *vierhundertelf*
14 *vierzehn*	60 *sechzig*	
15 *fünfzehn*	70 *siebzig*	

525 *fünfhundertfünfundzwanzig*

1000 *tausend*

2500 *zweitausendfünfhundert*

1984 *neunzehnhundertvierundachtzig* (in dates)

Ordinal numbers

To make the ordinal numbers (first, second, etc.) up to 19th, you add **-te** to the cardinal number. There are a few exceptions: first (*erste*), third (*dritte*), seventh (*siebte*) and eighth (*achte*).

1st *erste*	11th *elfte*
2nd *zweite*	12th *zwölfte*
3rd *dritte*	13th *dreizehnte*
4th *vierte*	14th *vierzehnte*
5th *fünfte*	15th *fünfzehnte*
6th *sechste*	16th *sechzehnte*
7th *siebte*	17th *siebzehnte*
8th *achte*	18th *achtzehnte*
9th *neunte*	19th *neunzehnte*
10th *zehnte*	20th *zwanzigste*

To make the ordinal numbers from 20th upwards you add **-ste** to the cardinal number.

*Ich bin auf **den zwanzigsten** Platz gekommen.*   I came in twentieth place.

When giving dates, use the dative: use *am* before the ordinal number and add **-n**.

*Ich habe **am zwölften** Dezember Geburtstag.*   My birthday is on the twelfth of December.

The time

To tell the time, you say *es ist* followed by:

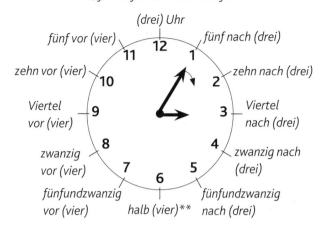

***Es ist **halb vier** means 'It's half three', not 'It's half four' – the *halb* indicates **half to the hour**, not half past.

To say at what time something happens, you use *um* followed by the above.

***Um** halb neun gehe ich in die Schule.*   I go to school at half past eight.

Verb tables

8 Verb tables

infinitive	present	imperfect	perfect	English
beginnen	beginnt	begann	begonnen	to begin
beißen	beißt	biss	gebissen	to bite
bewegen	bewegt	bewog	bewogen	to move
biegen	biegt	bog	gebogen	to bend
bieten	bietet	bot	geboten	to offer
binden	bindet	band	gebunden	to tie
bitten	bittet	bat	gebeten	to ask
blasen	bläst	blies	geblasen	to blow
bleiben	bleibt	blieb	geblieben*	to stay
brechen	bricht	brach	gebrochen	to break
brennen	brennt	brannte	gebrannt	to burn
bringen	bringt	brachte	gebracht	to bring
denken	denkt	dachte	gedacht	to think
dürfen	darf	durfte	gedurft	to be allowed to
empfehlen	empfiehlt	empfahl	empfohlen	to recommend
essen	isst	aß	gegessen	to eat
fahren	fährt	fuhr	gefahren*	to go, to travel
fallen	fällt	fiel	gefallen*	to fall
fangen	fängt	fing	gefangen	to catch
finden	findet	fand	gefunden	to find
fliegen	fliegt	flog	geflogen*	to fly
fliehen	flieht	floh	geflohen*	to flee
fließen	fließt	floss	geflossen*	to flow
frieren	friert	fror	gefroren	to freeze
geben	gibt	gab	gegeben	to give
gehen	geht	ging	gegangen*	to go

* Verbs which take *sein* in the perfect and pluperfect tenses.

infinitive	present	imperfect	perfect	English
gelingen	gelingt	gelang	gelungen*	to succeed
genießen	genießt	genoss	genossen	to enjoy
geschehen	geschieht	geschah	geschehen*	to happen
gewinnen	gewinnt	gewann	gewonnen	to win
graben	gräbt	grub	gegraben	to dig
greifen	greift	griff	gegriffen	to grasp
haben	hat	hatte	gehabt	to have
halten	hält	hielt	gehalten	to stop
hängen	hängt	hing	gehangen	to hang
heben	hebt	hob	gehoben	to lift
heißen	heißt	hieß	geheißen	to be called
helfen	hilft	half	geholfen	to help
kennen	kennt	kannte	gekannt	to know
kommen	kommt	kam	gekommen*	to come
können	kann	konnte	gekonnt	to be able to
laden	lädt	lud	geladen	to load
lassen	lässt	ließ	gelassen	to allow
laufen	läuft	lief	gelaufen*	to run
leiden	leidet	litt	gelitten	to suffer
leihen	leiht	lieh	geliehen	to lend
lesen	liest	las	gelesen	to read
liegen	liegt	lag	gelegen	to lie
lügen	lügt	log	gelogen	to tell a lie
meiden	meidet	mied	gemieden	to avoid
misslingen	misslingt	misslang	misslungen*	to fail
mögen	mag	mochte	gemocht	to like
müssen	muss	musste	gemusst	to have to
nehmen	nimmt	nahm	genommen	to take
nennen	nennt	nannte	genannt	to name

infinitive	present	imperfect	perfect	English
raten	rät	riet	geraten	to guess
reißen	reißt	riss	gerissen	to rip
reiten	reitet	ritt	geritten	to ride
rennen	rennt	rannte	gerannt*	to run
riechen	riecht	roch	gerochen	to smell
rufen	ruft	rief	gerufen	to call
schaffen	schafft	schuf	geschaffen	to manage
scheiden	scheidet	schied	geschieden*	to separate
scheinen	scheint	schien	geschienen	to shine
schlafen	schläft	schlief	geschlafen	to sleep
schlagen	schlägt	schlug	geschlagen	to hit
schließen	schließt	schloss	geschlossen	to shut
schneiden	schneidet	schnitt	geschnitten	to cut
schreiben	schreibt	schrieb	geschrieben	to write
schreien	schreit	schrie	geschrien	to cry
sehen	sieht	sah	gesehen	to see
sein	ist	war	gewesen*	to be
senden	sendet	sandte	gesandt	to send
singen	singt	sang	gesungen	to sing
sitzen	sitzt	saß	gesessen	to sit
sollen	soll	sollte	gesollt	ought to
sprechen	spricht	sprach	gesprochen	to speak
stehen	steht	stand	gestanden*	to stand
stehlen	stiehlt	stahl	gestohlen	to steal
steigen	steigt	stieg	gestiegen*	to climb
sterben	stirbt	starb	gestorben*	to die
stoßen	stößt	stieß	gestoßen	to push
streichen	streicht	strich	gestrichen	to paint
tragen	trägt	trug	getragen	to carry

infinitive	present	imperfect	perfect	English
treffen	trifft	traf	getroffen	to meet
treiben	treibt	trieb	getrieben	to do
treten	tritt	trat	getreten	to step
trinken	trinkt	trank	getrunken	to drink
tun	tut	tat	getan	to do
überwinden	überwindet	überwand	überwunden	to overcome
vergessen	vergisst	vergaß	vergessen	to forget
verlieren	verliert	verlor	verloren	to lose
verschwinden	verschwindet	verschwand	verschwunden*	to disappear
verzeihen	verzeiht	verzieh	verziehen	to pardon
wachsen	wächst	wuchs	gewachsen*	to grow
waschen	wäscht	wusch	gewaschen	to wash
weisen	weist	wies	gewiesen	to show
wenden	wendet	wandte / wendete	gewandt / gewendet	to turn
werben	wirbt	warb	geworben	to advertise
werden	wird	wurde	geworden*	to become
werfen	wirft	warf	geworfen	to throw
wiegen	wiegt	wog	gewogen	to weigh
wissen	weiß	wusste	gewusst	to know
wollen	will	wollte	gewollt	to want to
ziehen	zieht	zog	gezogen	to pull

Glossar

1 = **sehr gut**   very good

2 = **gut**   good

3 = **befriedigend**
satisfactory, fair

4 = **ausreichend**   sufficient,
pass (just)

5 = **mangelhaft**   poor,
unsatisfactory, fail

6 = **ungenügend**
extremely poor,
inadequate

A

die   **Aalsuppe**   eel soup

abbauen   to take down

das   **Abendessen (–)**   dinner,
evening meal

das   **Abenteuer (–)**   adventure

abfahren   to leave, to
depart

die   **Abfahrt (-en)**   departure

der   **Abfall (¨e)**   rubbish,
waste, (litter)

die   **Abgase**   exhaust fumes (pl)

abhängig sein von   to be
dependent on

abholen   to pick up,
to collect

die   **Abholzung (-en)**
deforestation

das   **Abitur (-e)**   German
school leaver qualification
(A-Level equivalent)

abkühlen   to cool

abnehmen   to lose weight

abnehmen   to decrease

das   **Abschlusszeugnis (-se)**
school leaving certificate

abschreiben   to copy

der   **Abstellraum (¨e)**   store
room

abstinent   teetotal

die   **AG (-s)**
**(Arbeitsgemeinschaft
(-en))**   extra-curricular
activity

die   **Ahnung (-en)**   idea

keine Ahnung haben
to have no idea

akzeptieren   to accept

alarmierend   alarming

der   **Albtraum (¨e)**   nightmare

alle zwei Stunden   every
two hours

allerlei   all sorts of

das   **Alter**   age

die   **alternative
Energiequelle (-n)**
alternative energy source

altmodisch   old-fashioned

das   **Altpapier**   waste paper

die   **Altstadt**   the old part
of town

die   **Ampel (-n)**   traffic light

sich   **amüsieren**   to enjoy
oneself

an   on

anbauen   to grow
(something)

anbieten   to offer

das   **Andenken (–)**   souvenir,
memento

ändern   to change

anders   different(ly), in a
different way

anfangen   to start

das   **Angebot (-e)**   range, offer

angenehm   pleasant,
agreeable

die   **Angewohnheit (-en)**   habit

die   **Angst (¨e)**   fear

angucken   to look at,
to watch

ansehen   to look at,
to watch

sich   **anhören**   to sound

der   **Anrufebeantworter (–)**
answering machine,
messaging service

der   **Anschluss (¨e)**   connection

anspruchsvoll   demanding

anstatt   instead of

anstrengend   hard work,
effortful

die   **Anwendung (-en)**
application, app

anziehen   to attract

sich   **anziehen**   to get dressed

die   **Apotheke (-n)**   pharmacy

die   **Arbeitserfahrung (–)**
experience of work

das   **Arbeitspraktikum
(-praktika)**   work
experience

der   **Arbeitstag (-e)**   working
day

sich   **ärgern (über)**   to get
annoyed (about)

arm   poor

der   **Ärmelkanal**   (English)
Channel

die   **Armut**   poverty

das   **Artensterben**   species
extinction

der   **Aschermittwoch**   Ash
Wednesday

atemberaubend
breathtaking

die   **Atempause (-n)**   a pause
for breath

atmen   to breathe

auf   on (top of)

auf die Nerven gehen   to
get on one's nerves

auf keinen Fall   under no
circumstances

der   **Aufenthalt (-e)**   stay

die   **Aufgabe (-n)**   task, job

aufgeben   to give up

aufgeregt   excited

aufhören   to stop

aufnehmen   to record

aufpassen   to watch out,
to take care, to pay
attention

aufräumen   to tidy up

aufregend   exciting

das   **Aufstehen**   getting up

aufstehen   to stand up, to
get up

aufwachen   to wake up

aufwachsen   to grow up

der   **Aufzug (¨e)**   lift

der   **Augenblick (-e)**   moment

die   **Aula (Aulen)**   school hall

die   **Ausbildung (-en)**   (job)
training, education

aus der Mode kommen   to
go out of style

der   **Ausflug (¨e)**   trip,
excursion

ausfüllen   to fill in

ausgestattet equipped

ausgezeichnet excellent

auskommen (mit) to get on (with)

das **Ausland** foreign country, abroad

ausprobieren to test, to try out

Auspuffgase exhaust fumes (pl)

ausreichend sufficient(ly)

die **Ausrüstung (-en)** equipment, kit

aussehen to look like, to appear

der **Außenseiter (–)** outsider

außerdem besides, furthermore

aussteigen to alight, to get off(bus, tram, train)

aussterben to die out, to become extinct

der **Austausch (-e)** exchange

Austern oysters (pl)

ausüben to practise (a profession)

ausverkauft sold out

die **Auswahl (-en)** selection, choice

ausziehen to move out

sich **ausziehen** to get undressed

die **Autobahn (-en)** motorway

der / die **Azubi (-s) (Auszubildende)** apprentice, trainee

B

die **Bäckerei (-en)** bakery, baker's shop

Backwaren baked goods (pl)

baden gehen to bathe, to swim

die **Badewanne (-n)** bathtub

der **Bahnsteig (-e)** platform

der **Bär (-en)** bear

der **Bart (¨e)** beard

der **Bauarbeiter (–)** construction worker (m)

die **Bauarbeiterin (-nen)** construction worker (f)

bedienen to serve

bedrohen to threaten

bedrohlich threatening

die **Bedrohung (-en)** threat

bedürftig needy

befahren to drive on

sich **befinden** to be situated

befriedigend satisfying

begleiten to accompany, to be with

behandeln to treat, to handle

beherrschen to master, to manage, to control

beide both

bekannt well-known, famous

der / die **Bekannte (-n)** acquaintance, friend

bekommen to get, to receive

die **Beleidigung (-en)** insult

beliebt popular

berichten to report

der **Beruf (-e)** job, profession

der **Berufsberater (–)** careers adviser

die **Berufspraxis (-praxen)** work experience

die **Berufsschule (-n)** vocational training school

berühmt famous

beschreiben to describe

besichtigen to sightsee, to visit, to have a look

die **Besichtigung (-en)** visit, tour

besonders special, particularly, especially

besprechen to discuss

bestehen to pass (an exam / test)

bestellen to order

bestimmt certainly

der **Besuch (-e)** visit

betreuen to look after, to supervise

betroffen affected

betrunken drunk

die **Bettdecke (-n)** blanket, duvet

beunruhigend worrying

die **Bevölkerung (-en)** population

die **Bewegung (-en)** movement, exercise

sich um ...**bewerben** to apply for

die **Bewerbung (-en)** application

bewerten to assess, to rate

bewundern to admire

bewusstlos unconscious

die **Beziehung (-en)** relationship

die **Bibliothek (-en)** library

der **Bildschirm (-e)** screen

der **Biomüll** organic waste

bis until, to

ein bisschen a little, a bit

blau machen to play truant, to skip school

das **Blei** lead

die **Blockflöte (-n)** recorder

blöd stupid

der **Boden (¨)** soil

der **Bodensee** Lake Constance

das **Boot (-e)** boat

böse evil, naughty, angry

das **Brathähnchen (–)** roast chicken

die **Bratwurst (¨e)** (fried) sausage

das **Brauch (¨e)** custom, tradition

brauchen to need

der **Bräutigam (-e)** bridegroom

brechen to be sick, to break

breit wide

brennen to burn

der **Brennstoff (-e)** fuel

der **Brief (-e)** letter

der **Briefträger (–)** postman

die **Briefträgerin (-nen)** postwoman

das **Bücherregal (-e)** bookshelf

die **Buchhandlung (–)** bookshop

das **Bundesland (¨er)** state (of Germany)

bunt brightly coloured

die **Burg (-en)** castle

der **Bürgersteig (-e)** pavement

der / die **Büroangestellte (-n)**
office worker

die **Bushaltestelle (-n)**
bus stop

C

die **Chemikalie (-n)** chemical

Chips crisps (pl)

der **Cousin (-s)** cousin (m)

die **Cousine (-n)** cousin (f)

die **Currywurst (¨e)** spicy
sausage

D

das **Dach (¨er)** roof

der **Dachboden (¨en)** attic,
loft

der **Dachstein (-e)** roof tile

dagegen against, opposed
to something

daher that is why

damals back then, in those
days

der **Dampfer (–)** steam boat

dann und wann now and
then

darüber hinaus
furthermore, moreover

Daten data (pl)

das **Datum (Daten)** date

dauern to last

dazu in addition

decken to cover

das **Denkmal (¨er)** monument

der **Eingang (¨e)** entrance

der **Zauberer (–)** magician

deshalb therefore,
because of that

deswegen because of that,
therefore

deuten to interpret

(Deutsches) Rotes Kreuz
(German) Red Cross

deutschsprachig
German-speaking

die **Diät (-en)** diet

dicht dense

dick thick, fat

die **Diele (-n)** hallway

das **Ding (-e)** thing

das **Dings** thingy

der **Direktor (-en)** head
teacher (m)

die **Direktorin (-nen)** head
teacher (f)

das **Doppelhaus (¨er)**
semi-detached house

das **Doppelzimmer (–)** double
room

die **Dose (-n)** can

draußen outside, outdoors

drinnen inside

das **Drittel (–)** a third

die **Drogenberatungsstelle (-n)**
advice centre for drug
addicts

der **Druck (-e)** pressure

duftend sweet-smelling

die **Dummheit (-en)** stupid
thing, foolishness

das **Düngemittel (–)** fertiliser

dünn slim

durchfallen to fail (exam /
test)

Durst haben to be thirsty

sich **duschen** to have a shower

E

ebenfalls as well

echt real, genuine

die **Ecke (-n)** corner

die **Ehe (-n)** marriage

eher rather

ehrenamtlich voluntary

ehrlich honest

eifersüchtig jealous

eigen own (adj)

eigentlich actually, really

sich **eignen** to be suitable

die **Einbahnstraße (-n)**
one-way street

einchecken to check in

eine Menge a lot of, lots

einen Sinn für Humor
haben to have a sense of
humour

einfach simple

das **Einfamilienhaus (¨er)**
detached house

der **Einfluss (¨e)** influence

der **Eingang (¨e)** entrance

der **Einkauf (¨e)** purchase

einladen to invite

einmal once

einschlafen to fall asleep

einschlafen to go to sleep

einschränken to limit

die **Einschränkung (-en)**
restriction

einsteigen to get in / on

die **Eintrittskarte (-n)**
admission ticket

einverstanden agreed

der **Einwohner (–)** inhabitant

das **Einzelzimmer (–)** single
room

einzig single, only

das **Elektroauto (-s)** electric
car

das **Elektrogeschäft (-e)** shop
for electrical goods

der **Elternteil (-e)** parent

die **E-Mail (-s)** email

der **Empfang (¨e)** reception
(hotel)

empfehlen to recommend

endlich finally, at last

die **Energiesparlampe (-n)**
energy-saving bulb

eng tight, close

entdecken to discover

entfernt away

enthalten to contain

entlang along

sich **entscheiden** to decide

die **Entscheidung (-en)**
decision

sich **entschuldigen** to
apologise

entsetzlich terrible, awful,
appalling

sich **entspannen** to relax

entspannend relaxing

entspannt relaxed

enttäuscht disappointed

entweder ... oder ...
either ... or ...

die **Entziehungskur (-en)**
rehab for drug addiction /
alcoholism

sich **erbrechen** to be sick

die **Erde** Earth

das **Ereignis (-se)** event

erfahren to learn, to find
out

die **Erfindung (-en)** invention

der Erfolg (-e) success

erfolgreich successful

erfrieren to freeze to death

erhitzen to heat

die Erholung (-en) recovery, revival, relaxation

sich erinnern to remember

erklären to explain

erlaubt allowed

erleben to experience

das Erlebnis (-se) experience

erleiden to suffer

die Ermäßigung (-en) discount, reduction

ermüdend tiring

die Ernährung (-en) food, nourishment, nutrition

eröffnet opened

erproben to try out

erreichen to reach

erscheinen to appear, to seem

erst only

erstarren to set

erstaunlich amazing

der erste Weihnachtstag Christmas Day

der / die Erwachsene (-n) adult

erwarten to wait, to expect

erzählen to tell, to narrate

es geht um it's about

es gibt there is / are

es macht nichts it's OK, it doesn't matter

die Etage (-n) floor, storey

etwas Positives something good

das Exemplar (-e) example

F

die Fabrik (-en) factory

die Fähigkeit (-en) ability, skill

die Fähre (-n) ferry

die Fahrkarte (-n) ticket

der Fahrkartenautomat (-en) ticket machine

der Fahrkartenschalter (–) ticket office

der Fahrpreis (-e) fare

der Fahrradverleih (-e) bicycle hire

die Fahrradvermietung (-en) bicycle hire

der Fahrradweg (-e) bicycle track / lane

das Fallschirmspringen parachuting

die Familie (-n) family

der Fasching another word for carnival

die Fastenzeit period of fasting, Lent

Fastnacht another word for carnival

faszinierend fascinating

faul lazy

die Faulheit laziness

das Fechten fencing

die Feier celebration

feiern to celebrate

das Feld (-er) field

das Fertiggericht (-e) ready meal

fest fixed, solid

festlich festive

die Festlichkeit (-en) celebration

das Festnetz (-e) landline

das Fett (-e) fat

fettleibig obese

das Feuerholz firewood

die Feuerwehr (-en) fire service

die Feuerwehrfrau (-en) firefighter (f)

der Feuerwehrmann (¨er) firefighter (m)

das Feuerwerk (-e) firework(display)

die Figur (-en) character (in film / novel)

der Film (-e) film

filmen to film

der Fink (-en) finch

die Fläche (-n) area

fleißig hard-working, industrious

fliehen to flee

die Flimmerkiste (-en) gogglebox, TV

die Flucht (-en) escape

der Flüchtling (-e) refugee

das Flüchtlingslager (–) refugee camp

der Flughafen (¨) airport

flüssig fluid, liquid

die Folge (-n) result, outcome, consequence

folgen to follow

das Formular (-e) form

der Fotoapparat (-e) camera

die Freiheit freedom

die Freiwilligenarbeit voluntary work

der Fremdsprachenassistent (-en) language assistant (m)

die Fremdsprachenassistentin (-nen) language assistant (f)

sich freuen (über) to be happy (about)

sich freuen auf to look forward to

der Freundeskreis (-e) circle of friends

die Freundin (-nen) (girl) friend

die Freundschaft (-en) friendship

die Frikadelle (-n) meatball

frische Luft schnappen to get a breath of fresh air

der Friseur (-e) hairdresser (m)

die Friseurin (-nen) hairdresser (f)

froh happy, glad, pleased

früh early

der Frühling spring

das Frühstück (-e) breakfast

sich fühlen to feel

der Führerschein (-e) driving licence

die Führung (-en) guided tour

funktionieren to work, to function

die Fußgängerzone (-n) pedestrian precinct

die Fußspur (-en) footprint

füttern to feed

G

der Gang (¨e) corridor

ganzjährig all year round

die Ganztagsschule (-n) school that lasts all day

der Gärtner (–) gardener (m)

die **Gärtnerin** (-nen) gardener (f)

das **Gebäude** (–) building

geben to give

das **Gebet** (-e) prayer

das **Gebiet** (-e) region, area

der **Gebirgssee** (-n) mountain lake

die **Geburt** (-en) birth

gechipped microchipped

das **Gedicht** (-e) poem

gedreht shot (a film)

geduldig patient

die **Gefahr** (-en) danger

gefährdet endangered

gefährlich dangerous

gefallen to please (to like)

die **Gefangenschaft** captivity

die **Gegend** (-en) area, region

geheim halten to keep secret

das **Gehirn** (-e) brain

gehören (zu) to belong to

die **Geige** (-n) violin

die **Geister** spirits (pl)

das **Geld** money

die **Gelegenheit** (-en) opportunity

gelernt fully trained

der / die **Geliebte** (-n) loved one

gemein mean

gemeinsam shared, in common, together

die **Gemeinschaft** (-en) community, group

gemischt mixed

gemütlich cosy, comfortable

genannt named, called

genau exact, exactly

Genf Geneva

genießen to enjoy

das **Gerät** (-e) device, gadget, appliance

geräumig roomy, spacious

das **Gericht** (-e) dish, meal

die **Gesamtschule** (-n) comprehensive school

das **Geschäft** (-e) shop

das **Geschäft** (-e) business, shop

die **Geschäftsfrau** (-en) businesswoman

das **Geschenk** (-e) present, gift

geschieden divorced

die **Gesellschaft** (-en) society

gesellschaftlich social

gespannt tense

das **Gespenst** (-er) ghost

gestreift striped

die **Gesundheit** health

die **Gewalt** violence

gewiss certain, some

gießen to pour

giftig poisonous

glatt smooth, sleek

gleich (the) same, equal

gleich immediately, in a minute, equal

das **Gleis** (-e) track, platform

die **Glocke** (-n) bell

das **Glück** happiness

Glück haben to be lucky

glücklich happy

glücklicherweise fortunately, luckily

der **Glühwein** mulled wine

die **goldene Hochzeit** golden wedding

gratis free of charge

der **Grillabend** (-e) barbecue

grillen to barbecue

der **Grillplatz** (¨e) barbecue area

großartig great

die **Großeltern** grandparents (pl)

die **Großmutter** (¨) grandmother

der **Großvater** (¨) grandfather

die **Grünanlage** (-n) green area, park

der **Grund** (¨e) reason

die **Grundschule** (-n) primary school

gruselig spooky

das **Gute** the good thing

gute Vorsätze resolutions (pl)

das **Gymnasium** (Gymnasien) grammar school

H

der **Haartrockner** (–) hairdryer

der **Hafen** (¨) harbour, port

das **Hähnchen** (–) chicken

die **Halbpension** half board

die **Handschuhe** gloves (pl)

hässlich ugly

hastig in a rush

der **Hauptbahnhof** (¨e) main railway station

das **Hauptgericht** (-e) main course

die **Hauptrolle** (-n) starring role, main role

die **Hauptschule** (-n) type of secondary school

die **Hauptstadt** (¨e) capital city

die **Hauptverkehrszeit** (-en) rush hour

der **Haushalt** (-e) household

der **Hausmeister** (–) caretaker (m)

die **Hausmeisterin** (-nen) caretaker (f)

die **Hauswirtschaft** (-en) home economics

heftig heavy, severe

heilig holy

der **Heiligabend** Christmas Eve

der **Heiligedreikönigstag** Epiphany / 6th January

herausbringen to release (record etc.)

die **Herausforderung** (-en) challenge

der **Herbst** (-e) autumn

herkommen to come from, to originate from

herrlich marvellous, magnificent, glorious

herstellen to make, to produce

hervorragend excellent, outstanding

das **Herz** (-en) heart

herzförmig heart-shaped

heutzutage nowadays

die **Hexe** (-n) witch

hilflos helpless

hilfsbereit helpful

die **Himbeere** (-n) raspberry

hinter   behind

das Hochhaus (¨er)   high-rise block of flats

hochladen   to upload

hochwertig   valuable

holen   to fetch, to get

das Holz   wood

der Honig   honey

hübsch   pretty

Hunger haben   to be hungry

die Hupe (-n)   horn, klaxon

I

der Identitätsklau   identity theft

ignorieren   to ignore

im Freien   outside, in the open air

im Voraus   in advance

in allem   in every way

in der Regel   in general

in die Brüche gehen   to break up

in Verbindung (mit)   in contact (with)

das Industriegebiet (-e)   industrial area

informiert   informed

der Ingenieur (-e)   engineer (m)

die Ingenieurin (-nen)   engineer (f)

der Inhalt (-e)   content

die Insel (-n)   island

insgesamt   in total, altogether

sich interessieren für   to be interested in

der Internat (-e)   boarding school

isolierend   isolating

J

das Jahrhundert (-e)   century

jeder / jede / jedes   each, every

jederzeit   at any time

jobben   to (do casual) work

der Jogurtbecher (–)   yogurt pot

jonglieren   to juggle

der Jugendclub (-s)   youth club

der / die Jugendliche (-n)   young person

das Juweliergeschäft (-e)   jeweller's shop

K

der Kalender (–)   diary, calendar

die Kalorie (-n)   calorie

die Kälte   cold

die kalte Schulter   the cold shoulder

der Kamin (-e)   fireplace

kaputt   broken

der Karfreitag   Good Friday

der Karneval   carnival

die Karriere (-n)   career

die Kartoffel (-n)   potato

der Karton(-s)   cardboard, cardboard box

der Kassierer (–)   cashier, bank clerk (m)

die Kassiererin (-nen)   cashier, bank clerk (f)

die Katastrophe (-n)   disaster

das Kaufhaus (¨er)   department store

der Kaugummi (-s)   chewing gum

die Kegelbahn (-en)   bowling alley

kegeln   to bowl

keinen festen Wohnsitz haben   to have no fixed abode

keineswegs   in no way

der Keller (–)   cellar

der Kellner (–)   waiter

die Kellnerin (-nen)   waitress

kennenlernen   to meet, to get to know

die Kerze (-n)   candle

die Kette (-n)   chain

die Kettenreaktion (-en)   chain reaction

der Kindergarten (¨)   nursery

das Kinderheim (-e)   children's home

kinderlos   childless

kindisch   childish

der Kirchturm (¨e)   church tower, spire

kitschig   cheesy

klappen   to succeed, to work

die Klassenarbeit (-en)   test

die Klausur (-en)   test

kleben   to stick

das Kleidergeschäft (-e)   clothes shop

der Kleiderschrank (¨e)   wardrobe

der Klempner (–)   plumber (m)

die Klempnerin (-nen)   plumber (f)

die Klimaanlage (-n)   air conditioning

der Klingelton (¨e)   ringtone

der Koch (¨e)   cook (m)

die Köchin (-nen)   cook (f)

die Kochkurs (-e)   cookery course

der Koffer (–)   suitcase

die Kohle   coal

komisch   funny, comical, odd

die Komödie (-n)   comedy

die Konditorei (-en)   confectioner's

der König (-e)   king

das Königreich (-e)   kingdom

konsumieren   to consume

kontrollieren   to control

sich konzentrieren   to concentrate

das Konzert (-e)   concert

der Kopfhörer (–)   headphones

das Kopfkissen (–)   pillow

körperlich   physical

korrigieren   to correct, to mark

kostenlos   free of charge

das Kostüm (-e)   costume

das Kraftwerk (-e)   power station

das Krankenhaus (¨er)   hospital

die Krawatte (-n)   tie

der Krebs (-e)   cancer

die Kreuzung (-en)   crossroads

der Krieg (-e)   war

das Krokodil (-e)   crocodile

die Küche (-n)   cuisine, kitchen

der Kühlschrank (¨e)   fridge

sich kümmern (um)   to take care of, to look after

der Kunde (-n) customer (m)
die Kundin (-nen) customer (f)
die Kunstgalerie (-n) art gallery
der **Kürbis (-se)** pumpkin
die Küste (-n) coast

L

das Labor (-e) laboratory
lächerlich ridiculous
der Laden (¨) shop
die **Lage (-n)** position
langweilig boring
der Lärm noise
die Laterne (-n) lantern
leben to live
das Leben (–) life
der Lebensbund (¨e) bond, union for life
Lebensmittel food (pl)
das Lebensmittelgeschäft (-e) grocer's shop
lebensnotwendig vital
der Lebensraum (¨e) habitat, living space
der Lebensstil (-e) lifestyle
die Leber liver
lebhaft lively, busy
ledig single, unmarried
lehren to teach
das Lehrerzimmer (–) staffroom
lehrreich educational, informative
leiden to stand, to bear, to suffer
ich kann … nicht leiden I can't stand … / I don't like …
das tut mir leid I'm sorry
leider unfortunately
die Leinwand (¨e) the big screen, cinema
die Leistung (-en) achievement
leistungsstark powerful (battery, processor)
das Licht (-er) light
lieb kind, lovely
liebevoll loving, affectionate

die Linie (-n) line, number (tram, bus)
der LKW (-s) (Lastkraftwagen) HGV, lorry
der LKW-Fahrer (–) lorry driver (m)
die LKW-Fahrerin (-nen) lorry driver (f)
locker casual, relaxed
der Löffel (–) spoon
der Lohn (¨e) wage
sich **lohnen** to be worth it
das Lokal (-e) bar, pub
lösen to solve
losgehen to set off
die Lösung (-en) solution
der Löwe (-n) lion
die Luftverschmutzung air pollution
Lust haben, etwas zu tun to feel like doing something

M

der Magen (¨) stomach
die Magermilch skimmed milk
magersüchtig anorexic
der Mann (¨er) man, husband
die Mannschaft (-en) team
der Marktplatz (¨e) marketplace
der Maßstab (¨e) standard
die Mauer (-n) wall (outside)
der Mechaniker (–) mechanic (m)
die Mechanikerin (-nen) mechanic (f)
der Meeresblick (-e) sea view
die Meeresfrüchte seafood (pl)
mehrere several
meist mostly, usually
die Menge (-n) crowd
die Mensa (-s) dining hall, canteen
merken to notice
merkwürdig remarkable
die Metzgerei (-en) butcher's shop
mies rotten, lousy
die Miete (-n) rent
mieten to rent

die Mikrowelle (-n) microwave oven
mindestens at least
der Mindestlohn (¨e) minimum wage
der Missbrauch (¨e) misuse, abuse
missbrauchen to misuse, abuse
das Missverständnis (-se) misunderstanding
miteinander with each other, together
das Mitglied (-er) member
mitmachen to join in
mitnehmen to take with (you)
das Mittagessen (–) lunch
mitteilen to announce
das Mittelmeer Mediterranean Sea
mitten in in the middle of
die **mittlere Reife** school-leaving certificate usually taken after the sixth year of secondary school
mobben to bully
die Modekette (-n) fashion chain
die Modemarke (-n) fashion brand
die Möglichkeit (-en) possibility
morgen tomorrow
der Morgen (–) morning
die Moschee (-n) mosque
die Mühe (-n) trouble
mühsam arduous, laborious, with difficulty
Mumm haben to have courage
München Munich
mündlich oral
die Muscheln mussels (pl)
mutig brave, courageous

N

der Nachbar (-n) neighbour (m)
die Nachbarin (-nen) neighbour (f)
nachdenken to think something over

die **Nachprüfung (-en)** re-sit

die **Nachricht (-en)** news, message

nachsitzen to have a detention

nachts at night

der **Nachttisch (-e)** bedside cabinet

die Nase voll haben to be fed up with something

die **Natur** nature

der **Neoprenanzug (¨e)** wetsuit

das **Netzwerk (-e)** network

der **Neubau (-ten)** new build

neugeboren newborn

neulich recently

das **Nickerchen (–)** nap

nirgendwo nowhere

der **Notausgang (¨e)** emergency exit

die **Note (-n)** mark, grade

der **Notendruck** pressure to get good marks

nötig necessary

notwendig necessary, essential

der **Nutzer (–)** user

O

obdachlos homeless

das **Obdachlosenheim (-e)** hostel for homeless people

die **Oberfläche (-n)** surface

das **Obergeschoss (-e)** floor, storey

die **Oberstufe (-n)** sixth form

der **Obst- und Gemüseladen (¨)** greengrocer's shop

öffentlich in public

öffentliche Verkehrsmittel public transport (pl)

die **Öffnungszeiten** opening times (pl)

ohne Zweifel without doubt

die **Ohrringe** earrings (pl)

die **Oma (-s)** granny, grandma

der **Onkel (–)** uncle

der **Opa (-s)** grandad

das **Opfer (–)** victim

der **Ort (-e)** place

der **Ostersonntag** Easter Sunday

die **Ozonschicht (-en)** ozone layer

P

das **Paar (-e)** couple

die **Panne (-n)** breakdown, puncture, flat tyre

der **Papagei (-en)** parrot

der **Parkplatz (¨e)** parking space

der **Partner (–)** partner (m)

die **Partnerin (-nen)** partner (f)

der **Passagier (-e)** passenger

das **Passwort (¨er)** password

die **Pause (-n)** break

peinlich embarrassing

das **Personal (–)** staff

die **Pflanze (-n)** plant

pflegen to care for

der **Pfleger (–)** care worker (m)

die **Pflegerin (-nen)** care worker (f)

das **Pflichtfach (¨er)** compulsory subject

die **Plattenfirma (-en)** record company

plaudern to chat, to talk

pleite skint, broke

der **Plüschbär (-en)** teddy bear

die **Praline (-n)** chocolate (in a box of chocolates)

der **Preis (-e)** price

preiswert cheap, value for money

preiswert good value for money, cheap

die **Priorität (-en)** priority

privat private

probieren to try out

probieren to try

der **Prospekt (-e)** brochure, leaflet

prüfen to check

die **Prüfung (-en)** exam

pünktlich punctual, on time

die **Pute (-n)** turkey

R

der **Rabatt (-e)** discount

der **Radiomoderator (-en)** radio presenter (m)

die **Radiomoderatorin (-nen)** radio presenter (f)

sich **rasieren** to shave

der **Ratschlag (¨e)** piece of advice

der **Ratschlag (¨e)** advice

das **Rätsel (–)** puzzle

rauswerfen to throw out

die **Realschule (-n)** type of secondary school

die **Rechnung (-en)** bill

die **Regel (-n)** rule

regelmäßig regular(ly)

der **Regenwald (¨er)** rainforest

der **Regisseur (-e)** director

reichen to range

die **Reihe (-n)** series (films / books)

das **Reihenhaus (¨er)** terraced house

die **Reinigung (-en)** dry-cleaner's

das **Reisebüro (-s)** travel agency

der **Reisebus (-se)** coach

der / die **Reisende (-n)** traveller

die **Reisetasche (-n)** travel bag

das **Reiseziel (-e)** destination

der **Reiz (-e)** attraction, appeal

reparieren to repair

der **Rettungsdienst (-e)** emergency service

das **Rezept (-e)** recipe

der **Rezeptionist (-en)** receptionist (m)

die **Rezeptionistin (-nen)** receptionist (f)

richtig real, proper, correct

riechen to smell

das **Risiko (Risiken)** risk

riskant risky

der **Rohstoff (-e)** raw material

die **Rolle (-n)** role

die **Rolltreppe (-n)** escalator

der **Rotwein** red wine

ruhig quiet, calm

rund um die Uhr 24/7

rund um die Welt all around the world

die **Rundfahrt (-en)** tour, round trip

S

die **Sache (-n)** thing, stuff

die **Sackgasse (-n)** cul-de-sac

die **Sahne** cream

die **Sammlung (-en)** collection

der **Sänger (–)** singer (m)

die **Sängerin (-nen)** singer (f)

sauber clean

sauer sein to be cross / annoyed

die **S-Bahn (-en)** suburban (fast) railway

das **Schach** chess

schaden to damage

schädlich damaging, harmful

schaffen to get, to achieve, to manage

der **Schatten (–)** shade, shadow

schattig shady

der **Schauspieler (–)** actor

die **Schauspielerin (-nen)** actress

sich **scheiden lassen** to get divorced

schenken to give (a gift)

der **Scherz (-e)** joke

schicken to send

die **Schildkröte (-n)** tortoise, turtle

das **Schinkenbrot (-e)** ham sandwich

der **Schlafsack (¨e)** sleeping bag

die **Schlägerei (-en)** fight, brawl

das **Schlagzeug** drums

die **Schlange (-n)** snake

Schlange stehen to queue

das **Schließfach (¨er)** locker

schlimm bad

das **Schloss (¨er)** castle

schmelzen to melt

der **Schmerz (-en)** pain

... schmerzen haben to have ... ache

sich **schminken** to put on make-up

der **Schmuck** jewellery

schmutzig dirty

die **Schublade (-n)** drawer

der **(Schul)abschluss (¨e)** qualification

der **Schüler (–)** pupil, school student (m)

die **Schülerin (-nen)** pupil, school student (f)

der **Schulhof (¨e)** school yard, playground

der **Schulleiter (–)** head teacher (m)

die **Schulleiterin (-nen)** head teacher (f)

das **Schulsystem (-e)** school system

die **Schüssel (-n)** bowl

der **Schutz** protection

schützen to protect

schwänzen to play truant, to skip school

schwatzen to chat

schwierig difficult

das **Schwimmbecken (–)** swimming pool

das **Segelboot (-e)** sailing boat

die **Sehenswürdigkeit (-en)** tourist attraction, sight

die **Seilbrücke (-n)** rope bridge

seit for (a period of time), since

das **Sekretariat (-e)** admin office

der **Sekt** German sparkling wine

Selbstmord begehen to commit suicide

selbstständig independent

die **Selbstständigkeit** independence

selten rarely, seldom

sicher safe, secure, sure

die **Sicherheit** safety, security

die **Sicherheitseinstellungen** security settings (pl)

der **Sicherheitsgurt (-e)** safety belt, seat belt

sitzen to sit

sitzen bleiben to repeat a school year

die **SMS** text

sofort straight away, immediately

sogar even

der **Soldat (-en)** soldier

die **Soldatin (-nen)** soldier (f)

sich **sonnen** to sunbathe

sonnenreich sun-drenched

sonst otherwise, or else

sich **sorgen** to worry

sich **Sorgen machen** to worry

sowohl ... als auch ... both ... and ...

spannend exciting, thrilling

sparen to save

die **Sparkasse (-n)** (savings) bank

spazieren gehen to go for a walk

die **Speisekarte (-n)** menu

der **Speisewagen (–)** dining car, restaurant car (train)

spenden to donate

der **Spitzname (-n)** nickname

das **Sprachlabor (-e)** language lab

der **Sprachunterricht (-e)** language lessons

der **Spritzentausch** needle exchange

die **Stabilität** stability

die **Stadt (¨e)** town

der **Stadtbummel (–)** stroll through town, window shopping

der **Stadtrand (¨er)** outskirts of town

der **Stadtteil (-e)** part of the town

das **Stadtviertel (–)** district, part of the town

stammen aus to come from, to date from

ständig constantly

starten to take off

der **Stau (-s)** traffic jam

die **Steh-Party** drinks party (literally: standing party)

die **Stelle (-n)** job

sterben to die

der **Stern (-e)** star

der **Stiefbruder (¨)** stepbrother

die **Stiefmutter (¨)** stepmother

die **Stiefschwester (-n)** stepsister

der **Stiefvater (¨)** stepfather

die **Stimme (-n)** voice

das **Stockwerk (-e)** storey, floor

der **Stoff (-e)** material, subject matter

das **Strandbad (¨er)** bathing beach

der **Strandkorb (¨e)** wicker beach chair

das **Straßenfest (-e)** street party

der **Strauß (¨e)** bunch of flowers

der **Streich (-e)** trick

der **Streit (-e)** argument

sich **streiten** to argue

streng strict

das stimmt that's right / correct

der **Stubenhocker (–)** couch potato, stay-at-home (m)

die **Stubenhockerin (-nen)** couch potato, stay-at-home (f)

das **Stück (-e)** piece

die **Studie** study, research

der **Studienplatz (¨e)** university place

das **Studium (Studien)** studies

suchen to look for

die **Sucht (¨e)** addiction

die **Suppe (-n)** soup

die **Suppenküche (-n)** soup kitchen

süß sweet

T

der **Tabak (-e)** tobacco

täglich daily, every day

die **Tante (-n)** aunt

die **Tanzfläche (-n)** dance floor

der **Tarif (-e)** tariff, scale of charges

die **Tasche (-n)** bag

das **Taschengeld (-er)** pocket money

tauchen to dive

die **Technologie (-n)** technology

der **Teil (-e)** part

teilen to share

teilnehmen to take part, to join in

der **Teilnehmer (–)** participant

teilweise partly

die **Terrasse (-n)** terrace, patio

die **Theatervorführung (-en)** Theatrical performance

theoretisch theoretically

der **Tiefkühlschrank (¨e)** freezer

die **Tiefkühltruhe (-n)** chest freezer

der **Tierfreund (-e)** animal lover

das **Tierheim (-e)** animal shelter

der **Tierpark (-s)** animal park, zoo

das **Tischtennis** table tennis

tot dead

die **Touristikwebsite (-s)** travel website

die **Tournee (-s)** tour

der **Traumjob (-s)** dream job

der **Trauschein (-e)** marriage certificate

sich **trennen** to separate

der **Tropfen (–)** drop

trotzdem nevertheless, even so

die **Turnhalle (-n)** sports hall, gym

das **Turnier (-e)** tournament

typisch typical

U

üben to practise

über over, above, via

überall everywhere

überbevölkert over-populated

die **Überdosis (-dosen)** overdose

die **Überfahrt (-en)** crossing (sea)

übergeben to present, to hand over

die **Übernachtung (-en)** overnight stay

die **Übernachtung mit Frühstück** B&B

überprüfen to check, to monitor

überraschend surprising

überwinden to overcome

üblich usual

umbauen to rebuild

die **Umgebung (-en)** surrounding area, environment

der **Umkleideraum (¨e)** changing room

umsteigen to change (means of transport)

die **Umwelt** environment

sich **umziehen** to get changed

der **Umzug (¨e)** street procession

(un)angenehm (un)pleasant

unbedingt definitely

unbekannt unknown

unerfahren inexperienced

unerträglich unbearable

unerwünscht unwanted

ungerecht unfair

unglaublich unbelievable, incredible

unhöflich impolite

die **Universität (-en)** university

unkontrollierbar uncontrollable

unordentlich untidy

unter under

unterhaltsam entertaining

die **Unterkunft (¨e)** accommodation

unternehmen to do, to undertake

unternehmungslustig adventurous

der **Unterricht** lessons, teaching

unterrichten to teach

unterschiedlich different, varied

die Unterstützung (-en) support, help

unzuverlässig unreliable

der Valentinstag (-e) Valentine's Day

der Vegetarier (–) vegetarian (n)

vegetarisch vegetarian (adj)

veraltet outdated

die Veranstaltung (-en) event

verbessern to improve, to correct

verbringen to spend (time)

verderben to spoil

das Verhältnis (-se) relationship

verheimlichen to conceal, to hide

verheiratet married

verkaufen to sell

der Verkäufer (–) shop assistant (m)

die Verkäuferin (-nen) shop assistant (f)

der Verkehr traffic

der Verkehrsunfall (¨e) traffic accident

sich verkleiden to put on fancy dress, to dress up, to disguise oneself

verlassen to leave

sich verlassen auf to rely on

die Verletzung (-en) injury

verlieren to lose

verlobt engaged (to someone)

die Verlobung (-en) engagement

vermeiden to avoid

veröffentlichen to publish

die Verpackung (-en) packaging

verpesten to pollute

die Versammlung (-en) assembly

verschieden various, different

sich verschlechtern to get worse, to deteriorate

verschmutzen to pollute

verschwenden to waste

die Verschwendung waste

verschwinden to disappear

versetzt werden to be moved up to the next year group

verständnisvoll understanding (adj)

verstehen to understand

sich verstehen (mit) to get on (with)

der Versuch (-e) attempt

versuchen to try

vertreiben to drive out, to expel

die Verwandten relatives (pl)

verwenden to use

verwöhnt spoiled (e.g. child)

verzichten auf to do without, to give up

der Vielfraß (-e) a greedy eater / glutton

vielleicht perhaps

der Volkstrauertag Remembrance Day

die Vollpension full board

vor in front of, before, outside

vorbeikommen to call in, drop by

vorbereiten to prepare

vorhersagen to predict

vorlesen to read (aloud)

der Vorort (-e) suburb

vorsichtig careful(ly)

die Vorspeise (-n) starter

sich vorstellen to introduce oneself, to imagine

das Vorstellungsgespräch (-e) job interview

der Vorteil (-e) advantage

der Wagen (–) float (in a procession)

wählen to choose

das Wahlfach (¨er) optional subject

wahnsinnig crazy

wahrscheinlich probably

die Waise (-n) orphan

die Wand (¨e) wall (inside)

wandern to hike

die Wanderung (-en) hike

das Warenhaus (¨er) department store

warnen vor to warn about

der Wartesaal (-säle) waiting room

Was darf es sein? what would you like? (in a shop / restaurant)

sich waschen to get washed

die Waschküche (-n) utility room

der Wasserhahn (¨e) tap

die Wasserverschmutzung water pollution

wechseln to change

wecken to awaken

der Wecker (–) alarm clock

weder ... noch ... neither ... nor ...

der Weg (-e) way, path, route

wegen because of

wegen Betriebsferien geschlossen closed because of holiday (firm / shop / attraction) (pl)

wegtreiben to drive away

wegwerfen to throw away

die Weihnachtskarte (-n) Christmas card

der Weihrauch frankincense

die Welt (-en) world

die Weltbevölkerung (-en) world population

die Weltkarte (-n) world map

weltweit worldwide

sich wenden an to turn to

weniger fewer, less

(das) Werken D&T (Design and Technology)

die Werkstatt (¨en) garage

wichtig important

wieder again

wiederholen to repeat

wiederkommen to come back

wiederverwerten to recycle

Wien   Vienna

(das)   **Wildwasserschwimmen**
white-water swimming

die   **Wirklichkeit (-en)**   reality

die   **Witwe (-n)**   widow

der   **Wohnblock (-s)**   block of
flats

wohnen   to live, reside

die   **Wohnfläche (-n)**   living
space, floor area

die   **Wohnung (-en)**   flat,
apartment

der   **Wohnwagen (–)**   caravan

sich   **wünschen**   to wish for

der   **Wunschzettel (–)**
Christmas list, wish list

Z

zahlreich   numerous

sich   **die Zähne putzen**   to clean
one's teeth

das   **Zeichen (–)**   character (in
text)

zeigen   to show

die   **Zeit**   time

sich   **die Zeit nehmen**   to take
your time

zeitgemäß   contemporary,
up to date

der   **Zeitpunkt (-e)**   point in
time, moment

der   **Zeitraum (¨-e)**   period of
time

die   **Zeitschrift (-en)**   magazine

das   **Zelt (-e)**   tent

zerstören   to destroy

das   **Zeugnis (-se)**   school
report

das   **Zinn**   tin, pewter

zögern   to hesitate

zu dritt   three (of us)

zufrieden   content, happy

zugeben   to admit

die   **Zukunft**   future

zukünftig   future (adj)

zum Entspannen   for
relaxing

zum Glück   fortunately

zunehmen   to put on
weight

zunehmen   to increase, to
put on weight

zur Verfügung stehen   to
be available

zurückgehen auf   to go
back to

zurückkehren   to return

zurzeit   at present

zusammen   together

zusammenbleiben   to stay
together

zusammenkommen   to
get together

der   **Zuschlag (¨-e)**   extra
charge, supplement

zustellen   to deliver

zuverlässig   reliable

der   **Zweck (-e)**   purpose

das   **Zweibettzimmer (–)**   twin
bedroom

der   **zweite Weihnachtstag**
Boxing Day

zwischen   between

zwischendurch   between
meals

Acknowledgements

Cover image: Travel Ink/Getty Images
Artwork by Q2A Pvt. Ltd.

The publisher would like to thank the following for permissions to use their photographs/artwork:

p16(T): Syda Productions/Shutterstock; p16(TC): Nopporn/Shutterstock; p16(BC): Jacek Chabraszewski/Shutterstock; p16(C): Carollux/Shutterstock; p18: Education Images/Universal Images Group/Getty Images; p20(TL): Auremar/Shutterstock; p20(TR): SergiyN/Shutterstock; p20(B): Lakov Filimonov/Shutterstock; p24(T): Zurijeta/Shutterstock; p24(B): Iryna Prokofieva/Shutterstock; p30: Nenetus/Shutterstock; p31: Syda Productions/Shutterstock; p32(B): Sascha Preussner/Shutterstock; p32(T): SpeedKingz/Shutterstock; p33: Cobalt88/Shutterstock; p34: Prach Trapmanee/Shutterstock; p36(T): SpeedKingz/Shutterstock; p36(B): Rido/Shutterstock; p42(L): Monkey Business Images/Shutterstock; p42(R): IVL/Shutterstock; p47(B): Soloviova Liudmyla/Shutterstock; p47(T): Monkey Business Images/Shutterstock; p48(T): Carlos Tischler/REX/Shutterstock; p48(BL): Diversepixel/Shutterstock; p48(BR): Katalinks/Shutterstock; p50: Moviestore/REX/Shutterstock; p51: Gts/Shutterstock; p52(T): ElenaGaak/Shutterstock; p52(TC): Robert Neumann/Shutterstock; p52(C): Simone Voigt/Shutterstock; p52(BC): Liv friis-larsen/Shutterstock; p52(B): Nitr/Shutterstock; p58: Dennis Grombkowski/Bongarts/Getty Images; p59: HuHu/Shutterstock; p65: Nejron Photo/Shutterstock; p66(T): ImageBroker/Alamy Stock Photo; p66(B): Relax Images/REX/Shutterstock; p68(T): Apollofoto/Shutterstock; p68(C): Allies Interactive/Shutterstock; p68(B): Joat/Shutterstock; p69: Juergen Sack/iStockphoto; p70(T): Jim Barber/Shutterstock; p70(B): LoloStock/Shutterstock; p81(T): 26kot/Shutterstock; p81(B): Peter Titmuss/Shutterstock; p82(T): Roman Sigaev/Shutterstock; p82(TC): Paul Vasarhelyi/Shutterstock; p82(BC): Bildagentur Zoonar GmbH/Shutterstock; p82(C): Art Konovalov/Shutterstock; p84(A): Marko Poplasen/Shutterstock; p84(B): Runzelkorn/Shutterstock; p84(C): Pavel Dudek/Shutterstock; p84(D): FooTToo/Shutterstock; p84(E): Acilo/iStockphoto; p84(F): 360b/Shutterstock; p85(TL): Adisa/Shutterstock; p85(CL): PhillipsC/Shutterstock; p85(TC): Nataliya Kuznetsova/Shutterstock; p85(C): Alzbeta/Shutterstock; p85(TR): Javier Brosch/Shutterstock; p85(BR): Karen Walker/Shutterstock; p85(B): Iriana Shiyan/Shutterstock; p86: Stephan Zabel/iStockphoto; p87: Moskwa/Shutterstock; p88(L): Sorbis/Shutterstock; p88(CL): Dotshock/Shutterstock; p88(C): Adisa/Shutterstock; p88(CR): Vvoe/Shutterstock; p88(R): Bikeriderlondon/Shutterstock; p89: Blend Images/Shutterstock; p90(T): Querbeet/iStockphoto; p90(C): Marvellousworld/iStockphoto; p90(A): Creation/Shutterstock; p90(B): Joyfull/Shutterstock; p90(C): Pi-Lens/Shutterstock; p90(D): Robert Kneschke/Shutterstock; p90(E): Philip Lange/Shutterstock; p90(F): Ralf Gosch/Shutterstock; p98: Christian Aslund/Getty Images; p99(T): Arnoaltix/Shutterstock; p99(B): Lee Snider Photo Images/Shutterstock; p100: KatarzynaBialasiewicz/iStockphoto; p102(T): Aleksandr Markin/Shutterstock; p102(B): Nikamo/Shutterstock; p108: Kuco/Shutterstock; p113(T): Aragami123345/iStockphoto; p113(B): Monkey Business Images/Shutterstock; p114(L): Mattomedia Werbeagentur/Shutterstock; p114(CL): Tupungato/Shutterstock; p114(C): Claudia Otte/Shutterstock; p114(CR): Diego Cervo/Shutterstock; p114(R): Strahil Dimitrov/Shutterstock; p115: Maciej Noskowski/iStockphoto; p116: TinnaPong/Shutterstock; p119: Chat Des Balkans/Shutterstock; p120: Photographee.eu/Shutterstock; p126(A): Prill/Shutterstock; p126(B): Lassedesignen/Shutterstock; p126(C): Nueng audok/Shutterstock; p126(D): Eric Isselee/Shutterstock; p126(E): Stockcreations/Shutterstock;

p126(F): Narinto/Shutterstock; p126(G): Mike Richter/Shutterstock; p126(H): Nordling/Shutterstock; p126(TL): Rocter/iStockphoto; p126(TR): Shockfactor.de/Shutterstock; p126(C): BreatheFitness/iStockphoto; p128(L): Tatiana Popova/Shutterstock; p128(R): Buena Vista Images; p128(C): Cate_89/Shutterstock; p130(B): Martinwimmer/iStockphoto; p130(T): Canadastock/Shutterstock; p131: Daniel M Ernst/Shutterstock; p132(L): Rainer Lesniewski/Shutterstock; p132(R): Hiroshi Higuchi/Getty Images; p138(T): Pinggr/Shutterstock; p138(B): Black Moon/Shutterstock; p139: Izabela Habur/iStockphoto; p143(T): Kristo-Gothard Hunor/Shutterstock; p143(B): Peter Probst/Shutterstock; p144(T): Nito/Shutterstock; p144(TC): Monkey Business Images/Shutterstock; p144(BC): Wavebreakmedia/Shutterstock; p144(B): AstroStar/Shutterstock; p146(L): Monkey Business Images/Shutterstock; p146(R): ImageBroker/Alamy Stock Photo; p147(TL): Liz Leyden/iStockphoto; p147(BL): Steve Debenport/iStockphoto; p147(TC): Steve Debenport/iStockphoto; p147(BC): Ultramarinfoto/iStockphoto; p147(TR): Agencja Fotograficzna Caro/Alamy Stock Photo; p147(BR): John Fedele/Blend Images/Getty Images; p148(TL): Mark Bassett; p148(TR): Ute Grabowsky/Photothek/Getty Images; p148 (B): Ismail Çiydem/iStockphoto; p150: Edyta Pawlowska/Shutterstock; p151: Monkey Business Images/Shutterstock; p152: Monkeybusinessimages/iStockphoto; p153: Michaeljung/Shutterstock; p158: Milan Markovic/iStockphoto; p159: KatarzynaBialasiewicz/iStockphoto; p160: Lucky Business/Shutterstock; p161: Nullplus/iStockphoto; p162(T): Photographee.eu/Shutterstock; p162(B): SpeedKingz/Shutterstock; p163: Lisa S./Shutterstock; p164(T): Tsian/Shutterstock; p164(A): Stephen Derr/Getty Images; p164(B): John Birdsall/REX/Shutterstock; p164(C): Picture Partners/Alamy Stock Photo; p164(D): Rob Lewine/Tetra Images/Corbis; p164(E): Hero Images/Getty Images; p165: Kzenon/iStockphoto; p171(T): Arek_malang/Shutterstock; p171(C): Monkey Business Images/Shutterstock; p171(B): Yeko Photo Studio/Shutterstock; p175(T): Tyler Olson/Shutterstock; p175(B): Vadim Ratnikov/Shutterstock.

The publisher and authors are grateful to the following for permission to reprint extracts from copyright material:

p24: www.sueddeutsche.de from Süddeutscher Verlag; p48: de.wikipedia.org under Creative Commons Licence CC-BY-SA-3.0; p50: www.filmstarts.de from Nicolas John and Webedia Group; p76: www.vis.bayern.de, Verbraucherportal VIS Bayern, from A. Hiebl; p102: www.gesundheit.de from Gesunheit.de; p114: www.umweltbundesamt.de from Federal Environment Agency, Germany; p114: www.eu-koordination.de from DNR, based on data from ec.europa.eu; p130: www.wien.info from Vienna Tourist Board; p170: www.zeit.de from Zeitverlag; Source: Von Maren Söhring, 23. Februar 2010, 7:00 Uhr / Quelle: ZEIT Campus 2/2010. Zeitverlag.

The publisher and authors would like to thank the following for their help and advice:

Audio recordings produced by Colette Thomson for Footstep Productions Ltd; Andrew Garratt (sound engineer).